UNDERSTANDING SPORTS COACHING

Successful sports coaching is as dependent on utilizing good teaching and social practices as it is about expertise in sport skills and tactics. *Understanding Sports Coaching* offers an innovative introduction to the theory and practice of sports coaching, highlighting the social, cultural and pedagogical concepts underpinning good coaching practice. Now in a fully revised and updated new edition, the book explores the complex interplay between coach, athlete, coaching programme and social context, and encourages coaches to develop an open and reflective approach to their own coaching practice. It addresses key issues such as:

- power and the coach–athlete relationship
- viewing the athlete as a learner
- instructional methods and reflection
- how our view of ability informs assessment
- coaching philosophy and ethics.

Understanding Sports Coaching also includes a full range of practical exercises and case studies designed to encourage coaches to reflect critically upon their own coaching strategies, their interpersonal skills and upon important issues in contemporary sports coaching. This book is essential reading for all students of sports coaching and for any professional coach looking to develop his or her coaching expertise.

Tania Cassidy is Senior Lecturer in Pedagogy, University of Otago, New Zealand.

Robyn Jones is Professor, Cardiff School of Sport, UWIC, Wales.

Paul Potrac is Senior Lecturer in Sports Coaching, Unitec, New Zealand.

UNDERSTANDING SPORTS COACHING

THE SOCIAL, CULTURAL AND PEDAGOGICAL FOUNDATIONS OF COACHING PRACTICE

Tania Cassidy, Robyn Jones and Paul Potrac

Routledge
Taylor & Francis Group

LONDON AND NEW YORK

First published 2004 by Routledge

This edition published 2009 by Routledge
2 Park Square, Milton Park, Abingdon, Oxon OX14 4RN

Simultaneously published in the USA and Canada
by Routledge
270 Madison Ave, New York, NY 10016

Reprinted 2008, 2009 (twice)

Routledge is an imprint of the Taylor & Francis Group, an informa business

© 2004, © 2009 Tania Cassidy, Robyn Jones and Paul Potrac

Typeset in Bell Gothic by
Keystroke, 28 High Street, Tettenhall, Wolverhampton
Printed and bound in Great Britain by
TJ International Ltd, Padstow, Cornwall

British Library Cataloguing in Publication Data
A catalogue record for this book is available from the British Library

Library of Congress Cataloging-in-Publication Data
Cassidy, Tania, 1964-
Understanding sports coaching : the social, cultural and pedagogical foundations
of coaching practice / Tania Cassidy, Robyn Jones and Paul Potrac. – 2nd ed.
p. cm.
Includes bibliographical references and index.
1. Coaching (Athletics) 2. Coaching (Athletics)–Philosophy. 3. Coaches (Athletics)–
Training of. I. Jones, Robyn L. II. Potrac, Paul, 1974- III. Title.
GV711.C34 2008
796.07'7–dc22   2008004726

ISBN10: 0–415–44271–0 (hbk)
ISBN10: 0–415–44272–9 (pbk)
ISBN10: 0–203–89292–5 (ebk)

ISBN13: 978–0–415–44271–8 (hbk)
ISBN13: 978–0–415–44272–5 (pbk)
ISBN13: 978–0–203–89292–3 (ebk)

In memory of Frederick and Marie O'Neill

▼ CONTENTS

▼ ACKNOWLEDGEMENTS

Many people have knowingly, or not, contributed to the ideas presented in this book. We acknowledge the hundreds of undergraduate students who, over the years, have enrolled, willingly or not, in PHSE 201 and now PHSE 101. They have been the catalysts for the book, as well as the 'guinea pigs' for the ideas in some of the chapters. We thank the representative coaches of the Otago Rugby Football Union who participated in the CoDe programme and, as a result, trialled some of the ideas discussed in this book. Their enthusiasm was infectious and feedback on the ideas invaluable.

TC: To my extended family and friends, thank you for keeping me sane, for your love and for making me smile. A special thank-you to Georgia, Jake, Toby and Zach for giving me a reason to play.

RJ: To Theresa, Savanna, Seren and Sian

PP: To Mum, Dad, Lisa and Susana

ACKNOWLEDGEMENTS

INTRODUCTION

Welcome to the second edition of *Understanding Sports Coaching*, which expands on the first in many ways. It contains fresh material in terms of updating and building upon concepts previously mentioned, while also including some new ones. The details of these changes are contained and explained throughout this opening chapter. In relation to the chapter's structure, there follow two vignettes. The first is entitled 'How it all started', and describes how we came to write the book. The second, entitled 'How it moved on', brings the story of the project up to date. Then, the aims of the book, why we believe it is needed, for whom it is principally written and how it is organized are articulated. The traditional model of coaching is then outlined, before the case is made for greater consideration to be given to social, cultural and pedagogical factors if coaching is to be more holistically understood and practised. Indeed, building on the earlier discussion, this section provides a detailed rationale for the book. Finally, a personal postscript ties the complex experiences we had as joint authors to the subject of coaching as a whole, where numerous agendas must be somewhat fused and directed towards a joint goal.

HOW IT ALL STARTED

Tania

For some years I had been lecturing at the School of Physical Education at the University of Otago, New Zealand (which could equally be described as a department of human movement, exercise science or kinesiology), where I taught a compulsory pedagogy course to approximately 220 undergraduates. The course had not been particularly popular with students, the most common objection being 'I'm not going to be a teacher, so why do I have to do pedagogy?' Over the years I tried different strategies in an effort to make the course more obviously relevant without compromising its educational content. Many times I stressed that while the subject matter focused on educational and, to a lesser degree, sociological concepts, the course was appropriate to movement specialists in general, since the notions and ideas discussed govern much human behaviour. Until the fifth year of teaching the course I had, in the main, relied on the students themselves to make the links between the concepts examined and an area that particularly interested them if they were not considering becoming teachers. It was clear from the student evaluations that this strategy was not successful.

In 2002 I decided to contextualize the course within the field of sports coaching. I based this decision on the assumption that most of the students would have had some experience of being coached or of being a coach, hence could better relate to the subject and the linked conceptual matter. It was also much easier to engage with contemporary issues using a sports coaching context, given the coverage of sport by the media and its omnipresence in modern-day society. To hook the students in the first lecture, I asked them to list the characteristics of the person they considered to have been their best teacher. Then, I asked them to do the same for someone they considered to have been their best coach. When the two lists had been compiled and compared, it became obvious that they shared many characteristics. It was my intention that the students, through completing this task, would begin to see the connection between pedagogy and the wider world of sport.

In the second lecture I introduced another exercise aimed at guiding the students to further recognize the invisibility of critical sociological and educational ideas in the sports coaching context, and to see how this void could be detrimental to coaches and athletes. First, I presented the following scenario: each student was the coach of a team of elite athletes who could call upon unlimited resources. Although on paper this was a very good team, that fact was not reflected in its performances. I asked the students to list the professionals or specialists they could call on in an effort to improve the team's performance. When collated, the final list contained a predominance of health and sport scientists such as physiotherapists, nutritionists, fitness trainers, biomechanists, motion analysts and exercise physiologists, and when a social scientist was included, it was in the form of a sports psychologist. There was no mention of considering the coach as an educator, and therefore no suggestion that a specialist could examine the educational and social practices of coaching. Plainly, the students' conception of the coaching role remained a narrow one, and while their lack of recognition did not surprise me, it did get me thinking about why this might be so.

Robyn

When Tania and I shared a 'working coffee' one day, she told me of her intended strategy to hook students into pedagogy through the use of the sports coaching context. She asked if, as a lecturer in coaching, I knew of any potential texts or readings that would be informative for the course and the slant it was taking. Unfortunately, I knew only too well that there was no published material that adopted a sociological and educational approach to coaching, although my developing work with a small group of others was beginning to theorize and provide empirical support for such a position. Not much earlier, I had begun to teach my sports coaching units using sociological and educational concepts. I did this because I believed that coaching is ultimately a social endeavour, and while sport-specific physiological and psychological tools are necessary, if coaches lack the sensitivity to act appropriately within a dynamic social and learning environment, they will struggle to achieve their intentions of improving the quality of experience and performances of their charges.

Additionally, it seemed to me that very few people who enrol in coach education or sport science programmes actually learn much about the messy reality of coaching and how best to deal with it. Unsurprisingly, then, despite the amount of information given about various aspects of the process on such courses, the impact on subsequent coaching practice remains minimal. Common rebuttals heard are 'That just wouldn't work for me', or 'It's OK in theory, but what if . . . ?' Consequently, tried and trusted methods gleaned from experience have tended to override both the integration of academic knowledge into coaching practice and the innovation that reflection upon such applied knowledge can produce. In short, many coaches, wary of stepping outside a comfort zone of given drills and discourse, tend to coach the way they were coached. For this reason, coaching has often come to characterize a repetitive one-dimensional circle, as opposed to a progressive three-dimensional spiral.

Paul

Having previously worked extensively with Robyn on a critical examination of the coaching process, I was more than happy to agree to become involved in the unfolding project. With academic roots in the sociology of sport, I needed no convincing of the relevance of 'social things' to sports coaching. Furthermore, from my previous work with elite coaches it seemed to me that they often did use sociological and educational concepts in their practice, but in a haphazard, almost accidental way. If such strategies could be better formalized and acknowledged, I had no doubt that practice could be improved, with something akin to the mythical 'X' factor being achieved!

Working together

Our joint belief in the value of both sociological and educational ideas to the coaching process was the germ of this project. As the three of us talked further about how relevant such concepts are to pedagogy, we became convinced that a book outlining this stance was necessary so that students could better develop a sociologically and educationally informed sense of what it means to be a coach. This text is our response to that perceived need.

HOW IT MOVED ON

Tania, Robyn and Paul

Although we obviously knew that sales of *Understanding Sports Coaching* had gone quite well, we were nevertheless a little surprised and very pleased when Sam Grant, then a commissioning editor from Routledge, asked us how we felt about delivering a second edition. The stated requirement was that at least 25 per cent of the developed text had to comprise new material. Following a brief but intense flurry of emails, we agreed on following up the invitation and began to draw up a proposal.

The first edition had obviously struck a chord with readers internationally. This was not only in the United Kingdom and New Zealand, where, as authors, we are based, but also in, among other places, South Korea and Norway, where it has been translated and used extensively as an undergraduate text. Consequently, we recognized that in many ways we did not want to change too much within a second edition, particularly regarding the underlying message of the book as expressed in the title. Still, there was plenty of scope for development, in terms of both updating existing chapters and developing new ones. Indeed, since 2004, when the first edition appeared, although psychological investigations of coaching have continued, an appreciation of the social, cultural and pedagogical foundations of coaching practice has really taken root. This has been most clearly seen in the published literature that has used such a framework to ground its understanding of coaches and coaching. It is a movement that attests to the growing influence of such thought in exploring and explaining coaching practice.

As ever, there was plenty of enthusiastic debate between us over which chapters and concepts we should amend, develop or cut. Here, the tyranny of distance (as mentioned in the Postscript to this chapter) remained and had to be dealt with. Similarly, as each of us had developed our own independent paths of inquiry since writing the first edition, we constantly had to check our standpoints on several issues to ensure a consistency of message. We knew, however, that the important thing was not to agree universally on all points, but to present thought-provoking notions and concepts to readers about the issues that we believe underlie coaching practice. To help us negotiate these sometimes choppy waters, in addition to our own reflections there were helpful reviews to draw upon and other colleagues to talk to.

Eventually we decided upon amending and developing a number of chapters quite substantially; for example, those related to Chapter 2: 'Instructional methods and pedagogical strategies', Chapter 3: 'Quality in coaching', Chapter 5: 'Learning and development', Chapter 7: 'Understanding athletes' identities' and Chapter 10: 'Assessment and ability in coaching'. This was done to reflect not only recent writings in the areas concerned, but also our own developing thoughts and theories in relation to them. Other chapters meanwhile were introduced as new material (i.e. Chapter 12, 'Theory, practice and professionalism in coaching', and Chapter 13, 'Power and the coach–athlete relationship'), some were moved to different parts of the book (namely Chapter 8, 'The discourses of coaching'), while still others were cut altogether. Finally, those chapters not subject to substantial surgery were updated as appropriate. All of these decisions were driven by our collective purpose to provide a more comprehensive view of the social, cultural and pedagogical foundations that underpin coaching practice. Our aim in this second edition, then, is the same ambitious one that drove us in the first.

Despite the substantial revisions made between and within both chapters and parts, we still do not claim to have provided all the answers in this complex field of social inquiry. What we do hope to have produced is a more up-to-date, complete view of the major themes currently being discussed, debated and researched by many coaches and coaching scholars. We would be interested to hear what you think!

AIMS OF THE BOOK

Recent empirical research (Jones *et al.* 2004; Potrac 2001) indicates that good coaches can evaluate and rationalize their actions. They think about, and are aware of, their practice before, during and after the event, reflecting in some depth about plans, actions and consequences. Taking our lead from such findings, we believe that if coaches are to understand why they are doing what they are doing, and if they are to appreciate the limits and possibilities of their practice, it is useful for them to have a grasp of social, cultural and educational concepts. The principal aim of this book is to highlight some of these concepts and to link them directly to the practice of coaching, as we believe that they fundamentally inform it.

We recognize that good coaches probably already use some educational and sociological concepts in their practice, which, in turn, wield considerable influence on their general coaching styles. However, the adoption of these concepts often occurs implicitly rather than explicitly and, as a consequence, leaves coaches unaware of the assumptions that inform their practices. Indeed, this was a driving issue behind Jones's (2006a) recent text *The Sports Coach as Educator*, in which socially related pedagogical theories were explicitly presented in the context of coaching, thus illustrating the close relationship between the two activities of coaching and pedagogy. By not questioning and hence not critically engaging with their actions, coaches make it difficult to systematically develop their programmes for the maximal benefit of athletes; they also make it difficult for themselves to fully understand the ethical, moral and political consequences of their practice. Given that coaching does not occur in a social vacuum (Schempp 1998; Jones 2000), we also believe that the social and educational values that construct the person of the coach need careful and thoughtful consideration if coaches are to act in enlightened, effective and sensitive ways (Jones 2000). Similarly, recognizing the constraints and possibilities for practice enables coaches to become aware of the suppressed culture of coaching rather than only of its visible, formal face as presented through dominant discourses (i.e. ways of talking about it) (Grace 1998).

Recent work has also emphasized the reflective activities and qualities of top-level coaches. For example, a study by Irwin *et al.* (2004) concluded that elite gymnastic coaches' knowledge was principally founded on reflecting upon critical discussions with colleagues and peers. Similarly, Gilbert and Trudel (2006) used Schön's (1983) framework to highlight how coaches can and should use reflection to develop their knowledge in a realistic way. The value of reflecting for coaches, as well as the dangers of unquestioningly adopting it, thus building on the work of Gilbert and Trudel (2006), will be discussed in depth in the following chapter (Chapter 1, 'Reflection'). The purpose of introducing the notion here is to present reflective practice as a central means or principle for how this book should be read. That is, although we naturally believe that the concepts presented within the text are indicative of good practice, to be implemented appropriately, reflection upon them is necessary – reflection in relation to their extent, frequency and timing. Subsequent action, of course, is inevitably dependent on the beliefs held by the individual coach in question with regard to what is being reflected upon, and the context.

We recognize that building a purely theoretical case for the inclusion of sociological and educational concepts into coaching practice would, in all probability, have a limited impact on the practice of sports coaches. In an effort to give this book a wider application, we have provided practical exercises and thought-provoking questions at the end of each chapter, to link the discussed concepts to coaching practice. We hope that the exercises provided will resonate with coaches, as they are grounded in the messy reality of coaching itself. The aim of these exercises, then, is twofold. First, it is to illustrate how the sociological and educational concepts discussed can be workably integrated into general practice and wider coach education programmes. Second, it is to encourage coaches to personally reflect on, and engage with, the technical, moral, ethical and political issues that occur in their own coaching contexts. We hope that the exercises will make a small contribution to closing the gap between theory and practice.

WHY IS THE BOOK NEEDED?

The principal rationale for writing this book comes from our difficulty as lecturers, researchers and coach educators in finding coaching literature that is informed by sociological and educational perspectives. There continues to be relatively little available literature that questions some of the taken-for-granted practices in coaching and acknowledges the complex reality within which coaches work (Côté et al. 1995; Bowes and Jones 2006). This situation, however, is being increasingly questioned (see Cross and Lyle 1999; Strean 1998; Jones 2000; Lyle 1999b), with a call for coaching to be recognized as multivariate, interpersonal and dynamic; for the social to be reintroduced within social cognition (Brustad and Weiss 1992). Such a stance implores us to avoid treating coaches as 'cardboard cut-outs' (Sparkes and Templin 1992: 118), and athletes as non-thinking pawns. Indeed, the past decade has witnessed a growing number of coach educators and academics who are prepared to engage with the sociology of coaching (see Jones and Armour 2000; Jones et al. 2004). Equally, there are a number who focus on the pedagogy of coaching (e.g. Kidman and Hanrahan 1997; Martens 1997). However, with the principal exceptions of Jones (2006a) and Bergmann Drewe (2000), this latter group predominantly concentrate on rather simplified 'how to' methods and effective coaching models. This approach differs from our interpretation of pedagogy, which we view as a problematic process that incorporates the interaction between how one learns, how one teaches, what is being taught (Lusted 1986) and the context in which it is being taught (Cassidy 2000). The key to adopting this view lies in making coaches aware of the social and educational dynamics that have created (and continue to create) their identities and philosophies, and hence their abilities to perform (Armour and Jones 2000). Developing such an awareness in coaches provides them with the ability to evaluate information from a range of sources, and the confidence and courage to take responsibility for their decisions.

We contend that a growing number of coaches want to develop athletes who can make decisions and adapt to changing situations on the field or court (Kidman 2001). Such a stance implicitly supports the view that learning is less the reception of acts and facts, and more a social practice that implies the involvement of the whole person in relation not only to specific activities but also to social communities. In this respect, we agree that 'the study and education of the human is complex' (Zakus and Malloy 1996: 504) requiring sensitivity, subtlety and subjectivity. If coaches want to produce responsible decision-making athletes, then it is useful for them to adopt coaching practices that take account of, and can facilitate, such a socially determined goal.

The significance of this book lies partly in response to Knudson and Morrison's (2002) call for a reality-based integrative approach to human movement. It is a position rooted in the belief that a socio-cultural pedagogic approach is imperative for understanding such a complex and dynamic activity as coaching, where, invariably, the whole is considerably greater than the sum of the constituent parts. Within this approach, the coach is viewed as a holistic problem-solver involved in the planning, prioritization, contextualization and orchestration of provision in an ever-changing environment. In this respect, it differs from the traditional approach to studying coaching from rationalistic subdisciplinary perspectives.

Adopting such a framework means that our discussion calls on theoretical ideas from disciplines that take account of the problematic human factor as well as real-life sports coaching scenarios, as we seek to develop a more credible view of the coaching process. As we touched upon earlier, despite our belief in and commitment to the position taken in this book, we acknowledge that the concepts selected for discussion do not comprise all the related sociological or educational theory available, or all that could be applied to sports coaching. Rather, we have selected concepts that reflect our preferences, and those that we consider could most directly assist coaching practitioners.

WHO IS THE BOOK FOR?

The book is principally written for sports coaching students, whose numbers are rapidly rising as programmes related to coach education, sports science, kinesiology and physical education proliferate in higher education institutions. It is also aimed at the physical education teacher education market, the students of which invariably become involved in coaching school sports teams. For undergraduate students of coaching, it can serve as an introductory manual to illustrate the social, cultural and educational nature of coaching, and how interacting educational and sociological philosophies can inform professional practice. Additionally, the book may assist beginning postgraduate students to make links between theory and practice, and further develop their recognition that coaching can and should be a reflective endeavour. Since many sports science students are also working coaches, the book holds the potential to give such practitioners a greater awareness of the factors that influence their coaching, hopefully stimulating them to further evaluate their own practices, and, where necessary, consider alternatives.

We believe the book is applicable to coaches at any level: those working with children through to mature international athletes. Indeed, the concepts discussed within it are relevant to any coach who wishes to maximize the sporting experience for his or her charges, whatever the context might be. This is because coaching, in whatever guise it is packaged, is essentially a social, educational enterprise. It is social in that it involves human interaction, and educational in that it extends from learning to have fun and mastering basic skills to knowing about the minute intricacies of body adjustment and tactical awareness so necessary for success in elite sport (Jones 2006b). Finally, the book will be useful in developing coach education programmes, some of whose coordinators are presently evaluating the content of their courses to see how they can better equip coaches to deal with the complex socio-pedagogic nature of their work.

HOW IS THE BOOK ORGANIZED?

The framework of this book is informed by our belief that coaching is fundamentally a social, cultural and pedagogical practice that comprises the interconnections between the teacher, learner, content (Lusted 1986) and context (Cassidy 2000). Although we are aware that the term 'pedagogy' could be taken as including both social and cultural aspects, we decided to keep them separate to emphasize the importance of each component within the totality of coaching. Consequently, to fully understand (and achieve) quality coaching practice (resulting in intended and appropriate athlete learning), we need to take account of individual coach biographies, their socialization and their personal interpretations of such practice within their respective working environments – a perspective that takes account of social and cultural factors on coaches' delivery and general interactive behaviours. Hence, the book is divided into four parts dealing respectively with the coach, the athlete(s), the content and the context. Each part contains a number of relevant chapters, with each chapter concluding with a set of questions and suggested readings.

Specifically, Part One explores the coach in relation to the concepts of reflection (Chapter 1), instructional methods and pedagogical strategies (Chapter 2), quality in coaching (Chapter 3), and the developing of a coaching philosophy (Chapter 4). Part Two deals with the athlete(s). Here, we discuss understanding the learning and development process (Chapter 5), and the development of young athletes (Chapter 6). This latter chapter is written by Dr Lisette Burrows, from the University of Otago. Dr Burrows is respected for her knowledge of developmental issues in the physical education context and we thought her insights would be useful for sport coaches, especially those working with children and young people. Also included in Part Two is a chapter on understanding athletes' identities (Chapter 7). Part Three focuses on coaching content, and includes chapters on the discourses of coaching (Chapter 8), coaches' content knowledge (Chapter 9) and assessment in coaching (Chapter 10). Finally, Part Four explores ethical issues associated with coaching (Chapter 11), professionalism within coaching (Chapter 12) and, finally, the nature of power in coach–athlete relationships (Chapter 13).

Although the analysis has been presented in a linear format, many of the concepts discussed have cross-chapter relevancy, highlighting the interdisciplinary nature of the subject matter. At relevant points, to assist in making the interconnections between the coach, athlete(s), content and context, we will direct readers to complementary discussion in other chapters.

THE TRADITIONAL MODEL OF MULTIDISCIPLINARY COACHING AND COACH EDUCATION

Without restating the case made in earlier work (Potrac *et al.* 2000; Jones 2000), suffice it to say that traditional views of coaching have located it within a bioscientific, product-orientated discourse. Consequently, coaching knowledge has been seen as unproblematic, with coaches viewed as mere technicians involved in its transfer (Macdonald and Tinning 1995). The discourse has been one related to 'processing' and 'packaging' athletes, in attempts to attain ever higher levels of 'output' (Bale and Sang 1996; Jones *et al.* 2006). According to Bale and Sang (1996: 21), such terminology and the behaviour it engenders have resulted in the reducing of athletes 'to inanimate objects, as things, to be recorded and ranked'. The implication is that the power to succeed is vested firmly in the individual (as long as they have the potential) if only they are prepared to train hard enough.

A principal contributor to this picture of athlete as 'machine' has been the education programmes set up for, and attended by, coaches. Here, conceptual views about the coaching role are shaped, as are perceptions about the 'valuable' knowledges needed to coach successfully. Such programmes have been almost exclusively multidisciplinary in nature, containing discrete units within detached and parallel disciplines devoted to certain aspects of coaching knowledge (e.g. physiology, nutrition, psychology). Although much useful information has been contained within the structure, attending coaches have been left to make the cross-subject connections for themselves, which, research suggests, they have consistently failed to do (Saury and Durand 1998; Jones *et al.* 2004). Such findings give support to the claim that the current structure remains fragmented and disjointed (Jones 2000). Indeed, we can liken it to a 'smorgasbord of disconnected facts and experiences' (Locke 1985: 10), which is hardly likely to produce consistent excellence in such a complex area of human relations as coaching. Additionally, for many, it appears that such programmes lack credibility since, by separating theory from practice, they routinize and simplify high-level tasks (Macdonald and Tinning 1995). It is a tendency towards deskilling the practitioner, in terms of both human and cognitive interaction as it assumes that knowledge is 'clean', sequential and given (Jones 2000).

An inherent problem with such an approach to knowledge is that the learning contained within it takes place in an expressive climate that is placid and neutral, causing coaches to suffer from 'reality shock' when they actually start working. Such programmes have the potential to produce limited two-dimensional coaches (Sparkes and Templin 1992), who, driven by piecemeal mechanistic considerations, are unable to comprehend and thus adapt to the multifaceted and wide-ranging human context (Jones 2000). This focus has created a distorted framework that is unable to take account of, and therefore clashes with, the unique and 'hybrid' nature of athletes (Shogan 1999), whose distinctive identities are created from many different practices and positions (Hall 1996). Hence, we argue that there is a need for greater balance within a more integrated framework to better prepare coaches for the complexities of their role. This issue was neatly conceptualized in an article by Burt (1998), albeit in the wider context of the contribution of 'kinesiology' as a subject for solving social problems. It was suggested that kinesiology was too narrowly conceived in rigidly separated subdisciplines and too divorced from its central reality-based mission to properly deal with its stated aims. It was urged, instead, to focus on the quality of practitioners it produces, and hence to fulfil its potential in dealing with and overcoming real-life problems. Echoing Jones (2007), we issue a similar rallying call to coaching 'science'; indeed, the time may well be right to either better 'contribute or fall back' (Burt 1998: 80).

COACHING HOLISTICALLY – OR AT LEAST WITH SOCIAL, CULTURAL AND PEDAGOGICAL CONSIDERATIONS IN MIND

Although the value of holistic coaching has been increasingly recognized in recent times, this has tended to remain at the level of abstract thought and generalized support. To avoid a similar oversight, we begin this section by defining what we mean by the term 'holistic coaching'. The *Concise Oxford Dictionary* definition of the term 'holistic' is a consideration 'of the whole person, including mental and social factors' (Oxford 1991: 562). Even though this sets us on our way, we would like to be more wide-ranging in our definition in asserting that the person is also an emotional, political, spiritual and cultural being. To coach holistically, then, is to coach with all of these considerations in mind. Although this inevitably leads to discussion about appropriate and workable boundaries for the coaching role, we consider that if such factors affect athletic performance and enjoyment, then they should warrant consideration within the coaching remit.

Taking a holistic approach to coaching as such, as you have no doubt recognized, is not literally in line with the stated aim of this book. This is because the text does not take into account the rationalistic thought that has characterized much psychological, physiological and biomechanical writing on coaching. This is not to say we do not support the concept of the need to coach holistically. In fact, we very much believe that coaches should treat each situation, inclusive of its many variables, on its merits, assess it, carefully weigh the options and choose the most appropriate course of action. To do so, a coach must draw on many knowledge sources and decide, with insight, how to amalgamate and utilize them in what fashion, when and where. Our goal here, however, is to redress the balance a little away from the predominant bioscientific view of coaching, and to highlight the need to also take account of the personal, emotional, cultural and social identity of the athlete if maximal performances are to be obtained.

The purpose here, then, is to raise awareness in coaches and students of coaching about factors that need to be considered if the goal of coaching holistically is to be achieved – factors which have remained for too long hidden in the depth of the activity. Through questioning current assumptions surrounding the extent and nature of the coaching role and how we prepare coaches for it, the book aims to redefine and extend what it means to coach. This redefinition is based on recognizing the centrality of cultural and social relationships within the coaching process (Jarvie 1991; Jones 2000, 2007; Schempp 1998). Since such relationships are influenced by factors that are situational, political, ideological and moral in nature, we believe that coaches should carefully consider them, and therefore take a more holistic approach to coaching in order to realize the full potential of their athletes. The goal, then, is to increase coaches' sensitivities to individual athletes' needs and identities, allowing them to better manage the relationship between the individual and the social context, which in turn supports learning (Langley 1997).

The argument in support of such a position is based on recognizing coaching as intellectual as opposed to technical work, requiring higher-order thinking skills to deal with the humanistic, problematic and dynamic nature of the tasks involved. The case is summarized around three principal issues: the need for coaches to consider (1) cultural factors, (2) the development of social competencies, and (3) the pedagogical contextualization of practice, if lasting improvement is to occur. In making the case that Kenyan middle-distance athletes are culturally as opposed to naturally produced, Bale and Sang (1996: 17) stated that 'running can mean different things to different cultures'. They argued that sport participation and achievement should be firmly placed within the context of culture if they are to be properly explained. The same could be said of coaching. Douge and Hastie (1993: 20) agreed that 'effective leadership qualities may be unique to a social fabric', while Schempp's (1998) declaration that 'our social worlds offer no immunity to sports fields or gymnasia' provides further evidence of the belief that knowledge of culture and related social factors should be prime considerations for coaches. Such a stance also supports Cheffers' (1997: 4) philosophical lament that 'no individual is an island', and further emphasizes the need to coach contextually for meaningful progress to occur. For instance, in the context of Aotearoa/New Zealand, expecting a Mäori athlete to engage in direct eye-to-eye contact is problematic, since for Mäori looking an older person in the eye is a sign of disrespect (Durie 1998). Alternatively, Mäori are often more impressed by the unspoken signals conveyed through subtle gesture (e.g. a raised eyebrow), with words in some situations being regarded as superfluous and even demeaning (ibid.). Within the cultural context, then, learning is considered both an individual and a social process, with meanings being constructed both in the mind of the learner and through his or her community of practice (Langley 1997). Consequently, we need to be culturally sensitive; that is, to develop social competencies when coaching – as culture exerts a considerable influence over identities and motivations, particularly when it comes to influencing others.

Indeed, in order to deal with the fundamental nature of their work, Schempp (1998) advocated that coaches should focus centrally on the problems and realities of human interaction above other concerns of content. This would sensitize them to the unique dynamics of the local situation and enable them to act accordingly (Jones 2000). To improve such competencies, we need to think and move beyond the obvious, and insightfully consider why our 'coaching fortunes' are as they are.

The process involves carefully considering the reasons behind the behaviour of ourselves as coaches and the athletes in our care, in the constant search for alternative, improved options.

Recent research (Jones *et al.* 2003, 2004; Saury and Durand 1998) has suggested that elite coaches, although not educated to do so, have a tendency to coach contextually. That is, they appear to utilize flexible planning strategies within detailed set routines that permit improvised adaptation to the evolving situation at hand. Such practice is based on the belief that definitive standards cannot be applied outright, as they often conflict with other structural constraints within the coaching situation, and are often witnessed in relation to reacting to athletes' particular needs (Saury and Durand 1998). Consequently, in what clearly can be seen as a more holistic approach, such coaches were aware of the need to care for their athletes' well-being beyond the sporting arena, and of exercising social competencies to ensure the continuance of positive working relationships (Jones *et al.* 2003, 2004; Saury and Durand 1998). The message here is that coach–athlete relationships need to be carefully nurtured, and be flexible enough to deal with the multiple realities and needs that exist within the coaching process if athletes are going to reach their potential and success is to be achieved. What is more, such relationships should extend far beyond the immediate sports field or gym to encompass the whole person. Current practice, then, suggests that the coach is much more than a subject-matter specialist and a method applier (Squires 1999); rather, he or she is a person with multiple dimensions operating within given structural constraints in a dynamic social environment. From this perspective, coaching is fundamentally about making a myriad of connections between subject, method and other people to overcome the many and varied problems faced. We could not agree more.

POSTSCRIPT

We began the project of writing this book united in the belief that linking sociological and educational concepts to coaching practice would assist coaches and students of coaching to make some sense of the muddled realities of their work. What we did not foresee was that the practice of writing about coaching was just as messy and complicated as coaching itself.

We all came to the initial project with different experiences of coaching, writing and life. For example, Robyn had experience of being a performance-orientated coach, while Tania had experience of being a participation-orientated coach. Robyn had written a number of books, while Tania had not written any, and Paul was somewhere in between. Also, the context in which the ideas were being conceived, and tried, were different: one of us was working with undergraduate students who were specializing in coaching science, while the other two were working with students who were enrolled in more general human movement-type degree programmes. Paul and Tania were also trying some of the ideas with representative coaches. Added to the mix was the tyranny of distance. The project had been

conceived over a coffee with a colleague a few doors away in the same building, but, as each of us followed our individual academic careers, it was completed over a distance half the world away and in three different institutions. Our initial general consensus, then, very quickly became a distant memory as specifics were explored and uncovered.

The influence of these contextual factors became very evident the first time we swapped our 'draft' chapters. Suffice it to say, it did not look as though we were singing from the same hymn sheet. Over time, and with each other's help, the ideas became more harmonious again. The reason we share this experience is to highlight that even with the best of intentions and a reasonable level of theoretical and practical understanding, collective compromise and consideration in addition to individual determination are required to realize one's coaching goals.

SUGGESTED READINGS

Bergmann Drewe, S. (2000) 'An examination of the relationship between coaching and teaching', *Quest*, 52: 79–88.

Jones, R.L. (ed.) (2006) *The Sports Coach as Educator: Re-conceptualising Sports Coaching*, London: Routledge.

Jones, R.L. (2007) 'Coaching redefined: An everyday pedagogical endeavour', *Sport, Education and Society*, 12(2): 159–173.

Schempp, P. (1998) 'The dynamics of human diversity in sport pedagogy scholarship', *Sociology of Sport Online*, 1(1): Available at http://physed.otago.ac.nz/sosol/v1i1/v1i1a8.htm (accessed 20 April 2008).

PART ONE
THE COACH

CHAPTER 1

▼ **REFLECTION**

INTRODUCTION

In the past two decades the focus on reflection, or on becoming a reflective practitioner, has gained popularity in a wide range of contexts, including education (Smyth 1991), graphic design (Poynor 1994), art (Roberts 2001), engineering (Adams *et al.* 2003), medicine (Middlethon and Aggleton 2001) and coaching (Gilbert and Trudel, 2006). Increasingly, practitioners are being encouraged to 'stand back and reflect upon the construction and application of their professional knowledge' (Hardy and Mawer 1999: 2). The resurgence of interest can largely be attributed to the work of Schön (1983), who discussed reflection in relation to architecture, town planning, engineering and management. 'Reflection' is a term that has multiple interpretations, which include 'turning a subject over in the mind and giving it serious and consecutive consideration' (Dewey 1910: 3); having 'a capacity for autonomous professional self-development through systematic self-study' (Stenhouse 1975: 144); the study of other professionals; and the testing of ideas in practice (ibid.). While these and other interpretations exist (see Moon 2004), Smyth (1991) cautions against the consequences of reflection becoming commonplace. Two reasons are given for such caution. First, because it can be interpreted in so many different ways, it has the potential to lose its core meaning. And second, the popularity of the term has created a 'paradoxical situation' where reflection has come to be used in 'an unreflected manner' (Bengtsson 1995: 24).

When attempting to gain an understanding of the complexities associated with reflection, it is useful to consider Tinning's (1995: 50) point that 'if becoming reflective were simply a rational process then it would be easy to train . . . teachers [read coaches] to be reflective'. He argues that this is not so simple, however, because 'many of the issues' on which practitioners 'should reflect are not merely a matter of rational argument'; rather, they 'have a large measure of emotion and subjectivity embedded within them' (ibid.: 50). Many coaches learn how to coach as a consequence of being an apprentice to another coach, often a coach they admire, and base their own practices on those of their mentor. Not surprisingly, it can be challenging reflecting on, and possibly critiquing, taken-for-granted practices that are associated with valued memories that may also have become integral to a sense of self.

While there are people who support the increasing emphasis being placed on coaches becoming reflective practitioners (see Fairs 1987; Gilbert and Trudel 2001; Kidman 2001), Crum (1995) questions whether being a reflective practitioner should become standardized practice – in other words, should it become the 'norm'? While he debates this question in the physical education context, the issue has relevancy for sports coaches. According to Crum, the answer depends on the definition held of physical education or, in this case, coaching. If a practitioner holds a 'training-of-the-physical' view of coaching and believes his or her role is only to improve fitness and adopt a technical or utilitarian approach, then becoming a coach who reflects deeply is not going to be paramount. In contrast, if a coach holds a view that coaching is 'a teaching–learning process', does 'not focus on the body-machine . . . but on humans moving' and views coaching as a process that is 'socially constructed and historically situated', then he or she is required to reflect insightfully on a wide range of issues (Crum 1995: 15). Despite agreeing with Crum that it may not always be necessary for some coaches to reflect, we contend that it is still useful for all coaches to engage in some degree of reflection, even if it is only at the technical level (we discuss the various levels later in this chapter). This is because by reflecting on practice, a coach may expose his or her perceptions and beliefs to evaluation, creating a heightened sense of self-awareness, which in turn may lead to a 'certain openness to new ideas' (Hellison and Templin 1991: 9).

The aims of this chapter are twofold. First, it aims to introduce some of the ways in which reflection has been interpreted and discussed in the literature, in particular Schön's (1983) concept of 'reflection-in-action'. Second, it aims to provide a discussion of some of the issues to consider when becoming a reflective coach in the modern sporting context.

WHAT IS REFLECTION?

Many consider John Dewey to be the 'founder' of reflection. He contrasted routine behaviour with reflective thought, defining the latter as the '[a]ctive, persistent, and careful consideration of any belief or supposed form of knowledge in the light of the grounds that support it, and the further conclusions to which it tends' (1910: 6). According to Dewey (1966), those who adopt a reflective pose investigate the assumptions that inform their behaviour and accept responsibility for their actions.

Dewey (1916) suggested that before an individual can engage in reflective thinking, three personal attributes need to be present: open-mindedness, wholeheartedness and responsibility. These are defined as follows:

- Open-mindedness is 'an active desire to listen to more sides than one; to give heed to facts from whatever source they come; to give full attention to alternative possibilities; to recognize the possibility of error even in the beliefs that are dearest to us' (Dewey 1916: 224).
- Wholeheartedness, as the name suggests, refers to being 'absorbed' and/or 'thoroughly interested' in a particular subject.
- Responsibility refers to when the consequences of actions are not only considered but also accepted, thereby securing integrity in one's beliefs.

Over 80 years later, these attributes still appear to be relevant to contemporary coaches, as evidenced by Wayne Smith's (assistant coach to the All Blacks, the national rugby union team of New Zealand) description of the qualities needed to be a good coach. In his own words,

> the key thing I think is the openness to learning. I think coaches need to look at things on merit and understand that just because they've played the game, they don't know everything about it. . . . Having a passion to improve is important. Knowing that you are a part of the problem means that you can also be part of the solution.
>
> (Wayne Smith, in Kidman 2001: 43)

Although Dewey is considered the founder of reflection, the increased interest in the term in the past two and a half decades can be attributed to the work of Schön (1983, 1987), Zeichner (1983, 1987) and (Crum 1995). In contrast with Dewey's view of reflection, whose focus lay 'outside the action' and on 'future action rather than current action' (Eraut 1995: 9), Schön's (1983) interpretation of reflection takes practice into account. While Schön provided examples of practice from professions such as town planning and architecture, Zeichner did so from teaching and teacher education (Crum 1995). Hence, we consider the work of both Schön and Zeichner to be particularly useful when examining reflection in a coaching context.

In discussing the concept of reflection, Schön (1983: 50) introduces the notion of reflection-in-action, which describes what professional and lay people alike do in practice, namely 'thinking about what they are doing, even while doing it'. For example, a big-league baseball pitcher described the process of reflecting-in-action by explaining how in the midst of playing the game '[you get] a special feel for the ball, a kind of command that lets you repeat the exact same thing you did before that proved successful' (Schön 1983: 54). Further, Schön stressed that phrases such as 'keeping your wits about you', 'thinking on your feet' and 'learning by doing' highlight 'not only that we can think about doing but that we can think about doing something while doing it' (Schön 1983: 54).

REFLECTION

Schön (1983: 50) identified three general patterns prevalent within reflection-in-action. First, reflection is often initiated when a practitioner is 'stimulated by surprise'. Here, in the process of dealing with an unexpected phenomenon, a practitioner reflects on his or her understandings that are implicit in the action and then critiques, restructures and embodies the practice in future action. In other words, when something unexpected happens, 'they turn thought back on action' (ibid.: 50) and then try to deal with it. The second pattern prevalent in reflection-in-action was what Schön (ibid.: 268) called a 'reflective conversation with the situation'. What he meant by this was that while an 'inquiry begins with an effort to solve a problem . . . [t]he inquirer remains open to the discovery of phenomena' (ibid.: 268). In the process of attempting to solve the initial problem, a discovery is made that is incongruous with the efforts to solve the problem. If this happens, the inquirer then 'reframes' what is considered to be 'the problem' (ibid.: 268). Schön argued that one of the consequences of having such a reflective conversation with a situation is that it is possible for practitioners to achieve some degree of professional growth by reflecting in, and reflecting on, practice. For examples and a model of a reflective conversation occurring in a coaching context, see Gilbert and Trudel (2001, 2005, 2006).

The third pattern inherent in reflection-in-action was what Schön (1983: 62) termed the 'action-present'. He described this as the 'zone of time in which action can still make a difference to the situation' (ibid.: 62). While all processes of reflection have an 'action-present', it 'may stretch over minutes, hours, days, or even weeks or months, depending on the pace of activity and the situational boundaries characteristic of the practice' (ibid.: 62). For example, in the middle of a verbal exchange with an athlete, a coach's reflection-in-action may occur in a matter of seconds, but when the context is a season, the reflection-in-action may occur over several months. Hence, the duration and pace of when reflection occurs will vary depending on the context. Arguably, the way one interprets the 'action-present' will dictate whether the more generic reflection-in-action term is utilized or, alternatively, whether reflection-on-action (ibid.), or the later-developed retrospective reflection-on-action (Gilbert and Trudel 2001, 2005, 2006), is used in describing the reflective process.

From the above we assume that reflection-in-action enables practitioners (athletes and coaches) to engage in 'on-the-spot' experimentation (Eraut 1995). Yet they are not only reflecting-in-action, but also reflecting-on-action. While Schön (1983) viewed reflection-on-action as being integral to reflection-in-action, not everyone agrees. Gilbert and Trudel (2001, 2005, 2006), for instance, view them as separate types of reflection, with reflection-on-action occurring 'within the action-present, but not in the midst of activity' (2001: 30). A coaching example is when a coach reflects on an issue in between practice sessions. Another who also views reflection-on-action as separate from reflection-in-action is Bengtsson (1995), who suggests that the former type of reflection can also occur before the action and when the problems arise. Gilbert and Trudel (2006) go on to argue that reflection-on-action can be further broken down, and as a consequence they suggest a third type of reflection, which they call 'retrospective reflection-on-action'. They describe this type of reflection as 'that [which] occurs outside the action-present (e.g., after the season or after a coach's reflection can no longer affect the situation)' (2001: 30).

In this chapter we follow the lead of Schön (1983) by considering reflection-on-action to be integral to reflection-in-action, and accept his argument that the notion of reflection-in-action has emerged as a consequence of the limits of technical rationality. When one takes this standpoint, particular issues arise for the coaching community, and it is some of these that we focus on in the remainder of the chapter.

BECOMING A REFLECTIVE COACH: ISSUES TO CONSIDER

In the first edition of this book we had a section entitled 'Why is it useful to become a reflective coach?' That we decided to remove the section in this edition is testament to how much we believe the coaching community has 'bought into', at least rhetorically, the value of coaches becoming reflective practitioners. In the past decade, empirical evidence has highlighted the need to reflect upon one's own and others' coaching in developing good practice (see Cassidy *et al.* 2006a; Cushion *et al.* 2003; Gilbert and Trudel 2001, 2005, 2006; Jones *et al.* 2004; Kidman 2001, 2005; Knowles *et al.* 2001; Nelson and Cushion 2006; Saury and Durand 1998). Despite this acknowledgement, we recognize that reflecting on one's practice is not an easy or quick exercise. Indeed, there are many traditions, rituals and so-called norms associated with the coaching culture that act as constraints on one's willingness and ability to experiment with reflection. In the following section we explore some issues that both constrain and enable coaches to become reflective practitioners.

Issue 1: Expertise and professionalism

Drawing on anecdotal accounts, Lyle (2002: 245) contends that many coaches in professional sport are 'recruited almost exclusively from the performer base', with 'high value' being 'placed on lengthy experience, sport-specific skills and technical insight, to the exclusion of other knowledge and skills'. However, it is not only those who select coaches that consider technical expertise important. Not surprisingly, coaches themselves also value this knowledge, as evidenced by the following quote from Ian McGeechan (a former Scotland rugby union coach):

> I don't think that you can coach at this level without a reasonable technical knowledge, because a lot of the things that you do are technical, in that you have to see when something is right or wrong, you have to put something in place, or be part of a conversation or discussion which can put something in place. Now if you cannot be a full part of that, you would lose respect from the players.
>
> (Jones *et al.* 2004: 61)

Emphasizing sport-specific technical expertise over other attributes does little to assist those who wish to promote sports coaching as a profession. We are not suggesting that technical expertise is not important for a coach to possess. It is. But if coaching is to be viewed as a profession,[1] then the coaching community needs to recognize both the tacit knowledge of coaches and the expertise that is acquired over an extended period of overt education where the emphasis is on the development of cognitive skills (Lyle 1998). Four years later, when he was judging sports coaching against numerous criteria of professionalism, Lyle (2002: 310) observed that 'the realisation of the professionalisation of sports coaching is yet some way off', with more emphasis required on the 'interpersonal dimension' of coaching as well as on the 'process elements of the job'. He went on to say that while technical knowledge is a given, 'we need to build on the co-ordinating, managing, planning, decision-taking role, with appropriate levels of delivery expertise' (ibid.: 308). We would also add to this list the need to develop sociological and cultural sensitivities, so that coaches can make ever more informed decisions in the best interests of their charges. This is a point that will be explored in greater depth in the final chapter.

It is the association, and at times tension, that exists between professionalism and technical expertise that can constrain coaches who aim to become reflective practitioners (Schön 1983). For example, when a coach has become extremely skilful at the techniques associated with coaching, he or she can be viewed as a 'technical expert'. When this is the case, coaches may find that surprises occur less often, thereby preserving the perception of the coach as expert. Coaches will also experience fewer 'problematic situations if they prefer to follow a well established routine that prevents them from falling outside the boundaries of their comfort zone' (Gilbert and Trudel 2006: 115). If, over time, the coach begins to value unproblematic knowledge preservation, then uncertainties become a threat or an admission of weakness, and therefore something to be avoided. By avoiding coaching situations that may solicit surprises, a coach may miss the opportunity to reflect on his or her practice.

Issue 2: 'Thinking interferes with doing'

Another possible constraint on one's willingness to experiment with becoming a reflective coach is associated with a commonly held belief that 'thinking interferes with doing' (Schön 1983: 276). Schön describes at least three specific ways in

---

1 Early evidence of this is that one of the proceedings of the Eighth Commonwealth and International conference on Sport, Physical Education, Dance, Recreation and Health, held in Edinburgh in 1986 was entitled 'Coach Education: Preparation for a Profession'. Over the years the desire for professional status has only intensified as a consequence of improved career opportunities in coaching, coach education and access to coaching studies in tertiary institutions (Lyle 2002). This desire was still evident at the International Council of Coach Education conference held in Beijing in 2007.

which this is 'supposed' to happen. First, there is no time to reflect when in the middle of the action. We recognize that sometimes in a sporting context it is 'dangerous to stop and think' (ibid.: 278). For example, it would be difficult for a scrum-half in rugby union to stop and consider all the options when he or she is holding the ball at the back of the scrum. But as Schön (ibid.: 278) reminds us, 'not all practice situations are of this sort'. It is unlikely that a coach would find him- or herself in a 'dangerous' position if he or she chose to stop and think when in the middle of a coaching session. Hence, the argument that 'thinking interferes with doing' is less convincing when applied to coaching practice. That said, Jones *et al.* (2004) point out that the 'front' coaches put up is important in maintaining credibility. Therefore, it is possible that if a coach often visibly 'stopped and thought' it could be interpreted by athletes as uncertainty, thus putting at risk the coach's credibility as someone who knows what he or she is doing.

A second way in which thinking potentially interferes with doing is the perception that when we think about behaviour we overanalyse it and consequently lose the flow of the action. We acknowledge that it is possible, if there is an extended action-present period, that excessive time spent on thought can interrupt the flow of the action. However, coaches and athletes can be taught to provide information about action, and think about their behaviours respectively, in a very short period of time. For example, in tennis a coach can teach a skilled athlete to take a moment to plan the next shot. If the athlete correctly gauges the time for reflection and integrates the outcome of the reflection into the action, then it is likely that performance will be enhanced. Not only can a coach teach the athlete to 'take a moment', but a coach who is committed to becoming reflective can also use the same strategies to integrate reflection into his or her own coaching action.

A third way in which thinking could interfere with doing is that when we begin to reflect, it is possible that 'we may trigger an infinite regress of reflection on action, then on our reflection on action, and so on ad infinitum' (Schön 1983: 277). Schön contends that this fear of regressing into a state of continual reflection is derived 'from an unexamined dichotomy of thought and action' (ibid.: 280). To break down the dichotomy, Schön constructed the notion of reflection-in-action in such a way that 'doing and thinking are complementary' (ibid.: 280). They are complementary in the sense that '[e]ach feeds the other and each sets boundaries for the other. It is the surprising result of action that triggers reflection, and it is the production of a satisfactory move that brings reflection temporarily to a close' (ibid.: 280) until new issues trigger further reflection. For example, a coach observes that, despite being provided with explanations and demonstrations, an athlete continually fails to comprehend new drills or plays immediately. This surprises the coach because the athlete is an engaging, bright and articulate individual, and once the drills or plays have been practised a few times the athlete does not forget them. In an attempt to find out why this athlete is slow to respond, the coach discusses the observations with colleagues and, in the process, reflects on how he or she is presenting the material and what learning medium is being privileged. As a consequence of the discussions, the coach recognizes that athletes who are aural and visual learners are initially advantaged when the material is presented compared to those athletes who learn via their kinesthetic senses. In subsequent training sessions, the coach introduces the drills and plays via aural, visual *and* kinesthetic media and finds that the athlete who was initially slow to comprehend now understands what is expected as quickly as the others.

Thus, thinking does not have to interfere with the flow of the action, yet sometimes it does, albeit temporarily. For example, a golf coach might suggest that a player change his or her grip on the club. Here, it is reasonable to expect that there would be a loss of flow until the player becomes accustomed to the new grip. Similarly, if a coach changed the coaching method by including, for example, some problem-solving tasks, then it is reasonable to expect that there would be a loss of flow in the practice until the coach and athletes become accustomed to the expectations, rights and responsibilities associated with the new method.

Whether or not coaches are prepared to pay the price of a loss of flow and incur 'a temporary loss of spontaneity' (Schön 1983: 280) depends on their ability to construct a 'low-risk' environment in which to practise. We contend that, more often than not, the price is worth paying, since reflection-in-action is often initiated when a performance is unsatisfactory. As such, we agree with Schön (ibid.: 279), who asserts that the question then becomes 'not so much *whether* to reflect as what *kind* of reflection is most likely to help us get unstuck'. We have interpreted 'kinds' of reflection to mean levels of reflection, a topic that we discuss in more detail below.

Issue 3: Reflection is an insular process

While the scope for reflection is great, one of the concerns that we, and others, have with reflection is that the focus is potentially 'inwards' on the practitioners' own practice 'without sufficient attention to the social conditions that frame and influence that practice' (Zeichner and Liston 1996: 19). One way of moving away from thinking of reflection as only an internally focused process is to think of it as occurring on a number of different levels. Drawing on the work of those sociologists associated with the Frankfurt School, Van Manen (1977) argued for three levels of reflection: (1) technical, (2) practical and (3) critical. Although he identified three levels of reflection, Van Manen (ibid.) did not position one level as necessarily being better than another, recognizing that they can occur in conjunction with one another.

According to Van Manen (1977) and Zeichner and Liston (1987), a *technical* level of reflection can occur when a coach focuses on achieving set objectives and on the effective and efficient application of knowledge. Some questions a coach could ask at this level include:

- How can I make sure all the athletes hear me?
- What resources could I utilize to improve the teaching of this task?
- Did I achieve the goals I set for this session?

- How can I fix this problem?
- What part of the training could I change so that it finishes on time?
- What is wrong with the athletes? Why do they not want to do this drill or exercise?
- How can I better structure this drill or exercise?

Alternatively, a *practical* level of reflection occurs when a coach is aware of, and analyses, the athletes as people and the assumptions that he or she and the athletes bring to the coaching environment. It also occurs when the coach acknowledges the culture of the sport, is approachable and flexible, and recognizes the practical and educational implications of an action (Van Manen 1977, 1995; Zeichner and Liston 1987, 1996). Some questions a coach could ask that illustrate a practical level of reflection include:

- What is it about the way I have structured the session that does not appear to suit the athletes?
- What other ways can I get my message across?
- What messages are being portrayed by my posture(s) and what I am wearing?
- How are my experiences of being coached influencing what I do and my expectations?
- How does my behaviour reinforce stereotypes?
- What effect does each type of feedback have on what the athletes learn?
- What am I doing as a coach to include all learning media?

Finally, a *critical* level of reflection occurs when a coach focuses on the political, moral and ethical meaning of knowledge and the domination of various forms of authority. It occurs when the coach questions the worth of knowledge, works towards justice and equality, and problematizes the context in which the activity occurs (Van Manen 1977; Zeichner and Liston 1987). Some questions a coach could ask that illustrate a critical level of reflection include:

- Whose knowledge, and whose point of view, is represented in the knowledge being (re)produced in the training session?
- What do I do if one of the athletes is only 80 per cent fit but he or she is the best on the team? Do I play him or her when the team is up against the leaders in the competition?
- What do I do about those practices that are inequitable or unjust but are part of the team or club traditions?
- Why is there a difference between the type of feedback I give to the more skilled and less skilled members of the team?

We recognize that many conscientious coaches already ask themselves these sorts of searching questions. However, as we highlight throughout this book, it is not always easy to answer them rigorously and systematically because of multiple contextual pressures and constraints.

Another way of moving away from thinking of reflection as only internally focused is by incorporating some form of collegiality into the process. It may, however, be difficult for coaches who wish to be reflective practitioners to be part of a like-minded group, given the varied aspects of the sport culture that act as constraints in this regard. Yet a like-minded group does not need to be made up of co- or assistant coaches; it could be administrators, friends, parents, academics or even coaches from rival teams and clubs (for an example of the last of these, see Cassidy *et al.* 2006a). This is illustrated by Cassidy *et al.*'s (2006b) account of an eclectic group assisting each other to enhance their understanding of the coaching process. The forum comprised a siliconCOACH (a computerized two-dimensional video analysis tool for coaches) software developer and two university lecturers (one with an interest in pedagogy and sport coaching, and the other with interests in biomechanics and motor control). In the ensuing group discussions it was evident that when the software developer reflected on his practice, he did so at technical and practical levels. At the technical level he commented that 'often the features of the software are the result of technology becoming available rather than research into what is best for the user' (Cassidy *et al.* 2006b: 286). While reflection at the practical level did not specifically inform the development of subsequent siliconCOACH software, it did nonetheless raise 'possibilities for enhancing the utilization of the software for the benefit of coaches' teaching, athletes' learning [and] skilled movement' (ibid.: 287). The process of verbally articulating an observation or judgement to the group thus generated insight and provided another perspective on the situation, thereby facilitating the reflective conversation with the situation.

One tool that can support coaches to have a reflective conversation with their situation and with colleagues is Gilbert and Trudel's (2001) reflective model. The model was grounded in empirical data gained from youth sport coaches and has six components (coaching issues, role frame, *issue setting*, *strategy generation*, *experimentation* and *evaluation*), although it is the last four of these that specifically relate to the reflective conservation (Gilbert and Trudel 2006). Furthermore, expanding on their earlier work, Gilbert and Trudel suggested that four *conditions* influence the reflective conversation. They identify these as:

> (1) access to respected and trusted peers, (2) a coach's stage of learning (coaches with more experience are less likely to consult coaching material, instead relying on creative thought and joint construction), (3) issue characteristics (for challenging dilemmas it is more likely that coaches will consult during strategy generation, experimentation and evaluation) and (e) environment, for example, the support provided by the community.
>
> (ibid.: 119–120)

Another tool that can be used to support coaches to have a reflective conversation is action research. Despite incorporating the term 'research', action research was not devised for academics; rather, it was promoted as

> a form of *collective* self-reflective enquiry undertaken by participants in social situations in order to improve the rationality and justice of their

THE COACH

own social or educational practices, as well as their understanding of these practices and the situations in which these practices are carried out.
(Kemmis and McTaggart 1992: 5; emphasis added)

The action research process is made up of four phases (planning, acting, observing and reflecting) that are constantly repeated. Its process of longitudinal study in context involves basic cycles or spirals of observation, interpretation (including the integration of theory), action and reflection. This allows for the continuous construction and testing of theoretical explanations in practice, leading to improved understanding and learning (Tsai *et al.* 2004). The *plan* must be orientated around some future action and be flexible enough to cope with unforeseen circumstances. The plan should also assist the coach to realize new potential for action. The *action* is a carefully planned, and critically informed, variation of practice and is acknowledged as a 'platform for the further development of later action' (Kemmis and McTaggart 1992: 12). Action is also considered to be dynamic, 'requiring instant decisions about what is to be done, and the exercise of practical judgement' (ibid.: 12). The role of *observation* in the action research process is to document the effects of the action and to provide data upon which to reflect in the next stage of the process. Not only is the overt action observed, but so are 'the effects of action (intended and unintended), the circumstances of and constraints on action, [and] the way circumstances and constraints limit or channel the planned action and its effects' (ibid.: 13).

Reflection is based upon the data collected and is usually fostered by discussion with others (hence the collective character of action research). In order for these discussions to take place there is a requirement that some sort of systematic data collection take place. It is possible that one reason why many practitioners do not find it easy to reflect on their practices (other than maybe at a technical level) is that they do not have reliable data upon which to reflect. While data-collection strategies that are planned in advance do have limitations, such as its not being possible to document unplanned action and only being possible to record observable action, it is nonetheless useful for the coach to be aware of such strategies. Possibly the most obvious way of recording practices for future analysis is through the use of video or audio tape. Once this has been done, the coach then has the possibility of analysing the same footage repeatedly, each time looking and listening for different things and reflecting on different levels. While video and audio tape may be ideal ways to collect data, there are less technologically advanced methods that require little more than pen and paper and an extra set of eyes (which could belong to an assistant coach, manager, injured athlete or a parent). There have been many data-gathering strategies or systematic observational instruments developed for assessing teacher effectiveness (for examples, see Siedentop and Tannehill 2000) that can be adapted and used to collect data on coaches' practices.

While there are limitations to systematic observational instruments and strategies, they are still a useful entrée into the process of collecting data on coaching practice and can still be used to help coaches to reflect. However, Brewer and Jones (2002)

have warned against the unproblematic use of such instruments, questioning their construct validity. Here, they point to the need to secure accurate data through reliable instrumentation so that the subsequent reflective process becomes an effective and relevant one. Finally, Kemmis and McTaggart (1992: 13) contend that 'Crleflection has an evaluative aspect – it asks action researchers to weigh their experience – to judge whether effects (and issues which arose) were desirable, and suggest ways of proceeding'. The four steps mentioned may well be a process that all conscientious coaches go through. However, Kemmis and McTaggart (ibid.: 10) argue that when a practitioner is informed by action research, these steps occur 'more systematically and rigorously'.

CONCLUDING THOUGHTS

We began the chapter by stating that the notion of reflection has gained considerable popularity over the past two and a half decades, thanks largely to the work of Schön (1983). This book is but one example of how that popularity has been manifest in the sports coaching community. However, it is useful to recognize that despite the rhetoric about the proposed benefits of reflection, some environments are more supportive of practitioners becoming reflective than others. Schön believed that reflection was more likely to occur in an environment that prioritizes flexibility, acknowledges that there are multiple views on issues, appreciates the complexity of issues, and is non-hierarchical. This does not sound like your typical coaching context. Combine this with George and Kirk's (1988) claim (albeit made 20 years ago) that within the sport culture there exists a degree of anti-intellectualism, and it does not augur well for coaches to become reflective practitioners. Even if the anti-intellectualism is a thing of the past, in some sports coaching communities disdain still exists for anything that has been informed by any research other than the biophysical, which continues to pose a challenge for those who propose the development of reflective coaches.

However, it is not all 'doom and gloom' for those advocating the benefits of sports coaches becoming reflective practitioners. As the sports coaching community strives to become recognized as a profession, practices will change and questions will be asked of some traditional customs and sentiments. These may well come from coaches who have graduated with tertiary qualifications in coaching science (or the equivalent) and who have had the opportunity and the time to combine theory and practice, or from coaches working in the 'swamp of practice' (Schön 1983), or from a combination of both. Time will tell, but one thing is sure: coaching practice will change. The challenge is to make sure that the change is engaged with integrity and an open mind (which just happen to be two attributes of a reflective pose).

SUGGESTED READINGS

Cassidy, T., Potrac, P. and McKenzie, A. (2006) 'Evaluating and reflecting upon a coach education initiative: The CoDe of rugby', *The Sports Psychologist*, 20(2): 145–161.

Gilbert, W. and Trudel, P. (2001) 'Learning to coach through experience: Reflection in model youth sport coaches', *Journal of Teaching in Physical Education*, 21(1): 16–34.

Gilbert, W. and Trudel, P. (2006) 'The coach as reflective practitioner', in R.L. Jones (ed.) *The Sports Coach as Educator: Re-conceptualising Sports Coaching*, London: Routledge.

Jones, R.L., Armour, K.M. and Potrac, P. (2004) *Sports Coaching Cultures: From Practice to Theory*, London: Routledge.

Moon, J. (2004) *A Handbook of Reflective and Experiential Learning: Theory and Practice*, London: Routledge.

END-OF-CHAPTER TASKS

Van Manen (1977) argues that reflection could occur on three levels. Drawing on a sporting or activity context with which you are familiar:

1   Identify the three levels, then for each provide two questions you, as a coach, could ask yourself that would be consistent with the respective level of reflection.
2   Describe how the answers could assist you to improve your coaching practice.
3   Describe some of the issues that could both constrain you and, conversely, enable you to become a reflective practitioner.

REFLECTION

CHAPTER 2

▼ ## INSTRUCTIONAL METHODS AND PEDAGOGICAL STRATEGIES

INTRODUCTION

Those who have participated in sports, as either a coach, athlete or spectator, will have witnessed and/or experienced a variety of coaching methods. For that reason, many people have some knowledge about coaching and have opinions about what constitutes successful practice. Anecdotal evidence suggests that the majority of coaches can still be broadly classified as authoritarian. What we mean by this is that many coaches position themselves, or are positioned by others, as the 'boss' or 'expert' in the context. Arguably, this has consequences for the practices that occur. If we consider it important to increase the number of people participating in sport, reduce drop-out rates, enable people to gain more enjoyment and success from playing sport, and improve sporting performance, then maybe it is time to scrutinize the methods that have been taken for granted and explore other possibilities.

Many terms have been used to describe what it is that coaches actually do. Two that are often (perhaps incorrectly) conflated or used interchangeably are 'styles' and 'methods'. A spectrum of teaching styles was designed in the mid-1960s in an attempt to create some cohesiveness around teaching behaviour (Mosston 1966). The spectrum was designed not with the intention of prescribing specific teaching practices, but as a prompt for teachers to reflect on their teaching (Mosston 1972). It was contended that the 'beauty of the spectrum lay in its ability to awaken teachers to their potential for reaching more students than is possible with a less comprehensive approach to teaching' (ibid.: 6).

Thirty years later, Kirk *et al.* (1996) synthesized the spectrum in an attempt to make it more 'user-friendly'. They did this by grouping some of the related styles together, thus reducing the number on the continuum from 11 to five and changing the terminology from styles to methods. While Kirk *et al.* (1996) do not give a reason for this change, a possible one is that styles have come to be viewed as 'a manner of self-expression peculiar to the individual' (Tinning *et al.* 1993: 118), and potentially, therefore, very subjective. Adopting the term 'method' meant that the continuum became a more rigorous analytical framework, especially when a method is defined as being 'like a set of beliefs about the way certain types of learning can best be achieved . . . as much a statement about a valued form of knowledge as about procedures for action' (ibid.: 123).

Like Mosston's (1972) spectrum, Gilbert and Trudel's (2001) model of reflective conversation was designed to induce teachers to think about their practice. The model is based on empirical data and premised on the notion that the reflective conversation begins with a coaching issue. Once the issue is set, the 'coach proceeds to *generate a strategy* through one or more options' (Gilbert and Trudel 2006: 119; emphasis in original). Strategy in this context is taken as a plan of action, while methods are the beliefs that inform the plan. Gilbert and Trudel suggest that the options available to the coach include coaching repertoire, creative thought, coaching materials, seeking advice, co-constructing ideas, and reflecting on what he or she and other coaches are doing.

The aim of this chapter is to highlight and critically discuss several ways or methods of coaching. We shall begin by introducing the historical and contemporary links that exist between education and coaching. We shall then describe the characteristics of the various methods outlined by Kirk *et al.* (1996), and then discuss the possible consequences of each method for learners. The chapter concludes with an examination of the strategy commonly known as mentoring, which is adopted both formally and informally in coaching, as an example of how the outcomes of a strategy are dependent upon underpinning methods.

THE RELATIONSHIP BETWEEN COACHING AND TEACHING

It is generally acknowledged that historically there has been a strong relationship between teaching and the coaching of games. In the United States, in the early part of the twentieth century the teaching of physical education and that of athletics merged (Figone 2001). One consequence of this merger was that those who valued the educational aspect of school physical education were marginalized compared to those who placed importance on the interscholastic athletics programme (Templin *et al.* 1994). As coaching became the preferred role for many employers (Chu 1984), it also became the preferred role for many teachers (Figone 2001). In the United Kingdom, and in Commonwealth countries such as Australia and New

Zealand, the relationship between teaching and coaching did not manifest itself the same way. Here, the team games that originated in the English public (read private) schools were introduced both to the British masses and to the colonies at the end of the nineteenth century as a way of 'civilising the bodies of the children of the working classes' (Kirk 1998: 89).

This relatively common history of teaching and coaching, albeit a different one in the United States as compared with that in the United Kingdom and Common-wealth countries, may help explain why, when Gilbert (2002) grouped 611 coaching science articles into five categories, the three most popular had a strong connection to education: behaviour, cognition and measurement. This connection was further highlighted when Gilbert organized the articles within each category. For example, under behaviour he coded articles under feedback, communication, effectiveness, and instruction, which are all topics that have been, and continue to be, discussed in the educational literature. However, despite their obvious simi-larities, a number of publications have emerged on the theme of coach–teacher differences (for examples, see Lyle 2002). It appears that there is some effort, especially by those in sports circles, to stress the differences between coaching and teaching, arguably because of the 'higher value placed on sport as opposed to education in our society' (Bergmann Drewe 2000: 79). In recent times, such a stance has been increasingly criticized, with the growing recognition and accep-tance of coaching as an educational or pedagogical enterprise (see Cassidy *et al.* 2004; Cushion *et al.* 2003; Jones 2006a, b, 2007; Jones *et al.* 2004; Penney 2006; Wikeley and Bullock 2006).

In arguing against applying the education–training dichotomy to coaching, Bergmann Drewe (2000) suggests that it would be helpful if coaches, and others, regarded what they did as teaching. Viewing it this way might mean that coaches would be in a better position to educate the whole person, since teachers are expected to develop the cognitive (thinking), affective (feeling) and psychomotor (physical) domains of the children or people with whom they work. To date, however, many coaches typically focus on the psychomotor, with some recognition given to the cognitive, while little acknowledgement is made of the affective domain. This is despite the fact that many coaches work with relatively small numbers of athletes and spend a considerable amount of time with them. Bergmann Drewe (2000) contends that reorientating coaches' focus to education could have positive results in relation to the instructional methods adopted. For example, if coaches consider coaching to be a holistic practice that develops the cognitive, affective and psychomotor domains of athletes, they are more likely to treat athletes as knowledgeable and creative beings who are able to think for themselves.

We recognize that it is not easy and perhaps not possible to convince all coaches and administrators of the benefits of being an educator. This is because, particularly in the professional arena, coaches' job security is often tied to results, while even at the lower levels the culture of control is deeply embedded. To position themselves successfully as educators, however, coaches must try (to varying degrees) to forsake the immediate for longer-term developmental goals. In doing so, they should display a willingness to invest in their charges' holistic growth, which ought eventually to pay dividends in relation to improved sporting performances, too. One way towards achieving this goal is for coaches to reflect upon and know explicitly what they are doing, why they are doing it and what the consequences are of what it is they are doing. In the following section we shall discuss the characteristics of various instructional methods and the consequences of adopting each.

AN OVERVIEW OF METHODS

A spectrum of teaching styles (read methods) was designed in the mid-1960s in an attempt to create some cohesiveness around teaching behaviour (Mosston 1966). As was stated earlier, the spectrum was not designed with the intention of prescribing specific practices, rather as a prompt for teachers to reflect on their teaching (Mosston 1972). What follows is an overview of Mosston's methods as adapted by Kirk *et al.* (1996). Our rationale for providing this overview is that some readers may not be familiar with this range of methods and how they could be used in a sports coaching context. If coaches are not familiar with the scope and characteristics of the methods, it may be difficult for them to question current practice and make choices about the appropriateness of future action. It is important to remember that the characteristics associated with a particular method are not necessarily exclusive to that method, as, since the methods are positioned on a continuum, it is likely that those positioned next to each other will share some of the same characteristics. Kirk *et al* (ibid.) grouped their interpretations of Mosston's styles under the categorizations of direct, task, reciprocal, guided discovery and problem-solving methods. Each will now be discussed in turn.

The characteristics of the *direct* method involve the coach in:

- providing the information and direction to the group or individual;
- controlling the flow of information;
- privileging the demonstration (it can be given by the coach or the athlete, or be on video) (Kirk *et al.* 1996);
- giving little recognition to the diverse needs of the athletes;
- behaving in ways that can be categorized as managerial and organizational;
- setting goals that are specific and criterion based.

A coach adopting a direct method is a very common sight. When this method is used, the coach is positioned, or positions her- or himself, as the knowledgeable one. An example of this in a basketball context is where a coach wants to teach players how to dribble the basketball. After identifying five key elements of dribbling and demonstrating the skill, the coach outlines a drill that requires the players to practise dribbling in various poses, changing their pose on the sound of the whistle.

The characteristics of the *task* method include many of those of the direct method but also involve the coach in:

- designing the learning environment so that it has several different tasks (e.g. stations/circuits);
- designing the tasks so that each supports the objective of the session (e.g. effectively and efficiently passing the basketball);
- designing the session so that the tasks are performed simultaneously, not sequentially (i.e. small groups of athletes move through different stations after a pre-designated time period or when they have completed the task);
- organizing the content of the stations so that they are slightly shifted towards recognizing the needs of the athletes;
- designing the sessions so that the players can, at times, work independently from the coach (Kirk *et al.* 1996).

This method could be adopted in a soccer context where the aim is to improve the players' ball dexterity. To achieve this, the coach organizes the session so that there are a number of stations positioned around the field. The instructions at each station require the players to perform a different task. While the tasks are different (e.g. dribbling around cones, juggling the ball), they all reflect the aim of the session (i.e. to improve the players' ball dexterity). The players have five minutes at each station before they change (on the coach's command) to work at another station. When they are at the stations the players work by themselves or with team-mates, while the coach wanders around providing specific feedback or answering questions.

The characteristics of the *reciprocal* method reflect some of those evident in the previous two in that the coach is still responsible for selecting and sequencing the content. However, where the reciprocal method differs is that the coach now:

- requires the athletes to work with each other;
- designs the content of the session to suit the athletes' abilities and needs;
- matches the peers so that, ideally, one is more skilled and knowledgeable than the other;
- requires an athlete's peer to become responsible for demonstration and feedback;
- encourages athletes to develop feedback and social skills (Kirk *et al.* 1996).

Many semi-professional or professional teams have squads that are made up of the 'first-string' and the 'off-the-bench' players. This type of arrangement enables a coach to easily adopt a reciprocal approach to coaching. For example, a rugby union coach who wants to improve the ability of his players to throw the ball into the line-out could use the two hookers (the players who throw the ball into the field of play) to work together with the locks (generally those who catch the ball). While it could be expected that the more experienced players would provide the majority of the feedback, each athlete could take turns to provide performance-related feedback, as well as develop new, or adapt existing, throwing options to suit their respective strengths. The relationship between the less and the more experienced athlete is not one-way; rather, it can be viewed as reciprocal, hence the name of the method. Often, in the process of teaching or answering questions posed by the less experienced, the more experienced member in the relationship also learns (Royal Tangaere 1997). The reciprocal method reflects the New Zealand Mäori *tuakana–teina* view of learning, with *tuakana* meaning 'older sibling (brother to a boy or sister to a girl)' and *teina* a 'younger sibling (brother to a boy or sister to a girl)' (ibid.: 50). Since the *tuakana–teina* concept is related to both teaching and learning, 'it is an acceptable practice for the learner [read athlete] to shift roles and become the teacher [read coach] or for the teacher to become the learner' (ibid.: 50).

One way of incorporating the *tuakana–teina* concept into coaching is to encourage the more knowledgeable (although not necessarily the more senior) athlete to become the *tuakana* on, as well as off, the field to the less knowledgeable (*teina*). For example, when Daniel Carter (the incumbent New Zealand All Black fly-half) was 21 years old, he was interviewed about his meteoric rise. In the interview he talked about the way Andrew Mehrtens (a former Canterbury Crusaders and All Black fly-half) had assisted him in training sessions by being his partner in drills and providing him with insights into the game (TV3 2003). It was unclear whether the coach had formally mandated the *tuakana–teina* relationship or whether the athletes had arranged it themselves. Either way, from the perspective of the *teina* it was a useful arrangement.

In *Quality Teaching for Diverse Students in Schooling: Best Evidence Synthesis*, Alton-Lee (2003) reported that when 'cultural norms' such as *tuakana–teina* are integrated into learning contexts, not only are students' cultural and social development supported, but so too are their achievements. Furthermore, such practices as integrating cultural norms were recognized as important principles in developing a learning community 'whatever the cultural and language heritage of the learners' (ibid.: 30). Adopting *tuakana–teina* practices into the coaching environment also supports the claim made by Philips, McNaughton and MacDonald, albeit in the educational context, that 'there needs to be a closer matching between the cultural contexts of home and school' (in Alton-Lee 2003: 35). Such matching makes the athlete more comfortable and secure in the coaching context; perhaps more willing to try creative solutions to sporting dilemmas. Finally, incorporating *tuakana–teina* practice into coaching makes sense not only in terms of athletes' social and cultural development, but also, potentially, pedagogically. This was documented by Alton-Lee (ibid.: 35), who drew on international evidence to demonstrate the compatibility of *tuakana–teina* to the reciprocal method, with the latter, when used, showing 'a marked positive impact on higher student achievement'.

The following discussion focuses on the two next methods on Mosston's (1966) continuum (as adapted by Kirk *et al.* (1996)); guided discovery and problem solving. These methods have a strong relationship with learner-centred practices, which is reflected in their respective characteristics. The characteristics of the *guided discovery* method include the coach:

■ incorporating activities that require the athletes to become more independent of the coach;

- requiring the athletes to move through a series of tasks, in response to a number of questions, with the goal of discovering a *predetermined* solution (Kirk *et al.* 1996; emphasis added).

A guided discovery method can be seen in tennis when a player comes to the side of the court having completed the first set. At this point, the coach, who wants to improve the percentage of winning shots, asks the player some specific open-ended questions, for example 'What action could you take if your opponent lobbed the return to the middle of the court? Why?' or 'Can you tell me where you would place the ball if your opponent was standing on the baseline covering her backhand? Why?' or 'What happens when your opponent returns the ball to your backhand? How can you make the situation better?' (Thorpe 1997). While the coach knows the answer to each question (that is, there is a predetermined end), she or he encourages a response from the player, believing that the process of answering the questions will enhance the latter's understanding of the situation.

The coach's ability to ask meaningful and probing questions with the aim of extending players' knowledge often determines the success, or otherwise, of the guided discovery method. While many coaches do ask questions, the queries are often rhetorical (e.g. 'What do you think you are doing?'), or closed questions that only require a 'yes' or 'no' response. If coaches want to develop athletes who can make decisions and adapt to changing situations as they occur (Kidman 2001), then it is desirable to challenge athletes' cognitive capacities. Sanders (1966) adapted Bloom's taxonomy of Educational Objectives to devise a classification of cognitive level questions. It was Sanders' taxonomy that Butler (1997) drew on when investigating the questioning practices of coaches. In her study, Butler (1997) compared the questions coaches asked when adopting guided-discovery-type methods with those when adopting a direct method. She found those coaches adopting a guided discovery method asked not only more but also a wider range of questions. These ranged from memory-level questions that involved little cognitive involvement ('Why is this position called the triple threat?') to analytical and synthesis-level questions that required considerable cognitive involvement ('How could you increase your chances of scoring from a penalty corner?').

When coaches ask questions of their athletes, they may want to consider not only what levels of questions they ask, but also what the athletes' instructional and learning preferences are, since each learner has ideal ways of receiving and inter- preting information. There are numerous ways of ascertaining the instructional and learning preferences of an individual. Fleming and Bonwell (2001) developed a questionnaire to do just that (see VARK questionnaire n.d.). While acknowledging that we are generally influenced by five senses, Fleming and Bonwell (ibid.) chose to focus on three: hearing (aural), touching (kinesthetic) and seeing (visual). They named their way of viewing instructional and learning preferences VARK, an acronym for Visual, Aural, Read/Write and Kinesthetic. Typically, asking questions privileges those learners who prefer to learn through an aural medium. So, how can coaches ask in ways that support those athletes who have other learning preferences? One way is to ask questions with cue words that direct the learner to use their preferred media; for example:

- Visual: *Watch* the demonstration and then tell me what are the three phases of the kick.
- Aural: *Listen* to the sound of the skis on the snow when you turn. Why does the sound differ when you turn left?
- Read/Write: On the basis of your *reading* of these data, what could you do differently?
- Kinesthetic: What did your knees *feel* like when you carved that turn?

The important message here is that if questioning is going to be a meaningful and useful learning tool, it cannot be left to chance; rather, it has to be explicitly designed for the specific learner and desired outcome.

The characteristics of the *problem-solving* method are similar to those of guided discovery except that they include the coach in:

- establishing the problem, which may come from a situation the team or athlete has experienced;
- accepting that outcomes may be more varied;
- accepting that there is not necessarily one 'right' solution to the problem, although recognizing that some solutions are better than others;
- encouraging athletes to be responsible for the process of finding solutions;
- enabling work to be individualized or performed in groups;
- recognizing athletes' background knowledge and preferred pace of learning, and the medium through which they prefer to learn;
- recognizing that problem solving demands tasks that require more cognitive engagement (Kirk *et al.* 1996);
- having a 'debrief' at the end of the problem-solving scenario so that athletes can review what has been learned.

Adopting a problem-solving method does not mean that the coach abdicates all responsibility to the athletes. On the contrary, setting up appropriate real-life problem-solving scenarios, and expertly debriefing the scenarios at the completion of the exercise, requires knowledge of the content and context as well as considerable communication and interpersonal skills. In reviewing the literature, Alton-Lee (2003: 63) found that while pair, individual or group problem solving can provide students with 'the opportunity to scaffold their own learning through preparing, reflecting on, and/or practising a task before risking public participation', it is the whole-group discussion following this work that improves learners' achievements. Another factor identified as being influential in progressing students' long-term learning was the 'peer interactions during the negotiation and organization of group tasks' (ibid.: 64). Disagreements often occurred during the interactions. This, however, was viewed as a positive development that powerfully impacted on student cognition, not least because it provided a context for students to develop means to resolve conflict (ibid.).

A coach can adopt a problem-solving method when he or she wants the athletes to apply their understanding to a game-like scenario. For example, a netball coach may design a scenario along the following lines: the defensive players in the team are required to replicate the defensive pattern of the forthcoming opposition. The attacking team have the centre pass off and are told that the score is tied with 15 seconds left on the clock until the final whistle. The problem to be solved is: develop three options of breaking the defence and scoring a goal within 15 seconds. The coach tells the team that they have ten minutes to come up with some solutions. At the end of ten minutes the coach brings the group back together and proceeds to debrief. Here, the coach asks the team questions about what happened, what worked and what didn't, and what options they could try in the forthcoming match. Failure to conduct a debrief can really compromise the integrity of the method, as without it the approach can be perceived as supporting a *laissez-faire*, or anything goes, reactive strategy.

TAKING A CIRCUMSPECT VIEW OF METHODS

Choosing what method(s) to adopt is not like selecting a recipe

Coaches' choices of the working methods and practices they adopt are influenced by many factors. These include their apprenticeship and socialization, their skills and preferences, the content being taught, the context in which the coaching is occurring and their 'set of beliefs' (Tinning *et al*. 1993: 123). Often, coaches adopt particular methods they have experienced as a player or as a consequence of observing other coaches. This may work well if the model observed is a high-quality coach, but often that is not the case. The result is that undesirable coaching practices continue to be reproduced. Conversely, personal preference in terms of coaching method is important, as, in agreement with Siedentop and Tannehill (2000), we believe that practitioners need to believe in what they are doing. Consequently, although Jones *et al*. (2004) commented on how coaches often play roles for their athletes, this was not done insincerely; that is, the person coaching was not far divorced from the performance given. In this respect, many of the coaches interviewed by Jones *et al*. (ibid.) emphasized the importance of being 'true to yourself' as a coach and thus adopting appropriate strategies. This of course relates to a coach's personal philosophy of purpose and is explored in more depth in Chapter 4, 'Developing a coaching philosophy'.

The type of content being taught could also dictate what coaching method(s) to use. For example, it may not be appropriate to adopt a guided discovery or problem-solving method when teaching a complex and potentially dangerous dive to a novice. Similarly, a coach will more than likely use different method(s) when encouraging experienced athletes to develop a team-game defensive strategy for particular opponents as compared with when teaching the game to novices. The context in which the practice session occurs may also influence what method is adopted. For example, a tennis coach who is responsible for a large group of players over many courts may be more inclined to choose between task, reciprocal or problem-solving methods rather than a direct method because he or she may consider it a waste of time to bring the players back together each time a new shot has to be explained and demonstrated.

A coach's belief about decision making can also determine what methods are adopted in the training session. To firm up his or her thoughts about such an issue, a coach could ask self-questions such as 'Who makes the decisions in pre-training, during the training, and after the training?' 'How are they made?' 'In what circumstances are they made?' and 'For what purpose are they made?' If a coach believes that it is her or his role to dominate the decision-making process, then it is likely that that coach will adopt a direct method, which tends to reproduce existing knowledge, viewing athletes as passive learners. If, on the other hand, a coach believes it is possible to share the decision-making process with the athletes, then he or she may adopt a guided discovery method that can invite the production of new knowledge, with the athletes being seen as knowledgeable decision makers (Mosston 1992).

Although we have presented some of the methods here in isolation, almost as discrete options, we consider it unwise for coaches to view their selection as being synonymous with that of a fragmented recipe. Doing so reduces the opportunities for coaches to ask important questions of their practice, namely:

■   Who is being advantaged and disadvantaged by adopting a particular coaching method?
■   What are the consequences of adopting a particular coaching method?

When coaches ask themselves these and similar questions, they begin to reflect on their own coaching practice and how the given methods can best inform and develop it. Consequently, if a coach is interested in creating the best learning experiences for his or her athletes, then the methods 'must be exposed and open to scrutiny and challenge' (Tinning et al. 1993: 124). They are there to contextually think with, to mix up as the situation demands, not to unproblematically implement. One way of opening up the methods to scrutiny and challenge is to consider the hidden meanings or implicit learnings associated with them (we shall discuss the hidden curriculum in more detail in Chapter 9). Considering these possible hidden meanings within the methods is one way of answering the first question posed above, even if doing so raises more questions. For example, consider a situation where a coach who predominantly adopts a direct method asks the most skilful athlete in the team to demonstrate a desired skill. After the team has spent some time practising it, the coach then asks the other athletes to display their attempts to the whole group. What meanings could the athletes infer from this practice? What do the athletes learn when they listen to the explanation of the task? What do the athletes learn when the most skilful is picked to perform the demonstration? What do the athletes learn when they are asked to perform the skill in front of their peers? It is possible that what the athletes learn is that there is only one way to perform the skill; or that they are not particularly skilful at the task. Additionally, they could learn that it is somewhat embarrassing to perform the task, out of context, in front of their peers. In the following section we provide a more specific response to the question 'what are the consequences of adopting a particular coaching method?'

Consequences of the various methods for coaching practice

If we accept that methods are as much about 'valued forms of knowledge' as they are 'procedures for action' (Tinning *et al*. 1993: 123), then we need to be aware of the consequences associated with each method. There are numerous consequences of coaches adopting a *direct* method, five of which we identify here. First, athletes do not gain an understanding of the nuances of the game or activity, as they are not engaged as active learners but are expected to memorize and regurgitate information provided to them by the coach (Kidman 2001). Second, little new knowledge is produced since the coach controls the information flow. Third, young people may choose to leave sport because they are unable to have input into what and how they learn. Many expect to be able to provide input because of the learner-centred teaching philosophies and practices adopted in schools (Cassidy 2007a). Fourth, young people's problem-solving and creative ability will not be encouraged if they are exposed only to the direct method. Fifth, adopting the direct method in schools often has consequences for social relations within the group. Specifically,

> [w]hen single-task large group formats prevail, fixed academic hierarchies form influencing friendship patterns and academic status shaped by the teacher's public evaluations. Students become more competitive and less inclined to help, or associate with many other class members.
> (Bossert, in Alton-Lee 2003: 27)

We contend that similar consequences could occur in relation to physical hierarchies and status when the direct method alone is adopted in a coaching context. Nevertheless, coaches often adopt the direct method when they are teaching young and/or inexperienced athletes. The rationale for doing so is that those athletes do not have the knowledge or skills to play the game. This justification, however, is potentially flawed since much of the learning that occurs prior to starting school or to joining sports clubs occurs not via a direct method but through guided discovery and problem-solving.

Many of the consequences of a *task* method relate to the coach beginning to recognize that athletes are capable, to some degree, of self-management. Hence, opportunities arise for athletes to work away from the coach's direct gaze. This freedom, albeit rather limited, allows athletes to address their own needs, thereby potentially developing new understandings or knowledge. However, because the coach determines the content of the stations where the players work, the practices and hence the outcomes are still to a large extent coach driven. In terms of influencing the social make-up of the group, Bossert (in Alton-Lee 2003) claimed that the task approach, through engaging different students' strengths at different times, made friendship patterns and peer status more cooperative and fluid.

The consequences of adopting a *reciprocal* method relate even more to developing the social aspect of team dynamics. Having athletes work together and provide feedback to each other can improve their physical skills as well as their social and cognitive abilities. This is because in order to provide meaningful feedback to their peers, they have to carefully consider and develop movement analysis skills as well as communication skills. Since the coach sets the content of the session, adopting a reciprocal method can continue to reproduce existing knowledge, although, as a result of the interaction between the athletes, it is possible that new knowledge can be produced. Developing cognitive and social abilities is also a goal when adopting a *tuakana–teina* approach. Yet research conducted by Hohepa *et al*. (1996) questioned whether cooperative learning is ethnically preferable for Mäori students and raised the possibility of 'ethnic stereotyping'.

A potential consequence of adopting a *guided discovery* method is the development of the cognitive abilities of athletes. One strategy for developing cognitive abilities is for the coach to ask the athletes questions in an effort to arrive at a predetermined solution. This provides the athletes with an opportunity to answer the questions in ways that are unique to them, thus generating new and contextual knowledge. However, the practice of questioning is not so straightforward. For instance, because the coach asks the athletes questions about what they think is happening, and what could happen, the coach does not establish him- or herself as the 'expert'. A possible consequence of this is that some athletes, especially those who have been successful under a more orthodox approach to coaching, may question the coach's ability. Care must therefore be taken to explain the rationale behind the approach and its intended benefits.

Another issue that arises around the practice of asking questions relates to the level at which questions are asked. In synthesizing the literature, Alton-Lee (2003: 84) observed that findings highlighted 'the importance of scaffolding questioning to support and generate higher order thinking'. Here, it was interestingly concluded that

> [l]ow level and factual questions often provide better scaffolds for students to achieve higher order thinking than higher order or open questions. Higher order or open questions can confuse students, particularly students who do not bring the cultural capital of the school to their activities, and leave them without the metacognitive tools or information about question genre to achieve [the dominant culture's view of] sustained thoughtfulness.
>
> (ibid.: 84)

The importance of recognizing the cultural capital of the learners when deciding whether to adopt a questioning approach was reflected in a longitudinal ethnographic study by Jones (1991). Adopting the role of participant observer, she accompanied a class of 19 Pasifika girls whose parents had emigrated to New Zealand from five different Pacific Islands through junior secondary school. Jones contrasted the experiences of these girls with those of a class of middle-class Päkehä girls. (Päkehä is a term used to describe non-Maori New Zealanders, usually of European descent.) She found that there was a mismatch between the Pasifika girls' understanding of what constituted appropriate behaviour in school and the 'cultural requirements for success in schooling . . . this led them [i.e. the Pasifika girls] to refrain from asking questions, and to discourage teachers from asking them questions demanding interpretation' (Alton-Lee 2003: 36).

This aversion to the questioning approach has also been documented in a coaching context. When Wrathall (in Thompson *et al.* 2000) interviewed elite female Mäori athletes about their experiences of and their views on the sporting system in New Zealand a number of issues arose, one of which was 'communication and use of language'. From the data, it was clear that '[c]ommunication between the administrators and athletes brought out cultural differences in language' (Thompson *et al.* 2000: 247). For example, the athletes believed that 'Pakehas are very forward and are taught to question. It's all right for them to do it, while Mäori kids are ignored and tend to drop back and ask no questions even when they don't understand' (ibid.: 247).

And:

> I answered a question once; never again. They just looked at me like 'what planet are you on?' Now I just sit back with a blank expression on my face . . . you know, like don't ask me a question. It's far easier.
>
> (ibid.: 248)

Yet a study conducted by Alton-Lee and colleagues raised 'the question about the inappropriateness of failing to engage and challenge Mäori students because of a presumed sensitivity to a child's experience of being whakamä (experiencing shame and abasement – in this case, through being publicly selected to speak)' (in Alton-Lee 2003: 27). Raising this issue is worthy of consideration because generalizing about how all Mäori will react when asked to speak in public possibly reflects what Hohepa *et al.* (1996) described as 'ethnic stereotyping'. To limit the possibility of such stereotyping, it is important for coaches to acknowledge the desires and hopes as well as the motivations and fears of the people with whom they are working both as a group and individually.

The consequences of adopting the *problem-solving* method are similar to those associated with guided discovery, since they both have the goal of developing the cognitive abilities of athletes. Here again, then, care and consideration must be given to the type and tone of the guidance, which could well result in the ability of the coach being questioned, especially if he or she sets irrelevant problems and accepts all solutions.

ONE PEDAGOGICAL STRATEGY IN ACTION; WHY THE DIFFERENT OUTCOME?

In this section we discuss how the strategy of mentoring can be informed by different methods and consequently produce different outcomes. Many in the coaching community agree on the value of mentoring, yet there appears to be lack of a clear conceptual definition (Bloom *et al*. 1998). According to Alleman *et al*. (1984: 329), mentoring refers to a 'relationship in which a person of greater rank, experience or expertise teaches, guides and develops a novice in a profession'. Similarly, Merriam (1983) defines a mentor as a supporter, counsel and guide to a protégé, while for Fletcher (2000), mentoring is synonymous with guiding and supporting a trainee through difficult transitions. Recent research has indicated that while mentoring is already very much in operation within coaching, it is so without much success, arguably because in its current unstructured and uncritical form it only serves to reproduce the existing coaching culture and practice (Cushion 2001). To gain some insight into why this is the case it may be worthwhile to examine the methods that inform the practices of coaching mentors.

One of the common themes that come through the various definitions of mentoring is 'guidance'. We suggest that guidance is reflected in a concept of scaffolding, a notion that is increasingly used in the sports coaching literature (for examples, see Potrac and Cassidy 2006; Wikeley and Bullock 2006). Scaffolding is a metaphor used to describe the role of a more knowledgeable and capable individual in assisting and guiding the development and learning of another (Vialle *et al*. 2005). According to Vialle *et al*. (2005: 68), although the term 'scaffolding' is often attributed to Lev Vygotsky, it was first introduced by 'Wood, Bruner and Ross (1976) in an attempt to operationalise . . . [Vygotsky's] concept of teaching in the zone of proximal development'. As a consequence, scaffolding has often been viewed as a process that occurs only in learner-centred pedagogies that use methods such as guided discovery and problem solving. We, however, challenge this and argue that a coach using a direct method could equally scaffold an athlete's learning. How this can be done becomes clear if scaffolding is viewed as

> a changing quality of support over a teaching session, in which a more skilled partner adjusts the assistance he or she provides to fit the child's [read athletes'] current level of performance. More support is offered when a task is new; less is provided as the child's [athletes'] competence increases, therefore fostering the child's [athletes'] autonomy and independent mastery.
>
> (Vialle *et al*. 2005: 68)

The support could come from a skilled 'other' using a direct, reciprocal or guided discovery method, depending on the desired outcome. But as Vialle and her colleagues (2005: 68) correctly point out, '[o]bviously, not any kind of adult support can be regarded as scaffolding'. They suggest that in order for a teaching and learning practice to qualify as scaffolding, it needs to satisfy three criteria:

- It must enable the learner to complete a task he or she would not have been able to complete alone.
- It must have the learner reach a state of competence that will eventually enable them to complete the task alone.
- There needs to be evidence that the learner has achieved a higher level of competence as a consequence of having been scaffolded.

A possible explanation for Cushion's (2001) claim that much current mentoring in coaching appears only to reproduce existing practice could be related to the methods that inform the mentoring strategies used. If mentoring practices reflect the direct method, then it is possible that it will consist of little more than merely passing on 'survival tips' or 'the tricks of the trade'. Similarly, it could also be a reason why the personal knowledge and experience of the mentored are ignored rather than elevated or built upon (Snow 2001). Alternatively, for many the promise of mentoring lies in 'its capacity to foster an inquiring stance' (Field and Field 1994: 67), which in turn has the potential to inform insightful learning. Furthermore, quality mentoring involves doing something *with* as opposed *to* a trainee; it is seen as an investment in the total personal growth of the individual. If these are the desired outcomes, then when mentoring programmes are established it would be advisable for the mentors to be encouraged and supported to primarily adopt learner-centred practices that reflect reciprocal and guided discovery methods. Indeed, this was supported in a recent review of mentoring literature by Jones *et al.* (in press). In drawing on sources from management, nursing and business in addition to sports coaching, they concluded that good-practice mentoring consisted of a number of elements. These included those related to focusing on and identifying the needs of the person being mentored at the beginning of the relationship (Eby and Lockwood 2005), ensuring flexibility in the mentoring programme and thus accommodating the full range of possible mentoring relationships and methods (Busen and Engebretson 1999). Also, that the mentoring process should be a facilitative, nurturing one, not allowing mentors to dominate and produce cloned copies of themselves (Cushion *et al.* 2003; Layton 2005). Hence, it is plain that the adoption of a specific strategy is not enough to change practice, as the effectiveness of a strategy is dependent on the methods that inform it.

CONCLUDING THOUGHTS

We are well aware that there are plenty of reasons why some coaches find it difficult to embrace a variety of methods, and that coaches may not necessarily adopt a new method of coaching based on a convincing rational argument. This reluctance to change may be due, in part, to the culture associated with the sport or activity. It is possible that coaches may be reluctant to challenge taken-for-granted practices of a sporting culture, especially if they have been a successful participant in that culture. Even if coaches are prepared to challenge some of these practices, maybe as a consequence of enrolling in tertiary study or professional development or some eureka-type experience, it is possible that the athletes they are coaching or the administrators of the sport may not wish to change time-honoured traditions and customs. To overcome such barriers, coaches may have to 'prove' themselves to be adept at using the more orthodox methods associated with the culture of the sport or activity. By working adeptly within the orthodoxy, coaches may gain the necessary credibility to experiment with so-called alternative methods.

Gaining this credibility and capital may take some time. Even when coaches feel that the athletes and administrators are open to some innovation in relation to methods, it is still wise to tread slowly and carefully, as the latter two groups have been socialized into what it means to be a coach, and therefore have certain expectations. If these expectations are challenged 'overnight', it is possible that coaches could experience a degree of resistance. After all, as Tinning (1994: 17) emphasized, competition between different interest groups is not just philosophic jousting; 'it relates to people's careers, to department resources and growth, and to political affiliations'. With this in mind, it may also be useful for coaches to explain why they do what they do. It is also good practice to introduce the new method slowly, to allow athletes and administrators the opportunity to become used to the different practices and obligations placed upon them, and to feel comfortable about having different expectations of the coach.

SUGGESTED READINGS

Butler, J. (1997) 'How would Socrates teach games? A constructivist approach', *JOPERD*, 68(9): 42–47.

Jones, R.L. (ed.) (2006a) *The Sports Coach as Educator: Re-conceptualising Sports Coaching*, London: Routledge.

Kidman, L. (2001) *Developing Decision Makers: An Empowerment Approach to Coaching*, Christchurch, NZ: Innovative Press.

Thompson, S., Rewi, P., and Wrathall, D. (2000) 'Mäori experiences in sport and physical authority: Research and initiatives', in C. Collins (ed.) *Sport in New Zealand Society*, Palmerston North, NZ: Dunmore Press.

Tinning, R., Kirk, D. and Evans, J. (1993) *Learning to Teach Physical Education*, London: Prentice-Hall.

END-OF-CHAPTER TASKS

To complete the following tasks you are required to select at least one coach to observe. To make the tasks more meaningful, it would be useful if the coach were involved in a sport or activity in which you are interested. Preferably the coach will be working with more than one athlete. Prior to observing the coach you MUST ask their permission to do so. Once permission is given, ask the coach to describe the aim of the session.

1   Describe the methods that the coach adopted in the session. Provide examples and discuss the consequences for the athletes of adopting these methods.
2   Describe how you would design the session so as to achieve the same aim but using at least two methods that are different from that used by the observed coach. Provide examples and discuss the consequences for the athletes of using these methods.

CHAPTER 3

▼ **QUALITY IN COACHING**

INTRODUCTION

During the course of a season, various people make judgements of a coach. Athletes, parents, club members, employers, sponsors, owners of the club and supporters evaluate the quality of the coach on the basis of issues such as enjoyment, safety, win/loss record, and cost. These judgements influence people's perception as to whether or not the coach is good and/or effective. Contrary to popular practice, we believe using the terms 'good' and 'effective' interchangeably is counter-productive since each is based on quite different assumptions. In the past few decades the notion of effectiveness has become prevalent in coaching literature and rhetoric. The reason Lyle (2002) gave for this is that many coaches are pragmatists. However, pragmatism can be used as an excuse for maintaining the status quo, or at least a focus on technical and practical issues. As we shall illustrate in this chapter, the notion of the effective coach is increasingly being challenged, not only in the literature (see Lyle 2002) but also by some successful (performance-orientated) coaches (see Jones *et al.* 2004).

The aim of this chapter is to examine the term 'quality' within the context of sports coaching, the various ways it has been conceptualized and how it is currently being evaluated. Before we begin in earnest, however, we believe it is useful to discuss how the concepts of 'good' and 'effective' have previously been, and continue to be, used to judge the performances of coaches.

A GOOD COACH

More often than not, when someone inquires about a coach, one of the first questions is framed along the lines of 'Is she or he a good coach?' When 200 undergraduate students were asked to compile a list of characteristics that described a good coach they came up with a comprehensive inventory that included the following:

Patient	Flexible
Experienced	Organized
A good communicator	Not just a dictator
Knowledgeable about skills	Open-minded
Motivator	Has the ability to teach
Has a sense of humour	Punctual
A people manager	Has a loud voice
Adventurous	Uses time wisely

In compiling the list it became apparent that the students had a 'common-sense' understanding of what the term 'good' meant in this context. Their understanding reflected a dictionary definition, namely, having 'admirable, pleasing, superior or positive qualities' (Collins 1992: 549). It is not only undergraduate students who have such an understanding of, and interest in, what makes a 'good' coach, as evidenced by the large number of high-profile elite coach biographies and autobiographies that are purchased by the public at large every year. These biographies are popular not because they provide a detailed outline of the coaching sessions but because they tell a more subjective story of top-level coaching, with descriptions of what happened inside the changing rooms and away from the gymnasium or field.

This popular, or lay, notion of the 'good' coach is tied to coaching images of benevolent yet dictatorial, charismatic leadership. Judging coaches by such criteria, however, has never been part of formal coach evaluation. Since the 1970s there has been a push towards coaches becoming accountable not only to the athletes, and the families of athletes, but increasingly to a board of directors and sponsors. This development has been 'consistent with the adoption of corporate management models . . . and the prevailing climate of outcomes-driven economic rationalism' (Ingvarson and Rowe 2007: 1). These models and climate have raised issues such as accountability, standards, assessment, quality and effectiveness to an extent that such notions are now commonplace in the coaching context, as indeed is illustrated by the focus of some of this chapter. However, far from giving increasing credence to a rationalistic discourse, the ideas relating to effectiveness and quality discussed here are put forward from a socially realistic position giving weight to dynamic cultural and pedagogical processes in their workings.

AN EFFECTIVE COACH

In many cases, coaches are judged on easily objectified traits and actions rather than less easily measurable subjective characteristics. Although the general push

for effectiveness has been prevalent since the 1970s, there has been a focus, albeit limited, on effectiveness in the coaching literature as far back as the 1950s, when Friedrichsen (1956) studied the effectiveness of loop films as instructional aids in coaching gymnastics. Since then, grids have been developed to increase the effectiveness of coaching games (Bean 1976), coaching effectiveness programmes have been designed (Bump 1987), and guides written that have focused on helping coaches to know 'how to' teach sport skills effectively (Christina and Corcos 1988). In an effort to provide some conceptual clarity regarding coaching effectiveness and the effective coach, Lyle (2002) undertook a review of the written work that focused on these notions. One of the observations he made was that educational literature had influenced the research into coaching effectiveness and effective coaching. This was due in part to the development, and use, of systematic observational tools such as the Academic Learning Time-Physical Education (ALT-PE) instrument (Metzler 1979, 1989), which in the 1980s became a popular measure of teacher effectiveness. This had a strong influence on coaching literature, owing to its subsequent use of 'North American high-school and collegiate coaching samples, the borrowing of hypotheses from educational practice and a focus on the direct intervention role' (Lyle 2002: 261). One consequence of Lyle's review was that a valiant attempt was made to answer the question: are effective coaching and the effective coach the same concept? While he did not come up with a specific answer, Lyle (ibid.: 259) did recognize that the 'apparent certainty' that some have in relation to this issue 'continues to mask some important questions'. He went on to suggest that because of the lack of clarity that surrounds the terms 'coaching effectiveness' and 'effective coaching', it is necessary to consider alternative ways of judging coaching and coaches. While he identified and discussed a number of approaches such as process competence, value adding and data-led goal setting, we consider the notion of quality to be a particularly useful framework for doing so.

WHY QUALITY?

According to Ingvarson and Rowe (2007), the social, economic and technological changes that are occurring in many countries are requiring an increasingly skilled workforce. One consequence of this is that the delivery of high-quality education, particularly high-quality teaching, has become an imperative. The coaching community is not immune to these global changes, and the development of high-quality coaching has come to be viewed as important, too. This is evidenced by the growth in the number of coach education and development programmes administered by government agencies, sports bodies and the tertiary sector. Yet despite recognition of the need to produce quality teachers within education, there has been very little research focused on 'what teachers *should know* [subject matter content knowledge] and *be able to do*' [pedagogical content and procedural knowledge] (Ingvarson and Rowe 2007: 2; emphasis in original). We contend that the situation is even more dire in coaching.

Despite the limitations associated with the lack of research on what constitutes quality coaching and a quality coach, we have pragmatic and philosophical reasons for believing that a focus on quality coaching is preferable to a focus on effective coaching or the effective coach. Pragmatically, quality coaching can be considered to be amenable to a holistic approach to coaching. Adopting a holistic perspective enables the coach to consider the athlete as a human being, not just as a mechanical body or a commodity to do with as he or she pleases. If the athletes feel valued, then they are more likely to want to train hard and play well for the coach. The following two quotations from Graham Taylor (an ex-England soccer coach) and Bob Dwyer (an ex-Australian rugby union coach), respectively, highlight the way these coaches valued the intrinsic as well as the instrumental characteristics of coaching. (These characteristics will be discussed later in this chapter.)

> Unless people are willing to listen to you, unless you are prepared to listen to them and understand them as people, the best coaching book in the world isn't going to help you. It all comes back to the relationships that you have with your players and the trust that exists between you. That's just life.
>
> (Jones *et al*. 2004: 28)

> The total environment is essential, and the total environment is affected by as much what you do off the pitch as what you do on it. It's about developing a sense of confidence, self-worth, and well-being in the players, which can have a real effect on their performances.
>
> (Jones *et al*. 2004: 107–108)

Another pragmatic reason for focusing on quality in coaching is that the term is already associated with judgement, for example in quality management and quality control. Adopting it in a coaching context gives legitimacy that a considerably more vague notion such as 'good' cannot provide. Additionally, on a more philosophical point, Tinning *et al*. (2001: 303) remind us that the notion of 'quality' is not the 'end point but a process'; and what is more, it is a 'reflective process'. This means that when we focus on quality, two questions are placed in the foreground:

- What are the consequences of *what* I coach?
- What are the consequences of *how* I coach?

Furthermore, Tinning *et al*. (2001: 304) argued that a focus on quality requires practitioners to explore ways in which their practice can be made 'more meaningful, purposeful, just and enjoyable', thus helping them make a conscious effort to search for contradictions in their practice. Discovering the difference between what coaches think they are doing and what they are actually doing – in other words, between hope and happening – can highlight the contradictions. While it may be unrealistic to expect all ambiguities to be eliminated in coaching practice

– after all, it is a social process – at least acknowledging that contradictions that exist may assist in the development of quality in coaching.

CONCEPTUALIZING AND EVALUATING QUALITY

Before we try to develop methods for evaluating teacher quality, Ingvarson and Rowe (2007) suggest that it is useful to have a rigorous conceptual foundation that frames what we mean by quality. The process of conceptualizing the notion of quality in teaching – and, we would suggest, coaching – can be aided by asking the questions 'How do we decide what teachers [read coaches] should know and be able to do?' and 'On what bases should teachers be evaluated?' (ibid.: 6). Drawing on the work of both Scriven and Wheeler, Ingvarson and Rowe (ibid.: 6) identified the various conceptual foundations that have been used in the United States in the process of 'developing criteria for evaluating teachers'. While there are pros and cons for each foundation, it has been suggested that the most appropriate foundation for evaluating teacher quality is 'what the profession says teachers *should know* and *be able to do* – as specified in a set of professional standards' (ibid.: 7). We would contend that this would be equally appropriate to the coaching context. According to Ingvarson and Rowe (ibid.: 10), such standards fulfil at least three roles: they 'articulate professional principles and values', are tools to be used when making judgements, and 'provide the necessary context of shared meanings and values for fair, reliable and useful judgements to be made'.

Professional standards for coaching already exist in some countries. For example, in the United Kingdom the UK Coaching Certificate (UKCC) (UKCC n.d.), which is being led by Sports Coach UK (scUK), is based on, among other things, the National Occupational Standards (NOS) for Coaching, Teaching and Instructing. SkillsActive (the UK government-licensed Sector Skills Council for Active Leisure and Learning) developed the NOS in conjunction with partner organizations and experts in the active leisure and learning sector. The structure of the NOS is consistent across various levels, with a suite of units having been produced for each sector (National Occupational Standards n.d.). The structure of the units reflects the conceptual foundation for evaluating teacher quality described in the previous paragraph in that it specifies what a teacher should *know* and *be able to do*. For example, the Sport, Recreation and Allied Occupational sector, Level 1, unit D41 describes what a coach 'must do . . .' and states that the coach also has to show 'necessary knowledge and skills . . .' to meet the National Standard.

The NOS in the Coaching, Teaching and Instructing sector appear to reflect the features of a respected international development known as the National Board for Professional Teaching Standards (NBPTS). The standards enshrined in the NBPTS:

- . . . are developed by teachers themselves through their professional associations;
- . . . aim to capture substantive knowledge about teaching and learning – what teachers really need to know and be able to do to promote learning of important subject matter;

- ... are performance-based. They describe what teachers should know and be able to do rather than listing courses that teachers should take in order to be awarded registration or certification;
- ... conceive of teacher's work as the application of expertise and values non-routine tasks. Assessment strategies need to be capable of capturing teachers' reasoned judgements and what they actually do in authentic teaching situations.

(Ingvarson and Rowe 2007: 11)

Another reason why the NBPTS has received such acclaim relates to the methods used to gather evidence of teacher quality. One such method requires teachers to provide one sample of student work, two separate videotapes of their practice, and documentation of their contributions to the profession and the community. Another involves teachers completing six online exercises designed to gather evidence of subject-matter knowledge and pedagogical content knowledge (Ingvarson and Rowe 2007). These methods have been considered noteworthy because the constituent tasks:

- ... are authentic and, therefore, complex;
- ... are open-ended, allowing teachers to show their own practice;
- ... provide ample opportunity and encouragement for analysis and reflection;
- ... encourage teachers to exemplify good practice; and
- ... [assess] a cluster of standards.

(ibid.: 14)

Where professional standards on quality coaching are absent, there are other conceptual foundations upon which to evaluate the quality of a teacher or coach. One of these is 'what teachers should be doing' (Ingvarson and Rowe 2007: 6). We suggest that Carr's (1989) framework of quality teaching is useful when one is beginning to think about what 'coaches should be doing'. Here, Carr (1989) considered that a quality practitioner needed to be able to demonstrate both instrumental and intrinsic characteristics.

Instrumental characteristics can be viewed as those that focus on the practical and technical aspects of coaching. If we return to the list at the beginning of the chapter where the undergraduate students identified what they thought were characteristics of a 'good' coach, we can see that they included a number of instrumental characteristics. For example, they identified that a 'good' coach was required to have a loud voice, be punctual, be organized and be able to communicate ideas to the athletes. We agree that it is important for coaches to possess instrumental characteristics, especially if they want athletes to be engaged in meaningful physical activity in the training sessions.

Developing competency in instrumental aspects of coaching may assist coaches to increase the amount of time athletes are engaged in physical activity and decrease the time spent waiting around, receiving information and being managed. However, research conducted by Alton-Lee and Nuthall (in Alton-Lee 2003: 55) found that 'many behaviours traditionally classified in research studies as "on task" to be unrelated or inconsistently or even negatively related to learning outcomes'. An example of this in a coaching context would be a coach increasing the amount of time an athlete is physically active by getting him or her to do more laps in the warm-up. While that would increase the time the athlete spent being physically active, it would hardly be very meaningful to the athlete unless the coach had a specific aim of increasing cardiovascular fitness. There is no point in increasing the amount of physical activity in a session unless that activity is meaningful to the athletes and contributes to the learning outcomes of the session. Alton-Lee and Nuthall also found that 'many behaviours traditionally classified as "off task" were positively related to learning outcomes' (ibid.: 55). They gave the example of those students who when accessing 'information in a timely way', either through *talking* to teachers or peers or *moving* to gain reference material (practices often viewed in classrooms as 'off-task'), actually 'supported the learning process, and minimized time spent in confusion or time wasted' (ibid.: 55).

While it is important that coaches possess instrumental characteristics, there are limitations to focusing solely on these. As we have mentioned, and continue to mention, throughout this book, we value the ability of the coach to be reflective, not only technically and practically but also critically. If a coach solely relies on instrumental characteristics, then it is likely that there will be an overemphasis on technical and practical aspects and less emphasis on the subjective (social, affective and cognitive) aspects of the coaching process.

Intrinsic characteristics can be viewed as those that focus on the subjective (social, affective and cognitive) aspects of coaching. If we revisit the list of characteristics that undergraduate students identified as comprising a 'good' coach, included within it were intrinsic characteristics of a sense of humour, open-mindedness, patience and the ability to be a good motivator. We contend that it is important for coaches to possess these intrinsic characteristics if they wish to develop a positive working relationship with athletes. For example, Bob Dwyer (ex-Australian rugby union coach) was recently quoted on the importance of having a sense of humour.

> The players, I think, get enjoyment out of being able to mimic the [silly] things I do and say, so I leave them in my repertoire. I know they think some of the expressions are right funny, but I'm happy about that because I think they'll remember it and it gives them a laugh. It's all part of the psychology of coaching.
>
> (Jones *et al.* 2004: 50)

When other successful elite coaches (Steve Harrison, Hope Powell and Graham Taylor from association football, Ian McGeechan from rugby union, Di Bass from swimming, Lois Muir from netball and Peter Stanley from athletics) reflected upon their careers in coaching (Jones *et al.* 2004), it was evident that they too placed importance on the intrinsic characteristics of coaching practice. Their responses suggested that they believed coaching to be more than 'a process of passive instruction or training' (Carr 1989: 3) and, rather, to do with establishing fruitful working relationships with athletes through gaining and maintaining the latter's trust and respect.

Yet while it is important for coaches to possess intrinsic characteristics, there are limitations to focusing solely on these. Being the athletes' 'best mate' will not be enough to improve performance or even guarantee continued participation. The following quotation from an English premier league soccer coach highlights his belief that he would be in 'trouble' if he did not inject an element of technical instrumentality into his general caring philosophy.

> Footballers will test you . . . they will test you to see if you know. They usually pump you with questions . . . if I can't say why I want it done that way, if I can't give a good reason, then I've got trouble. You can't afford to lose players. So, you've got to know your subject . . . if you don't know your subject then you have real problems.
>
> (Potrac *et al.* 2002: 192)

It seems, then, that coaches must possess, and utilize, a mixture of instrinsic and instrumental practices in their coaching. Consequently, they must understand the athletes, care for them inside and outside the sporting environment, while also having a set of technical and tactical ideals that they can clearly implement in a competitive situation. When and how to use which strategy becomes a reflective issue, with awareness of unique contextual considerations coming to the fore.

CONCLUDING THOUGHTS

Most of us will have experienced at least one quality coach or teacher. If we can remember one such individual, it may also be possible to recount why he or she was a quality practitioner. Possibly the reason this coach or teacher was valued was that he or she made a connection with us. Whether this connection was the result of the coach's exceptional instrumental or intrinsic characteristics, anecdotal evidence suggests that quality coaches possess good recognition of, and attributes from, both categories. In contrast, many of us have knowledge of a coach who had tremendous technical ability (maybe as a consequence of being an elite athlete some years earlier) but who was not highly regarded as a coach. It is useful to be reminded that possessing good technical and even practical knowledge, in addition to having been an elite performer, does not automatically make such an individual a quality coach.

The notions of quality coaching and a quality coach are going to be with us for a while yet. We would argue that this is a result of the many technological, economic and social changes that are occurring worldwide and, in turn, require a more skilled workforce. A consequence of this demand is that mechanisms for judging who is

skilled or not, or who is considered to be a quality practitioner, are becoming increasingly sophisticated. One criterion for judging quality is the 'professional standard', which, like most evaluating mechanisms, can be well designed or not. Although we recognize that not everyone in the coaching community is going to have knowledge of, or access to, international best practice, we believe that by carefully reflecting on some of the concepts raised in this chapter, informed judgements can still be made as to what is quality coaching and who better reflects a quality coach.

SUGGESTED READINGS

Carr, W. (ed.) (1989) *Quality in Teaching: Arguments for a Reflective Profession*, London: Falmer Press.

Ingvarson, L. and Rowe, K. (2007) 'Conceptualising and evaluating teacher quality: Substantive and methodological issues', paper presented at the Economics of Teacher Quality Conference, Australian National University, 5 February.

Lyle, J. (2002) *Sports Coaching Concepts: A Framework for Coaches' Behaviour*, London: Routledge.

Tinning, R., Macdonald, D., Wright, J. and Hickey, C. (2001) *Becoming a Physical Education Teacher: Contemporary and Enduring Issues*, Frenchs Forest, Australia: Prentice-Hall.

END-OF-CHAPTER TASKS

1   Critically examine and then describe which sources have been the most valuable in terms of shaping your views and beliefs on quality coaching practice.
2   What do you consider to be quality coaching?
3   Describe to what extent your answer to question 2 has been influenced by your experiences of being coached by, and working with, other coaches. (Identify individuals who have served as positive and negative role models. What did they do? How did they do things? How have they influenced your current beliefs about coaching practice?)
4   Describe other sources of knowledge that have influenced your views on quality coaching practice.
5   Critically analyse what knowledge you consider to be important for a quality practitioner to possess. Compare and contrast your thoughts with those of Carr (1989), who proposed that a quality practitioner needed to demonstrate instrumental and intrinsic characteristics.

CHAPTER 4

▼ **DEVELOPING A COACHING PHILOSOPHY**

INTRODUCTION

It is widely accepted that what coaches do in their practice, and how they do it, tends to be shaped by their personal principles and values – attributes that are thought to comprise their respective coaching philosophies. It is also believed that clearly articulating one's philosophy is a prerequisite to good practice, as it provides direction and focus in relation to how one goes about doing the job of coaching. Indeed, a subsection and/or an accompanying 'reflective' exercise aimed at developing a coaching philosophy can be found in almost every related coach education publication or course.

Yet despite this official recognition that a philosophy has a direct impact on behaviour, many coaches consistently fail to engage adequately with the philosophic concept, not really grasping its relevance for, and accompanying influence over, practical problems. It appears that they just cannot see how investing in the process of developing and clarifying a clear philosophy can have an impact on their daily problems at work. Hence, the negative mantras of 'it'll never work in the real world' or 'we've never done it like that here before' continue to block tentative philosophic routes of inquiry. It is a situation reflective of coach educators and coaches situated at opposing theoretical and practical positions 'talking past one another', or even of coaches not talking (in terms of philosophizing) about coaching much at all (Green 2000). This lack of engagement appears to have been aggravated by the comparative lack of research done into the motives that drive coaches' actions (Wilcox and Trudel 1998), which has led to rather superficial and simplistic assumptions about the value of establishing and locating definitive philosophies within the overall coaching process.

The principal aim of this chapter is first to conceptualize what is commonly referred to as a coaching philosophy, before making the case for and 'signposting' how coaches can develop clear and credible philosophies. It therefore invites coaches to 'hike along a philosophic trail' (Kretchmar 1994: xiii) in order to hone their related skills before determining their own functional philosophies. The development of such skills is important, as coaches frequently encounter novel situations that require clear thinking and analysis. Similarly, a definitive personal philosophy is valuable as it can provide practitioners with both 'cause and compass' on which to base action (ibid.: xiii). However, in line with the book's theme, we emphasize that developing a philosophy, far from being a straightforward exercise, is quite problematic. It is a course of action fraught with ethical and moral questions, as the coaching process itself is grounded in various complex interpersonal dimensions and driven by multiple goals (Jones and Wallace, 2005; and see Chapter 11, 'Coaching ethics', for a fuller discussion of this issue). Consequently, we do not suggest that all coaches should possess one ideal philosophy and operate in a similar way, as there is no 'right' way to coach. In this respect, we agree with Lyle (1999a), who stated that when one is developing a philosophy, care must be taken that it does not turn into an insincere, tidy wish-list or model for coaching practice full of 'pat answers' that is perhaps at odds with one's underlying beliefs (Kretchmar 1994). We also recognize that, while based on principles, if a philosophy is to be deemed a credible and useful one, it should be flexible enough to take account of contextual factors. The objective of the chapter, then, is to raise awareness of the problematic nature of a philosophy and the need to engage in depth with that complexity, thus providing a framework to better develop one's own system of beliefs and practice. It is also to challenge coaches to examine and rethink personal biases and assumptions about the nature of coaching, and how they behave as coaches.

Following a section on the nature of a coaching philosophy and the need to create and clarify one, a discussion of the current literature and its shortcomings as it relates to developing a personal coaching philosophy will be undertaken. This, in turn, will be followed by suggestions of ways to cultivate more realistic coaching philosophies that take into account the contradictory social world within which coaches operate. In this respect, we are aware of the need to strike a balance between practicality and idealism; to develop philosophies that both promote dreaming and speculating, while being able to play an active role in solving real, everyday problems (Kretchmar 1994). Lyle's (1999a, 2002) work provides a general framework for this discussion, as he is one of the few scholars to have problematically engaged with developing and defining a functional coaching philosophy.

THE COACH

WHAT IS A COACHING PHILOSOPHY? AND WHY DOES A COACH NEED TO DEVELOP ONE?

We begin our answer to these twin questions by addressing another asked by many coaches in this context: 'What's the point of spending time on my coaching philosophy, when what I really need are practical coaching tips?' The answer lies in accepting the role of philosophy as a precursor to action, because every element of coaching (i.e. the what, why and the how of it) is affected by personal beliefs. An interesting analogy is to view one's philosophy as a pair of glasses, created by personal opinions, experiences and values, through which a particular perception of reality is filtered. It therefore has a direct bearing on how we understand the world, what actions we take, and why we take them. This definition of a philosophy appears to be common ground for many coaching scholars. For example:

A coaching philosophy is a set of values and behaviours that serve to guide the actions of a coach.

(Wilcox and Trudel 1998: 41)

A coaching philosophy is a personal statement that is based on the values and beliefs that direct one's coaching.

(Kidman and Hanrahan 1997: 32)

A coaching philosophy is a comprehensive statement about the beliefs that . . . characterize a coach's practice.

(Lyle 1999a: 30)

A coaching philosophy, then, can be considered to be a set of principles that guide an individual's practice. Consequently, an examination of it delves into the heart of coaches' actions, investigating why they coach as they do. According to Lyle (1999a), such an exploration should not be viewed as an 'optional extra' if we are to better grasp coaching practice, as it provides a framework within which its delivery can be understood.

The value of developing a philosophy is that it allows both coach and athletes a base from which to build and learn according to a consistent, coherent way of thinking. More specifically, it can help coaches clarify motives and provide direction to their coaching, while addressing what uniquely valuable contributions they might make as coaches (Kretchmar 1994). Without a definitive philosophy, behaviour can become too situation-specific, too reactive. A philosophy provides boundaries within which the coach–athlete relationship can be located. Writing one also has the potential to develop fresh ideas by encouraging us to think creatively and imaginatively about what we do as coaches and why we make these choices. For the individual, then, thinking through actions to determine their root cause can become an enlightening process, as the value systems that guide a person's coaching need to be understood if we are to equally comprehend his or her actions. Additionally, as coaching has the potential to be power dominated and harmful to athletes (Kidman and Hanrahan 1997), clarifying and adhering to a coaching philosophy can assist in reminding ourselves of why we coach, thus guarding against the excesses that circumstances may drive us to (Lyle 1999a). This is not to dispute that the coach–athlete relationship in many instances should be hierarchical and thus characterized by power, but to ensure that that power be used in a sincere, meaningful and progressive way (Kidman and Hanrahan 1997). (See Chapter 13, 'Power and the coach–athlete relationship', for a fuller discussion of this issue.)

We agree with many others in believing that, as a part of their training, coaches should become aware of their beliefs and how those deep-seated values influence their practice. Where we differ from most texts, however, is that we take issue with the largely unquestioned assumption that stated value frameworks or philosophies unproblematically guide a coach's actions. Alternatively, we are realistic about the range of behaviours open to coaches – a range that is often constrained by operating within a particular cultural tradition. Indeed, although a coach's behaviour will often reflect deep-seated beliefs, sometimes opposite pressures are also present, and complicate the decision-making process.

PROBLEMATIZING COACHING PHILOSOPHIES

Although we often assume that a philosophy is observable in behaviour, or that it should be, from empirical examinations we see that the connection is not as straightforward as much of the current coaching literature would have us believe (Lyle 1999a). This is because little account is taken of contextual pressures and constraints when writing philosophies. Consequently, when produced they lack the flexibility and credibility needed to be truly functional. For example, in a situation where a coach holds a developmental philosophy, does the less skilled child in the group, who is low on self-confidence and needs special attention, *really* receive the required time investment in relation to others? Usually not. On the other hand, even if the child did receive such attention, are his or her needs being unfairly prioritized over those of more talented children who equally deserve to have their abilities further developed and fulfilled? Not addressing such 'real' issues as the multiplicity of goals inherent in coaching leads only to a superficial adoption of stated values, which are then perceived as of no practical use to coaches (Jones and Wallace 2005). In this respect, 'philosophic statements often seem easy to make but hard to keep' (Lyle 1999a: 28). Subsequently, coaches appear to have little confidence in the validity of the philosophic process and the practical application of the resulting product. Despite being frequently committed to paper, then, philosophies are often discarded, or at best only paid lip service to, with coaches retreating into aspects of the process they can actually see or feel (Kretchmar 1994). This tendency was most recently found in a study by McCallister *et al.* (2000), where coaches, although able to clearly verbalize their philosophies, struggled both to articulate how they attempted to teach youngsters the stated outcomes and to demonstrate the actual implementation of them. Such a finding is consistent with

Stewart's (1993) belief that most coaches are effective at 'talking' rather than 'walking' a good philosophy.

Lyle (1999a) is one of the few scholars who has critically examined the assumption that coaching behaviour reflects philosophy, a notion that underpins much current coach education literature. He criticizes the view that the coach is free to allow any value framework to influence his or her behaviour, emphasizing that coaching practice can never be so objective. Rather, he contends that coaching is a social construction, developed from a personal set of beliefs, which, in turn, are derived from such sources as experience, observations and education programmes, among others. Although such beliefs are framed reasonably early in life, they remain susceptible to alteration as influencing networks and forces become ever more complex and compelling (Green 2002). Consequently, they are constantly pressured by many external factors, which compete with one's ability to implement a stated philosophy in influencing coaching behaviour (Stewart 1993). Such factors include the particular ethos of the organization or club where the coach is employed, a definitive coaching subculture, athlete expectations, and the pressures associated with getting results. A coach may feel the need to adhere to some or all of these expectations, or alternatively to fight against and subvert them within his or her practice. As a result, there could be various reasons that underlie coaching behaviour, ranging from an adherence to personal ethics, to a desire to fit in with the coaching culture, to meeting the needs of athletes and the employing organization. Here, then, lies the potential for conflict between stated beliefs, personal values and actual practice (Lyle 1999a). Little wonder that pedagogical philosophies, as well as actions, represent something of a compromise (Green 2002). To further complicate the issue, Lyle (1999a) noted that probably not all standards are applied in all aspects of coaching. For example, while coaches could appear willing to 'toe the party line' with respect to some policies, others are not treated with such reverence, particularly where the result has far-reaching consequences. It is a conflict between operational and fundamental ideology, and one that very often leads to some modification of the latter (Evans 1992). It is also a tension that many in coaching, particularly at the performance level, are very aware of, although it remains largely unaddressed and, therefore, unresolved.

Unfortunately, with the exception of the work of McCallister *et al.* (2000), the link between coaches' beliefs and their actions has rarely been examined through field studies (Wilcox and Trudel 1998; Jones *et al.* 2003). Additionally, the research that has been carried out has been based on the assumption that coaching behaviour is easily changeable, and thus has failed to deal adequately with the subtlety and scope of philosophies and their influence over practice (Lyle 1999a). At present, then, there is little evidence 'on which to evaluate the contribution of a coach's value system against other environmental factors' in relation to action (ibid.: 28). Indeed, according to Lyle (2000), there is no proof that how one coaches, as influenced by any particular philosophy, has any influence over performance. What has further hindered our understanding of practice in this regard is the simplistic aggregation of coaching styles or methods into the autocratic–democratic dichotomy. This model leaves little room for the fact that a coach may be more democratic in one area of practice while being more autocratic in another. The complexity here has been 'simplified for the sake of a "cleaner" research design', which may well mask important variations (ibid.: 29). Such a sentiment was echoed by the findings of Wilcox and Trudel (1998), who discovered that one-dimensional or superficial accounts of coaches' convictions, opinions or views may well be inaccurate, as coaches are likely to abide by different beliefs and principles in different situations. Hence, depending on the situation, coaches may favour one option over another, or look for a balance between them. Wilcox and Trudel (ibid.) concluded by calling for future investigations to avoid oversimplifying coaches' convictions and beliefs, and highlighted the need to help coaches develop philosophies that both reflect and leave room for these complexities.

The inadequacy of current thinking in relation to coaching philosophy also appears to be a result of the unquestioned focus given both to increased athlete involvement in the decision-making process and to their leadership preference. Although athletes may pronounce themselves to be more motivated as a consequence of such participation and perceptions, the optimum coaching environment is more complex than the need merely to make athletes happy. Lyle (1999a) also believes that current research could well have been influenced by popular perceptions of ethical standards when discussing the development of coaching philosophies. Hence, coaches, particularly if such philosophies are meant for public consumption, may feel pressure to cite more politically correct value statements than are actually observed in their practice. Indeed, coaches' notions of their philosophies appear more ideological than philosophical; that is to say, they are made up of seemingly mythical ideas of how they perceive they are supposed to act under a vague umbrella of 'good sportsmanship' or 'fair play'. The end result is the same: a simplified, sanitized list of statements that is not sufficiently refined to apply in the subtle, contradictory world of coaching.

Let us now examine, in a little more depth, some of the difficulties inherent in applying a definitive coaching philosophy to practice. Such a philosophy is usually given in the form of a declaration about an aspect of practice. For example, a statement regarding sincerity could be presented as 'I will be open and honest with my athletes' (Lyle 1999a). The values proclaimed are clear, but the circumstances in which they will be evident are not specified, giving the assumption that a sincere coach will always be honest and open with athletes. The problem with such a declaration comes not with its worthy intent, but with its practicality and appropriateness in all circumstances. It does not address the thorny issue of whether a coach *should* always be honest with athletes, for instance in terms of selection, opinions on performance, and the like. This, in turn, begs the question of whether there are certain situations where being less than honest is in the best interests of athletes or 'for the greater good' (Lyle 1999a). A principal problem here, then, is that the statement of intent is too far removed from the ambiguous and complex reality to have much effect.

Giving credence to Lyle's (1999a) considerations, recent research by Jones *et al.* (2004) found that, although acknowledging the value of honesty and trust in the coach–athlete relationship, elite coaches were not averse to using 'white lies' when they judged it to be in the best interests of the athlete or team. The point to be made is not that the coaches cited were unprincipled, but that they had found a way to be flexible within the confines of their respective philosophies. Consequently, they believed that what could be construed as a behavioural contradiction was, in fact, entirely consistent with overriding principles. These philosophies, then, although sincere and believed, were primarily functional ones that gave the necessary degree of credibility to be of use in guiding action. Perhaps this, then, is one way forward.

DEVELOPING FUNCTIONAL, FLEXIBLE PHILOSOPHIES

In order to generate more realistic and functional coaching philosophies, the first step is to acknowledge that they are very complex and complicated. Hence, they cannot be realistically created in a 30-minute workshop or through a 'quickie' self-reflective exercise since to make them credible they need careful and realistic consideration. Similarly, there is a need to move away from bland, generic statements written as if they were meant as ideals to aspire towards (Lyle 1999a), or reflections that are too abstract for addressing actual coaching needs in practice. Alternatively, philosophies should be highly individualized, grounded in reality and be based on personal objectives founded on experiences (Kidman 2001; Kidman and Hanrahan 1997). Indeed, the diversity of knowledge allied to personal idiosyncrasy means that coaches' practice will invariably differ – a creative individualism that should be encouraged. While one must acknowledge that there may be many means to the same end and that coaches will act according to their perception of the context, the clarification of purposes and guidelines encapsulated in a philosophy is still valuable as it leads to informed choices and better priorities. Such boundary definition is also beneficial as it lays the foundations for consistency (Kidman and Hanrahan 1997). Within this process, Lyle (2002) points to the need to consider and link issues of philosophy and behaviour. Hence, we need not only to differentiate between delivery style and core purpose, but also to sketch outlines of appropriate practice in relation to both. The important point here is that the objective is not to tie the coach down 'to a prearranged act, but to definitively guide action while maintaining the required flexibility to be contextual' (Lyle 1999a: 37).

Recent research into elite coaches' philosophies (Saury and Durand 1998; Jones *et al.* 2003) indicates an awareness of the need to remain flexible in practice, thus maintaining the ability to adapt to changing circumstances. It includes a belief that definitive standards cannot be applied outright, as they often conflict with other constraints inherent in the coaching situation (Saury and Durand 1998). However, and echoing the point made earlier, this does not mean that such coaches acted without principle. In explaining this apparent contradiction, Raffel (1998) draws a distinction between the 'principled' and the 'rule-guided' actor. While the latter would view practice as a set of prescriptions with which he or she is obligated to comply, the principled actor believes in the rightness of his or her actions, with practice clearly reflecting values. Consequently, there is room to explore and manoeuvre within a principled commitment to stated beliefs. Of importance is that principled individuals view their practice as something that is intrinsically worth doing – as something to actively further and not merely to comply with (Jones *et al.* 2004). In this sense, such coaches 'live' their own training sessions vicariously and emotionally, as they invest much of themselves in their practice (Saury and Durand 1998; Jones *et al.* 2004). It is the difference between being competent in relation to a philosophy and being *committed* to it.

Allowing flexible adherence within philosophical boundaries goes some way to explaining expert coaches' actions and their belief in applying sensitivity to unexpected and problematic tasks (Saury and Durand 1998; Côté *et al.* 1995). Indeed, according to Saury and Durand (1998: 264), the practice of such experts is 'very flexible and based on continuous step-by-step tuning to the context', albeit embedded in a deep knowledge of sport and a commitment to an established framework of behaviour. In this respect, the coaching process and coaching practice can be considered as 'regulated improvisation' (Bourdieu 1977: 79) that takes into account the particular challenges and tensions that are unique to it. Here, the particular is malleable within stated guidelines. Such practice was clearly evident in the accounts of expert coaches researched by Jones *et al.* (2004). For example, clear value statements were readily applied, while flexibility was acknowledged as vital to 'test the edges' of the underlying philosophy as it manifested itself in contextual practice (Lyle 2002). It appears, then, that top-level coaches are able to manage well the inevitable dilemmas between philosophy and practice, in that they are realistic and practical about their goals while retaining a strong personal set of values and standards (ibid.).

How should one go about developing such a functional, yet sincere, personal philosophy? As is stated in the introduction to this chapter, the aim here is not to provide 'correct' prescriptive thinking for all, but rather to assist coaches through a process by which they can arrive at their own individualized, personalized guides for action. A good place to start, however, is to utilize higher thinking skills in addressing fundamental issues about one's own personal involvement in coaching, while allowing more detailed reflective questions to emerge once the conceptual issues have been clarified. An important point to remember is that this process should be carried out in a systematic, careful and rigorous way, so as to give the findings definitive meaning. Here, Kretchmar (1994) suggests that we should use inductive, intuitive and deductive reasoning in developing philosophy, thus creating it from experience and reflection. This would give us a degree of security and confidence in its personal applicability. First, then, the following questions could be addressed:

- What is coaching, and why do I think that?
- Why am I a coach?

- Have my coaching motives changed? How? Why?
- Is there another way?
- Why are these athletes participating?
- Why did a particular coach have such a meaningful impact on me?
- What are my future hopes both for the athletes I coach and for myself as a coach?
- Are they 'my' athletes or am I 'their' coach?
- Who holds the power in a coach–athlete relationship?
- What is my role as a coach and why do I think that?

Although lists of similar questions appear in current coaching workshops, the superficiality with which they are engaged makes the exercise of little value. To create a worthwhile functional philosophy, such questions need to be carefully and sincerely addressed. For example, in examining the last of these questions ('What is my role as a coach?'), instead of merely brainstorming potential functions, we would implore coaches to address such issues related to role as: How do I 'play' the role of the coach? Whose expectations am I fulfilling? Why? Is there a case for me to expand and explore the boundaries of the traditional coaching role? Do I want to, and what are the implications of doing so? How can I allow my own personality to emerge through the coaching role? and Am I fulfilling myself within the coaching role? Through addressing these and other such carefully crafted questions to address both meaning and purpose, a deeper sense of a coaching philosophy and identity can emerge, one that is grounded in personal reality.

Once a philosophical framework has been established, or perhaps in tandem with it, more practical questions should be addressed so that the philosophy maintains a working credibility and usefulness for coaches. Such questions here could include:

- Is my approach educationally sound?
- Do the drills I use best serve the purpose for which they are intended (i.e. the objective of the session)? Why and how?
- Is the approach appropriate for the athletes?
- Is there a better way of doing what I'm doing?
- Can I explain and justify my coaching actions and decisions?
- How do I ensure that I follow my coaching philosophy?
- What happens if my coaching philosophy is challenged?
- How will I deal with the different values of other people (Kidman and Hanrahan 1997)?
- What is key about the interpersonal relationships I have with athletes?
- Are there situational compromises in the application of my stated values (Lyle 2002)?

Such reflective questions could be applied to all aspects of the coaching process, from pedagogical and motivational issues to those of planning, monitoring and organizing, to ensure that the philosophy developed is realized through behaviour. In many ways, it is important to commit the philosophy to paper for all to see, because a written document easily reminds everyone of the ethos of the sporting experience undertaken. It also forces the writer to organize his or her ideas and to defend a position. Of more importance, however, is the need to regularly re-examine and re-evaluate the philosophy, as our experiences constantly shape and evolve our thoughts. The philosophy should, therefore, be written in pencil, not in ink (Kretchmar 1994)!

CONCLUDING THOUGHTS

Writing a personal philosophy gives coaches the opportunity to identify and clarify what is important to them at the personal level. It is a chance to both consider the most appropriate destination for each of us, and to decide on the best route to get there (Kretchmar 1994). What needs to be avoided, however, when developing a philosophy, is the superficial adoption of public statements of intent that have little bearing on day-to-day practice. We advocate an in-depth engagement with the philosophic process, which can help us become aware of why certain decisions are made and actions taken. Indeed, the process is perhaps more important than the outcome, as involvement in it develops the clarity of thinking skills required for such a dynamic activity as coaching. To make a philosophy functional it should also take into account the external constraints on coaches' actions, thus appreciating the contextual complexity within which they work. Furthermore, perhaps we should pay close attention to the elite practitioners interviewed in the work of Jones *et al.* (2004), who not only believed in the value of clarifying philosophies as flexible guides to action, but sincerely tried to live their coaching lives through them. In conclusion, we believe that the time it takes to evaluate, understand, choose and develop a functional yet sincere philosophy would be well spent, with the result being better guided, more thoughtful and imaginative coaches (Kretchmar 1994).

SUGGESTED READINGS

Kretchmar, R.S. (1994) *Practical Philosophy of Sport*, Champaign, IL: Human Kinetics.
Lyle, J. (1999a) 'Coaching philosophy and coaching behaviour', in N. Cross and J. Lyle (eds) *The Coaching Process: Principles and Practice for Sport*, Oxford: Butterworth-Heinemann.
McCallister, S.G., Blinde, E., and Weiss, W.M. (2000) 'Teaching values and implementing philosophies: Dilemmas of the youth sport coach', *Physical Educator*, 57: 33–45.
Raffel, S. (1998) 'Revisiting role theory: Roles and the problem of the self', *Sociological Research Online*, 4(2). Available at http://www.socresonline.org.uk/4/2/raffel.html (accessed 20 April 2008).

END-OF-CHAPTER TASKS

1   What is the value of developing a coaching philosophy?
2   Discuss some of the difficulties inherent in applying a definitive coaching philosophy to practice.
3   What is a functional coaching philosophy, and why do we need one?
4   Address some of the 'foundational' philosophical questions listed on pp. 62–3.

PART TWO
THE ATHLETES

CHAPTER 5

▼ **LEARNING AND DEVELOPMENT**

INTRODUCTION

Learning and development are integral to coaching, yet both have ambiguous status in the coaching literature. For example, when Gilbert (2002) compiled his comprehensive annotated bibliography of coaching science, cognition was the second most common theme. However, when he coded the cognition articles by keywords, no article was identified as focusing on the learning process, or the athlete as learner. The concepts of learning and development also have uncertain status with practitioners and students of sports coaching, with some questioning the relevance of such theories and perspectives to their practices. However, since Gilbert conducted his review, and the publication of the first edition of this text, there has been an increased interest in learning within the coaching context (see, for example, Culver and Trudel 2006; Galipeau and Trudel 2006; Trudel and Gilbert 2004; and the 2006 Special Issue of the *International Journal of Sports Science and Coaching* entitled 'The Sport Coach as Learner'). Additionally, Trudel and Gilbert (2006) introduced Sfard's acquisition and participation metaphors on learning as a framework for gaining insight into how coaches learn to coach. The acquisition metaphor, as the name suggests, views learning as a process of acquiring basic units of knowledge and can be loosely aligned to a behavioural view of learning. The participation metaphor views learning as occurring in context involving interaction with others, and can be associated with cognitivist views of learning. We endorse Sfard's (1998) position that it is undesirable to favour one metaphor (or view of learning) unconditionally at the expense of the other.

While most people would agree that learning is an important aspect of the coaching process, there is not one universal definition of learning to be had. Similarly, there is no one definition of development. That said, there appears to be a consensus that development is associated, albeit in different ways, with experience, learning and maturation (Eggen and Kauchak 2004). The aim of this chapter is to describe some of the prominent theories of learning and perspectives of development. We believe that having some knowledge of the characteristics and assumptions of such theories and perspectives provides us with two opportunities. First, it provides us with a 'vocabulary and a conceptual framework for interpreting the examples of learning that we observe', and second, it 'direct[s] our attention to those variables that are crucial in finding solutions' (Hill, in Merriam *et al.* 2007: 277–278). In an effort to make the description of, and discussion on, the characteristics of learning and development relevant to students of sports coaching, we shall intersperse it with real and fictitious examples from the coaching context. We hope that the examples will assist readers become aware that what they often consider to be 'common-sense' practices are, in fact, informed by particular theories of learning and perspectives of development. We must point out that this chapter is not a detailed overview of the respective theories and perspectives; rather, it is an introduction to some of the key related concepts.

The chapter is organized into three broad sections: behaviourist orientations to learning, cognitive orientations to learning, and cognitive orientations to development. Within each of these sections we focus on two different theories or perspectives that are associated with that orientation. It has been suggested that there are 14 different versions of behaviourism (Ward 2006), but here we focus only on classical conditioning and operant conditioning. Classical conditioning focuses on observable behaviour and ignores all non-observable behaviour, whereas operant conditioning focuses on observable behaviour and behaviours associated with thinking and feeling. The second and third sections are organized under the heading of cognitive orientations to learning and development respectively. We use the term 'cognitive' rather than 'constructivist' because constructivism is connected to a 'philosophical explanation about the nature of learning' and is therefore 'not a theory but rather an epistemology' (Schunk 2004: 286). When we discuss cognitive views of learning, we focus on social cognitive theory and situated learning theory. When our attention turns to cognitive orientations of development, we discuss the cognitive development perspective and cultural-historical perspectives.

BEHAVIOURIST ORIENTATIONS TO LEARNING

As we said in the introduction to this chapter, knowledge of the characteristics and assumptions of learning theories can assist us to interpret our observations of learning and help us to find possible solutions to make the learning experience more generative (Merriam *et al.* 2007).

How do behaviourists define learning?

Thorndike, a psychologist in the first half of the twentieth century, 'almost single-handedly' defined and established educational psychology (Lefrançois 2000: 67). Over the course of his career, Thorndike developed a number of laws to explain learning, one of which was the Law of Effect. Here, he emphasized

> a relation between behavior and its consequences. If a stimulus that follows a response makes that response become more likely, we say that the response was reinforced. If the stimulus makes the response become less likely, we say that it was punished.
>
> (Carlson and Buskist 1997: 145)

Thorndike emphasized the 'association between stimulus and response as the basis of learning', believing that 'learning often occurs by trial and error' (Schunk 2004: 30). Thus, 'responses resulting in satisfying (rewarding) consequences are learned; responses producing annoying (punishing) consequences are not learned' (ibid.: 31). This view of learning is described as a functional account. However, later in his career Thorndike revised the Law of Effect because research had demonstrated that satisfiers (rewards) and annoyers (punishments) were not opposite, but comparable (ibid.). None the less, Thorndike's work was significant because it highlighted the importance of making an association in the process of learning. This ability to make an association is a key aspect of learning when viewed via classical conditioning (Eggen and Kauchak 2004).

Classical conditioning

John Watson is often thought of as the founder of modern behaviourism and was an early advocate of psychology as a science. He rejected Thorndike's functionalist view as unscientific because he considered satisfiers and annoyers to be 'subjective mental concepts that were unobservable and unmeasurable' (Schunk 2004: 42). However, before Watson rose to prominence, a Russian Nobel Prize winner (in 1904 for his work on digestion) became an instrumental figure in how we understand learning from a behaviourist orientation. Ivan Pavlov's experiments on dogs' salivation patterns had widespread implications for how behaviour and learning were understood. In a now famous experiment, Pavlov highlighted how dogs 'who have an innate (unlearned) tendency to salivate at the sight of food, could learn to salivate at the sound of a bell if, during a training period, the bell was regularly sounded just before they were given food' (Sigelman and Rider 2006: 36). Pavlov's finding was the catalyst for work to begin in a field that became known as classical conditioning. When one is adopting a classical conditioning view, learning is considered to have occurred when an individual produces an involuntary physiological or emotional response that is similar to a reflexive or instinctive response (Eggen and Kauchak 2004).

Within the classical conditioning there are four basic processes:

- unconditioned stimulus: an event or object that causes a reflexive or instinctive (unlearned) emotional or physiological response;
- unconditioned response: the reflexive or instinctive (unlearned) emotional or physiological response caused by the unconditioned stimulus;
- conditioned stimulus: an event or object that develops an association with the unconditioned stimulus;
- conditioned response: a learned emotional or physiological response that is similar in appearance to the unconditioned response (ibid.).

If we examine Pavlov's experiment in light of the four basic processes of classical conditioning, it becomes clear how the theory can assist us to understand learning. The food presented to the dogs was the *unconditioned stimulus*, which caused the dogs to salivate (*unconditioned response*). To condition the dogs it was necessary to produce a neutral stimulus for a period of time prior to presenting the *unconditioned stimulus* – that is, food. The neutral stimulus Pavlov used was a bell. Over time the dogs salivated at the sound of the bell prior to receiving the food. The bell became the *conditioned stimulus* and caused a *conditioned response* – that is, salivation.

Several decades following Pavlov's experiments, the Americans Watson and Raynor conducted another famous study, with a child called Albert. This experiment demonstrated how fears could be learned via classical conditioning. In the pre-conditioning phase they presented Albert with a rat (neutral stimulus). At this point Albert showed no fear of the rat. In the absence of the rat, a loud noise was made (*unconditional stimulus*), which is an unlearned or reflexive stimulus for fear. The loud noise resulted in Albert's becoming upset (*unconditioned response*), since children tend to become upset by loud noises. In the conditioning phase the rat and the loud noise were presented together on numerous occasions and consequently became associated with each other. In the post-conditioning phase, when the rat was presented to Albert without the loud noise he became upset. He had learned to become fearful of the rat. The rat had become the *conditioned stimulus* and caused a *conditioned response*; that is, fear. This experiment provided evidence of how Albert's behaviour had changed as a result of the experience and highlighted that the key aspect of learning via classical conditioning is 'making an association' (Eggen and Kauchak 2004: 197).

How does this assist us to make sense of our observations in a coaching context? As learning via classical conditioning occurs in the conditioning phase, if a coach wishes to change a response an athlete constantly gives in a certain situation then he or she should consider what stimulus is being associated with what behaviour. While classical conditioning can help explain how people learn by responding to stimuli – that is, by events preceding the behaviour (stimulus-response) – it does not help us to understand why people initiate behaviours or 'operate' as they do in their environment. One theory that can assist us to understand the latter is operant conditioning (Eggen and Kauchak 2004).

Operant conditioning

While Watson's work formalized behaviourism as a 'school of psychology', it was Skinner who became most associated with behavioural thought (Carlson and Buskist 1997). Skinner's contribution to our understanding of learning was through his research on what he called operant conditioning. The basic premise of operant conditioning is that '*an observable response changes in frequency or duration as the result of a consequence*' (i.e. response–consequence), with a consequence being any outcome that '*occurs after the behavior and influences future behaviors*' (Eggen and Kauchak 2004: 200; italics in original). Some of the basic processes of operant conditioning are reinforcement, punishment, extinction and scheduling. The way many coaches conduct their coaching sessions, systematically using reinforcement and punishment to modify the behaviour of players, is an example of what psychologists call behaviour modification.

Reinforcement results in the behaviour preceding it being strengthened; in other words, reinforcement increases the chances of a particular response occurring again (Schunk 2004; Sigelman and Rider 2006). Reinforcement can be positive or negative, with positive reinforcement being viewed as '*the process of increasing the frequency or duration of a behavior as the result of presenting a reinforcer*'; in other words, 'receiving something that increases behaviour' (Eggen and Kauchak 2004: 201; italics in original). Negative reinforcement, on the other hand, is '*the process of removing or avoiding a stimulus to increase behavior*' – that is, 'removing something that increases behavior' (ibid.: 201). Although often perceived as such, it is important to stress here that negative reinforcement is not a form of punishment.

A key characteristic of reinforcement is the 'reinforcer', which has been described as 'consequences that increase behaviours' (Vialle *et al.* 2005: 8). There are many different kinds of reinforcers. They include natural reinforcers (being placed in a group with a friend), social reinforcers (spending time with the coach), activity reinforcers (getting to participate in a favoured activity), tangible reinforcers (medals and certificates) and edible reinforcers (chocolate bars) (ibid.). However, it is worth noting that if a coach wants to increase a particular behaviour, it is not enough for him or her to hand out indiscriminately reinforcers such as a smile or praise since reinforcers are 'situationally specific' (Schunk 2004: 51). This was highlighted in a study carried out nearly 40 years ago, when Rushall and Pettinger (1969) explored the outcomes different reinforcers (money, candy or chocolate bars, a coach's attention and nothing) had on swimmers' productivity in training.

Like reinforcement, reinforcers can be positive or negative. A positive reinforcer will strengthen a behavior only if the learner desires the reinforcer (Vialle *et al.* 2005). Consequently, the coach will need to know what athletes desire and what motivates them. For example, an edible reinforcer such as a Snickers bar will not strengthen an athlete's behaviour if the athlete is allergic to nuts. We do not have the space in this chapter to discuss desires and motivation, but for those wanting to follow up on these areas we recommend Reiss (2000). A negative reinforcer also aims to increase behaviour but it does so by removing something the learner views as unpleasant (Vialle et al. 2005). As with the positive reinforcer, a coach needs to know what the athlete finds unpleasant. A coach may think letting players who performed well in training leave early so they can get a hot shower will strengthen the desired behaviour. But if a player likes staying after training to pack up gear because it gives him or her a chance to have quality time with the coach, then the negative reinforcer is not likely to work as intended.

For reinforcement to be effective, it is important for coaches to consider not only the types and kinds of reinforcers to use but also when to schedule reinforcement. An assumption of operant conditioning is that it is desirable to 'provide continuous positive reinforcement when a new skill or habit is first being learned, reinforcing every occurrence' (Sigelman and Rider 2006: 37). But as time goes by, and in an effort to 'maintain the behaviour', it is recommended that the valued behaviour is not reinforced on every occasion, but only intermittently and unpredictably. It has been suggested that when this type of scheduling occurs, the 'learner is likely to continue performing even if the reinforcement stops' (ibid.: 37).

Punishment is another basic process in operant conditioning and has been described as 'any consequence that occurs immediately after an action that *decreases* [or weakens] the frequency of that action' (Vialle et al. 2005: 13). It is useful for a coach who wants to use a punisher to be mindful that, just like reinforcers, punishers will have different meanings depending on the recipient, hence they cannot be used indiscriminately. There are two types of punishment. One is presentation punishment and occurs when a learner receives (or is presented with) a punisher that decreases behaviour (Eggen and Kauchak 2004). For example, suppose that a coach requires an athlete to perform ten press-ups as a consequence of fumbling the ball in a drill. Here the athlete is presented with a physical punisher. The second type of punishment is removal punishment and happens when a learner has something removed that decreases behaviour. For example, when something pleasant, such as playing on the team, is removed, the player may choose to decrease the behaviour that caused this form of punishment in the first place.

The final basic process of operant conditioning we mention is extinction, which has been described as '*the disappearance of a conditional response as a result of nonreinforcement*' (Eggen and Kauchak 2004: 204; italics in original). A common example of extinction is when a coach ignores the behaviour of athletes who are off-task, hoping they will return to being on-task once the reinforcement (the coach's attention) is removed.

COGNITIVE ORIENTATIONS TO LEARNING

Over the past 60 years, many scientists, from a range of different disciplines, have expanded their research interests into areas that are not readily or easily observable (Bush 2006). Consequently, many of the assumptions that informed behaviourist theories of learning are being challenged so that 'today the major theoretical perspectives [on learning] are cognitive' (Schunk 2004: 83). In this section we shall discuss two cognitive learning theories: social cognitive theory and situated learning theory. Cognitive theories can be broadly described as constructivist since they are based on the assumption that learners are 'active seekers and processors of information' (ibid.: 443). Hence, when cognitive theories are used as explanatory frameworks, recognition is given to interactions that occur between behavioural, personal and environmental factors.

How do cognitivists define learning?

Within the cognitive perspective, learning is considered to be 'an enduring change in behaviour, or in the capacity to behave in a given fashion, which results from practice or other forms of experience' (Schunk 2004: 2). According to Schunk (2004: 2), such a description 'captures the criteria' most cognitivists would 'consider central to learning', and highlights at least four assumptions upon which the cognitive perspective is based. First, learning cannot be directly observed; only the products of learning can be observed. Second, learning involves the 'capacity' to change since it is believed that people can learn without necessarily 'demonstrating' it 'at the time learning occurs'; in other words, learning is 'inferential' (Schunk 2004: 2). Third, behavioural change (or capacity for change) endures over time; thus, a modification that lasts only for a brief period (i.e. seconds) is not considered to be learned. Fourth, since learning occurs 'through practice or other forms of experience', when changes in behaviour occur due to hereditary factors, such as maturation, these changes are not considered to be learning (ibid.: 2).

Social cognitive theory

Albert Bandura and his colleagues, who conducted studies on observational learning, are considered the early challengers to behaviourist learning theories. Not surprisingly, given the widespread influence of Skinner, the early work of Bandura was informed by operant conditioning (Schunk 2004). However, over time Bandura's work became more 'socially orientated', focusing on 'how people influence each other' (Lefrançois 2000: 305), hence the interest in observational learning. Two key findings of the research that took issue with the assumptions of behavioural learning theories were 'that people could learn actions merely by observing others performing them [and] . . . reinforcement was not necessary for learning to occur' (Schunk 2004: 83). Observational learning is regarded as a cognitive form of learning because learners are required to pay 'attention, construct and remember mental representations . . . of what they saw, retrieve these representations from memory later and use them to guide behavior' (Sigelman and Rider 2006: 39).

When Bandura proposed the social cognitive theory (formerly called social learning theory; Sigelman and Rider 2006), a key tenet was that learning occurs either '*enactively* through actual doing or *vicariously* by observing models perform' (Schunk 2004: 86; italics in original). Enactive learning is the learning that occurs from the 'consequences of one's actions' (ibid.: 86), whereas vicarious learning occurs 'by observing the consequences of others' actions' (Eggen and Kauchak 2004: 217). Historically, modelling was considered to be nothing more than imitation of behaviour. However, it is now recognized to be more sophisticated and has been described as the cognitive, behavioural and affective changes that occur as a result of observing models (Schunk 2004). Different forms of modelling exist and can be broadly classified under three headings: direct (models who appear in person), symbolic (models represented in books, movies and TV, etc.) and synthesized (developing behaviours from combining previously observed acts) (Eggen and Kauchak 2004).

According to Bandura (1971), there are four interrelated subprocesses associated with modelling or observational learning: attention, retention, production and motivation. The process of attention is important since exposure to a model is not a guarantee that learning will occur. Rather, learners need to be encouraged to be discriminatory in where they place their attention as well as be able to 'recognize, and differentiate the distinctive features of the model's responses' (ibid.: 16). Retention requires observers to be 'active agents who transform, classify, and organize modeling stimuli into easily remembered schemes' (ibid.: 21). The process of production requires observers to translate modelled events into overt behaviours (Schunk 2004). Finally, motivation is important if the learned behaviour is to be enacted into an explicit performance.

Numerous suggestions have been made regarding which factors influence the effectiveness of models. For example, Schunk (2004) suggested that influential factors were model prestige and competence, outcome expectations, developmental status of learner, vicarious consequences, self-efficacy and goal setting. Drawing on social-psychological research, Bandura (1971) contended that models who have power, prestige, intelligence and are competent are copied to a greater extent than models who are considered to be subordinate. Eggen and Kauchak (2004) proposed that a model's effectiveness was dependent on three factors, namely perceived similarity, perceived competence and perceived status. Roberts *et al.* (1999) meanwhile identified four influential factors: modelling correct behaviour is more beneficial for learning than modelling incorrect behaviour; a high-status model will be more beneficial than a low-status model; observing a model that is similar to the self is more helpful than observing a model that is dissimilar; and live and videoed models are of equal benefit.

At first glance, some of the above factors may appear contradictory. For example, a high-status model is better than a low-status one, while observing a model similar to oneself is better than observing a model that bears no resemblance. But what happens if you are working with junior athletes with limited skills? On the one hand, coaches are told that the athletes will learn better if the model has high status (e.g. an elite athlete), but on the other hand the research suggests that athletes learn better if the model is similar to themselves. So how does a coach reconcile this discrepancy? One way is to provide several different models as well as different forms of modelling. Eggen and Kauchak (2004: 221) suggested that 'several models are more effective than a single model, or even a few, because the likelihood of finding a model perceived as similar increases as the number of models increases'. However, they still pointed out 'people are more likely to imitate models perceived as competent than those perceived as less competent, regardless of similarity' (ibid.: 221).

Situated learning theory

The notions that learning is a social enterprise and is influenced by our participation in daily life are key to Jean Lave and Etienne Wenger's situated learning theory. Lave and Wenger (1991) explored the meaning of situated learning in a range of different contexts and proposed that learning was a process that required involvement in a 'community of practice' (CoP). They suggested that CoPs are everywhere and that we are often involved in more than one of them, sometimes as a core member, sometimes on the periphery (Communities of Practice n.d.). While there is no expectation that all CoPs will be the same, Wenger et al. (2002) proposed that they do all share some common elements, specifically a domain of knowledge, a community of people, and shared practices.

Building on earlier work, Wenger (1998) suggested that there was a relationship between CoPs and identity, which caused him to view learning as a transformative experience or, as he liked to call it, an 'experience of identity'. He claimed that the process of learning in a community is a 'vehicle for the evolution of practices and the inclusion of newcomers while also (and through the same process) the vehicle for the development and transformation of identities' (ibid.: 13). Yet for learning to occur, Wenger believed that the community had to have some coherence or reflect the elements described above. In other words, participants have to mutually engage in a joint enterprise in which they have a shared repertoire. Thus, for Wenger, learning was not so much the acquisition of knowledge as a process of social participation.

Associated with CoPs is the concept of legitimate peripheral participation (LPP), which assists us to understand the learning process (Lave and Wenger 1991). LPP explains how newcomers become part of a CoP, thus becoming participants in a socio-cultural practice. When people join a CoP they often do so at the periphery, but as they become more competent they become fuller participants, with some eventually becoming old-timers. This process has been described as moving from the periphery of the community towards the 'centre'. Lave and Wenger go on to say that learning via LPP occurs regardless of the context, or even if there is no explicit intention that learning will occur.

When Trudel and Gilbert (2006) provided a detailed overview of coaching research, some of the uncovered work reflected Sfard's (1998) participation metaphor, which, we would argue, is a fundamental tenet of situated learning theories. Cassidy and Rossi (2006) claimed that the potential for utilizing the concept of communities of practice in coaching is 'profound', and provided examples of recent work to support their contention. For example, Jones et al. (2004) suggested that the concept of CoP could be generative when interpreting the views expressed by elite coaches. Additionally, in work that was explicitly framed using situated learning, Cassidy et al. (2006c) highlighted how elite netball players' interpretations of belonging to a team differed between those who are more centrally located within the community and those who are on the periphery. What is more, they found that the players' sense of belonging appeared fundamental to their desire and motivation to learn, develop and perform. Trudel and Gilbert (2006: 528) used LPP to explain the way many elite coaches 'proceed from athletes to assistant coaches where they may spend five or more years'. They explained the athletes' transition as going from being on the periphery of the coaching process to becoming a more legitimate member as an assistant coach and eventually an elite or head coach. Additionally, Galipeau and Trudel (2006) used situated learning to explain athlete learning, suggesting that it was beneficial to view coaches and athletes as comprising two distinct CoPs, and hence the need to 'nurture' a separate athlete CoP. Finally, Rynne et al. (2006) used situated learning to inform their discussion on issues associated with coaches' learning in the workplace.

In a professional development context, Cassidy et al. (2006a) and Culver and Trudel (2006) found that coaches benefited from the round table discussions with others in a community, yet voiced the need for facilitators to exert some control over the direction and length of the discussions if they were to be of optimal value. Such a notion is in keeping with the work of Wenger et al. (2002: 80), who contended, 'the most important factor in a community's success is the vitality of its leadership'. Cassidy and Rossi (2006) also discussed the implications of using the concept of CoPs to energize the notion of the apprenticeship in coach education. When discussing potential designs for learning in coach education, they were cognizant that learning 'cannot be designed'; rather, learning 'happens, design or no design' (Wenger 1998: 225). Nonetheless, Wenger suggested that learning can be designed *for*; that is, learning can be brought about by facilitating the conditions in which it can occur. It is a stance we would encourage coach educators to heed.

Lave and Wenger's (1991) work is not the only framework that recognizes the situatedness of learning. Increasingly, an emerging Canadian body of work is utilizing Moon's generic view of learning to understand how coaches learn (see Hussain and Trudel 2007; Ménard et al. 2007; Werthner and Trudel 2006; Wright *et al.* 2007). In describing a pictorial representation of Moon's view of learning, as it is applied to a coach's learning process, Werthner and Trudel (2006: 201) stated:

> [t]he coach's cognitive structure is at the centre of this figure and will change and adapt under the influences of three types of learning situations. In mediated learning situations, such as formalized coaching courses, the learning is directed by another person. In unmediated learning situations, there is no instructor and the learner takes the initiative and is responsible for choosing what to learn. Finally, there are the internal learning situations, where there is a reconsideration of existing ideas in the coach's cognitive structure.

Moon uses the metaphor of the network to explain her situated view of learning. She explains that in a network, 'learning can take place in many different ways with many diverse individuals or groups and is seen as more than just an accumulation of knowledge' (Werthner and Trudel 2006: 201).

COGNITIVE ORIENTATIONS TO DEVELOPMENT

As was mentioned in the introduction to the chapter, there are many different categories of development. In this section we touch only briefly on cognitive orientation to development, specifically the work of Jean Piaget and Lev Vygotsky. While there are some similarities between the ideas expressed by these two, there are also definite differences. For example, although both Piaget and Vygotsky viewed learning and development as quite separate, Piaget saw 'development as preceding learning' (Sigelman and Rider 2006: 196) whereas Vygotsky perceived learning as setting 'developmental process in motion' (Driscoll 2005: 255). In this section we discuss two cognitive perspectives on development that reflect the work of Piaget and Vygotsky respectively. In concluding, we very briefly introduce the work of Urie Bronfenbrenner, whose work in the 'social and cultural context of human development' we believe holds considerable potential for pedagogical practice (Drewery and Bird 2004: 23).

The cognitive development perspective

Jean Piaget was a Swiss scholar whose work throughout the twentieth century was, and continues to be, influential on how we understand cognitive development. He was interested in studying 'how humans acquire knowledge and use it to adapt to their world' (Sigelman and Rider 2006: 41). Possibly because of his background in zoology and philosophy, his theories reflect the assumptions of constructivism and structuralism. These assumptions are grounded in the view that cognitive development 'depends on four factors: biological maturation, experience with the physical environment, experience with the social environment and equilibration'

(Schunk 2004: 447). The first three factors are self-explanatory, but it is the 'concept of equilibrium and the need to achieve it [that] are the foundations of Piaget's theory' (Eggen and Kauchak 2004: 37). Equilibrium has been described as '*a state of cognitive balance between individuals' understanding of the world and their experiences*' (ibid.: 37; italics in original). To understand the concept of equilibrium it is useful to be familiar with its associated processes, namely organization, adaptation, assimilation and accommodation.

A sense of balance or equilibrium is important to our development, and this is realized when we understand new experiences. However, if we are unable to understand the new experiences, a state of disequilibrium occurs, which can cause some discomfort, hence the saying 'I am out of my comfort zone'. Yet it is the notion of disequilibrium that is considered to be 'a major energizing force in development' since it requires the employment of two separate but related processes to restore a sense of equilibrium, specifically organization and adaptation (Eggen and Kauchak 2004: 37).

As the name suggests, the process of organization relates to organizing the vast number of experiences we have every day to make sure we do not get swamped. In our effort to achieve equilibrium we organize these experiences into some form of systems or mental patterns that Piaget called schemes. It is this process of organization – that is, forming and using schemes – that helps us to understand our world (Eggen and Kauchak 2004). However, when we are acquiring experiences, existing schemes can become inadequate and, as a consequence, we are required to adapt. The process of adaptation occurs when schemes and experiences are adjusted in an effort to maintain equilibrium (ibid.). Adaptation occurs via 'two equally important and complementary processes: assimilation and accommodation' (Vialle *et al.* 2005: 26).

Assimilation is the initial process we use upon meeting a new situation and occurs when we attempt to fit (or assimilate) the new information into existing schemes (Vialle *et al.* 2005). For example, when Tania moved to Australia for her doctoral study and tried to understand Australian Rules football (Aussie Rules), she initially relied on her existing schemes; that is, her knowledge of other forms of football (rugby union and rugby league). Similarly, when she saw her first game of European handball, it was judged against other existing schemes: knowledge of sports she considered to be similar, such as basketball, netball and water polo. Accommodation is the second process and occurs when we experience something that cannot be assimilated into our existing schemes, resulting in our having to make changes to our schemes (ibid.). As we interpret new experiences, assimilation and accommodation are in 'constant flow', with equilibrium occurring when a balance is found between the two (ibid.).

Equilibrium was one of the mechanisms Piaget suggested was responsible for progression from one 'stage' to the next (Driscoll 2005). Piaget proposed that there are four major periods or stages of cognitive development: 'the sensorimotor stage (birth to age 2), the preoperational stage (ages 2 to 7), the concrete operations stage (ages 7 to 11), and the formal operation stage (ages 11 to 12 or older)' (Sigelman and Rider 2006: 42). The view that development is 'stagelike' has had, and continues to have, considerable purchase in the coaching community, especially in relation to coaching youth sport and sport development. It is to this we now turn our attention.

Increasingly, young people begin their formal sporting experiences at younger ages – a tendency known as early specialization. In examining this phenomenon, Côté and his colleagues observed that the elite athletes generally transitioned through three stages of development: 'the sampling years (age 6–12), the specializing years (age 13–15), and the investment years (age 16+)' (Fraser-Thomas *et al.* 2005: 27). In the sampling years the elite athletes had participated in various different sports. This number decreased until they made a commitment to just one in the investment years. Because of this and other research, Côté is wary of young people specializing too early, suggesting that

> if specialization occurs at a developmental inappropriate age, benefits (e.g., improved skills) are outweighed by physical, psychological, and social disadvantages (e.g., overtraining, injury, failure to develop transferable skills, decreased enjoyment, burnout, depression, decreased self-esteem, increased sensitivity to stress, fear of competition, sense of failure, missed social opportunities etc.
>
> (Fraser-Thomas *et al.* 2005: 28)

While we agree with the above sentiments, to problematize it a little we refer readers to read Chapter 6, where Lisette Burrows highlights the negative consequences of viewing development as having to occur in narrowly prescribed 'age-appropriate' stages. It is useful to keep her ideas in mind when considering the Long Term Athlete Development (LTAD) framework. While the LTAD is not promoted as a panacea, it is described as being helpful 'to "package" complex phases of child/adult development into a simple and flexible model' (Sport England South West n.d.). Yet development is complex. Despite one of the principles of LTAD being that it is athlete centred, it uses terms that do little to support such a stance. For example, in phases 3, 4 and 5 of the 'staged talent development model', descriptors are used such as 'Building the "engine"', 'Fine tuning the "engine"' and 'Maximising [the] "engine"' respectively. Using such mechanical phrases to describe developing athletes does not give a sense that an athlete-centred environment is being promoted or that much recognition is being given to contextual factors that influence development.

Cultural-historical development perspectives

Lev Vygotsky was a prominent Russian whose work in educational psychology in the early twentieth century was, and continues to be, revolutionary in that he viewed 'learning and development as culturally, socially and historically mediated' (Vialle

et al. 2005: 48). Vygotsky's cultural-historical theory of development is complex, so we shall only briefly touch on two features here: co-construction and the zone of proximal development (ZPD). We acknowledge that there are limitations to focusing only on one or two concepts and not the whole theory. For example, Vialle *et al.* pointed out that the ZPD

> should be understood in the context of the theory as a whole . . . otherwise the zone of proximal development can be interpreted as being a 'restricted view of learning processes and reduces the learner's role to one of passivity and dependence upon the adult'.
>
> (2005: 61)

Similarly, Schunk (2004: 296) observed that the 'emphasis it [the ZPD] has received in Western cultures has served to distort its meaning and downplay the complexity of Vygotsky's theory' (for comprehensive overviews of Vygotsky's work, see Daniels 2001; Kozulin *et al.* 2003; Moll, 1990; and Wink and Putney 2002). Despite recognizing these limitations, we consider it to be beneficial for coaches and students of coaching to be introduced to Vygotsky's work so that they can begin to use his and related ideas to reflect on their beliefs and practices regarding development.

Underpinning Vygotsky's theory of development was his belief in the importance of the people surrounding a child (and, we would suggest, any learner). He saw these people as being crucial in 'supporting and enhancing the child's development' (Drewery and Bird 2004: 21). However, Vygotsky's focus was not just on the child, but also on the effect the interaction between the child and the supporting adults and older peers had on this latter group. He saw development, then, as occurring in 'interactions between people', a process he called 'co-construction'. Co-construction reflected his belief that 'knowledge creation' is 'a dynamic process' (ibid.: 21). Another feature of Vygotsky's theory of development was the zone of proximal development, where he believed our higher mental functions take place. He described the zone of proximal development as '[t]he distance between the actual developmental level as determined by independent problem solving and the level of potential development as determined through problem solving under adult guidance or in collaboration with more capable peers' (Vygotsky 1978: 86). In other words, the zone of proximal development exists between what can be achieved by the learner alone and what can be achieved with assistance (Royal Tangaere 1997). The assistance can come in various forms: from others, in the transition from other-assistance to self-assistance, and from the self (Dunphy and Dunphy 2003).

A useful metaphor for understanding Vygotsky's perspective on the zone of proximal development is a staircase. Here, the zone of proximal development can be viewed as the vertical distance between the stair on which the learner is standing and the next highest stair. To reach the higher stair the learner collaborates with others and/or receives assistance by others to perform. Over time the collaboration or assistance is reduced as the learners internalize what is required to perform the activity. Once the internalization has occurred and the learner no longer needs assistance to perform the activity, it can be said metaphorically that the learner has reached the tread of the next stair. When this occurs, the zone of proximal development becomes the vertical distance to the next stair, and so on (Royal Tangaere 1997). Vygotsky did not view development as linear but, like a stair, inclusive of 'periodic crises and revolutions' (McMillan 1991: 33). He also viewed learning as setting the 'developmental process in motion' (Driscoll 2005: 255).

What does a cultural-historical perspective of development mean for coaching? The zone of proximal development is one concept that has been 'modified to create an important educational practice' (Drewery and Bird 2004: 23), which has become known as scaffolding. In Chapter 2 we discussed the practice of scaffolding in more detail as a means through which a range of different methods could be implemented. Additionally, Potrac and Cassidy (2006) discussed some strategies that a coach, as 'a capable other', could adopt to scaffold the development of athletes. Many of the scaffolding strategies they suggested principally related to the guided discovery and problem-solving methods (again, see Chapter 2, 'Instructional methods and pedagogical strategies', for a discussion of these).

Urie Bronfenbrenner, a Russian emigrant living in the United States, is viewed as being one of the key people who brought Vygotsky's work to the attention of the English-speaking world. Although his ecological theory of development is not as comprehensive as others previously discussed, his work is beneficial because he 'provides a useful extension of Vygotsky's ideas on cultural context' (Drewery and Bird 2004: 23). Bronfenbrenner's ecological model of development can be described as the 'influences surrounding the developing individual' (ibid.: 24). These influences go from *microsystems* (immediate environment, e.g. family, team-mates), through *mesosystems* ('connections that link microsystems' (ibid.: 24)) and *exosystems* (larger social systems, e.g. communities), to *macrosystems* (cultural patterns). The interconnectedness of the systems, going from micro to macro, can be explained by considering them as a set of nested Russian dolls. (Other names for a set of nested Russian dolls are matryoshka doll, stacking doll or babushka doll. They are a set of dolls of decreasing sizes placed one inside another.)

Bronfenbrenner's model holds that 'in order for effective development to occur, youth must experience long-term reciprocal relationships with others', who, in the coaching context, could be coaches and peers (Fraser-Thomas *et al.* 2005: 28). To date, no sport youth development model 'has embraced the notion that positive youth development through sport must be deliberately worked towards by coaches, parents, sport organizations, and policy makers' (ibid.: 231). Notwithstanding such a claim, Côté's Developmental Model of Sport Participation (DMSP) does begin to recognize that sport programmes need to be designed in ways that acknowledge young people's social, physical, psychological and intellectual development. In this respect the DMSP 'integrates many of the concepts suggested

. . . necessary to foster youth development' (ibid.: 31). For example, the model supports young people's involvement in 'a diverse number of activities during early childhood', thereby favouring diversification rather than specialization, and recommends a shift 'from deliberate play to deliberate practice [as the child moves] from childhood to adolescence' (ibid.: 31).

In a number of countries it appears that an increasing emphasis is being placed on sporting talent identification. This has implications for how development is viewed, even though 'there is little evidence that talent identification is the "key" to talent development' (Fraser-Thomas and Côté 2006: 5). Abbott and Collins (2004: 395) have argued for reconceptualizing the notion of talent so that identification and development processes are 'perceived to be dynamic and interrelated'. They also contend that a greater emphasis needs to be placed on the capacity of the young person to develop in sport. Because of the limitations of many current models of talent identification and development, they went outside the sporting domain to draw on models that were multidimensional and dynamic, where increased emphasis is placed on supporting 'the athlete at different stages of their development and not just serv[ing] as a selection agenda' (ibid.: 405). When one is using a multidimensional model for talent identification, consideration is given not only to the physical dimension, for example 'an early maturer in rugby who consistently scores tries due to their physical advantage' (ibid.: 405), but to athletes' social, psychological and intellectual dimensions. Abbott and Collins (ibid.: 405) suggested that key questions should be asked when assessing the development of the early maturer – namely, does he or she 'learn motor elements (e.g., passing) and perceptual elements (e.g., decision making) during the development phase' and does he or she 'show a commitment to their development, especially when faced with adversity'?

CONCLUDING THOUGHTS

As we stated in the introduction to this chapter, it was not our intention to position one orientation to learning and development as being better than another, nor was the chapter designed to provide a detailed overview of various theories and perspectives. Rather, it was our intention to make explicit connections between some key learning theories and perspectives on development with coaching practices and research. We hope that this chapter has assisted coaches, or aspiring coaches, to recognize as well as systematically and rigorously examine: (1) what view(s) of learning inform their practice; (2) how compatible their views, and subsequent practices, are with the learning outcomes they set athletes to achieve; and (3) how their views of development enable and constrain athlete potential. Additionally, we have tried to highlight that the learning process is complicated, and therefore cannot be unproblematically linked to coach instruction.

Lefrançois (2000) suggested that when one thinks about learning it is useful to recognize that the process is not the same for everyone. Instead, learning occurs across a range of circumstances, and the strength of the learner is in having an 'enormous range of competencies' (ibid.: 337). He reminded us that the learner is 'flexible rather than rigid, open rather than closed, inventive rather than receptive, changing rather than fixed, poetic rather than prosaic' (ibid.: 337). While Lefrançois' learner is an ideal, we nevertheless believe it is still worthwhile for coaches to consider the above characteristics when thinking about the athlete as a learner.

SUGGESTED READINGS

Cassidy, T. (2008) 'Clarifying the concept of communities of practice in sport: A commentary', *International Journal of Sports Science and Coaching*, 3(1): 19–21.

Cassidy, T., Potrac, P. and McKenzie, A. (2006) 'Evaluating and reflecting upon a coach education initiative: The CoDe of rugby', *The Sports Psychologist*, 20(2): 145–161.

Cassidy, T. and Rossi, T. (2006) 'Situating learning: (Re)examining the notion of apprenticeship in coach education', *International Journal of Sports Science and Coaching*, 1(3): 235–246.

Culver, D. and Trudel, P. (2006) 'Cultivating coaches' communities of practice: Developing the potential for learning through interactions', in R. Jones (ed.) *The Sports Coach as Educator: Re-conceptualising Sports Coaching*, London: Routledge.

Culver, D. and Trudel, P. (2008a) 'Clarifying the concept of communities of practice in sport', *International Journal of Sports Science and Coaching*, 3(1): 1–10.

Culver, D. and Trudel, P. (2008b) 'Clarifying the concept of communities of practice in sport: A response to the commentaries', *International Journal of Sports Science and Coaching*, 3(1): 29–32.

Cushion, C. (2008) 'Clarifying the concept of communities of practice in sport: A commentary', *International Journal of Sports Science and Coaching*, 3(1): 15–17.

Fraser-Thomas, J., Côté, J. and Deakin, J. (2005) 'Youth sport programs: An avenue to foster positive youth development', *Physical Education and Sport Pedagogy*, 10(1): 19–40.

Owen-Pugh, V. (2008) 'Clarifying the concept of communities of practice in sport: A commentary', *International Journal of Sports Science and Coaching*, 3(1): 23–27.

Rynne, S. (2008) 'Clarifying the concept of communities of practice in sport: A commentary', *International Journal of Sports Science and Coaching*, 3(1): 11–14.

Trudel, P. and Gilbert W. (2006) 'Coaching and coach education', in D. Kirk, D. Macdonald and M. O'Sullivan (eds) *The Handbook of Physical Education*, London: Sage.

Werthner, P. and Trudel, P. (2006) 'A new theoretical perspective for understanding how coaches learn to coach', *The Sport Psychologist*, 20: 198–212.

END-OF-CHAPTER TASKS

Drawing on a sporting or activity context with which you are familiar, describe:

1   Examples of reinforcement (positive and negative) and punishment (positive and negative) that you have experienced. Discuss some of the consequences of receiving or giving these forms of reinforcements and punishments.

2   The CoP where your participation has the greatest legitimacy. Explain how and why you have gained this legitimacy.

3   A situation where you have learned something as a consequence of re-establishing a sense of 'equilibrium'. Your description should identify the processes of organization and adaptation (the latter via assimiliation and accommodation).

4   A situation where you have learned or developed as a consequence of a process which Vygotsky called 'co-construction'. Reflect on this experience and explain some of the consequences (positive and negative) of developing this way.

5   A situation where you improved as a result of assistance or 'scaffolding' provided by others. Reflect on this experience and explain some of the consequences (positive and negative) of developing this way.

THE ATHLETES

CHAPTER 6

▼ 'DEVELOPING' ATHLETES

Lisette Burrows

INTRODUCTION

Last night on television I saw a young man graduate with an honours degree in science. The only thing that made the story 'newsworthy' was the fact that he was just 13 years old. We do not expect achievements like this from young boys. We expect teenagers to be experimenting, searching for their identity, and rebelling against their parents or caregivers. Graduating from university just does not fit our picture of what young people should be doing at 13. Similarly, when we coach a team of 5-year-olds in football we do not expect them to be executing finely honed passing, dribbling and kicking skills, positioning themselves strategically on the field or engaging in complex tactical play. We expect them to cluster around the ball like bees around a honey pot, because 'that's the stage they're at'. Both of these expectations arise from developmental assumptions. In this chapter I outline what I mean by 'developmentalism'. Next, I explain why thinking about children 'developmentally' in coaching situations can be problematic. Finally, I sketch some alternatives that may help coaches to practise in less 'developmental' ways.

DEVELOPMENTALISM – WHAT IS IT?

Developmentalist notions are readily found within orthodox psychological accounts of how people change. But they are also readily found within the everyday common-sense assumptions that parents, coaches, teachers and children share about human

change throughout a lifespan. Developmental statements 'make a claim about a person or group of people on the basis of age or "stage"'(Morss 2001: 2). 'He's too old for that', 'she's acting like a baby', 'she's a terrible 2' and 'grow up, Johnny' are examples of developmental statements we hear every day in homes, schools and on sports fields. 'Developmentally appropriate practice' and 'sequential learning' are developmental concepts that we might hear teachers, psychologists and programme developers using. Developmentalism is an umbrella term used by some critical psychologists (e.g. Baker 2001; Morss 1996) to refer to these kinds of statements and the assumptions that underpin them.

When we use developmental language we assume that people think and act in particular ways depending on their age and/or stage. We also assume that those ages and stages are universally recognizable; that is, if I say, 'Tom's a terrible teen', others will know what I mean. Chances are, in Western society at least, that people *will* know what a 'teen' means. Indeed, decades of experimental research in developmental psychology has 'proved' that teenagers exist, that they behave in particular ways (for example, they take risks, they are egocentric), and that all of this is very different from the world of 'grown-ups'. But are teenagers 'really' like that? Do all teenagers feel, act and think in similar ways? Is it necessarily the case that a 13-year-old thinks more about him- or herself than about others? Are all teenagers clumsy? Do they all eat lots of junk food? Are they all concerned with image? What happens to our theories of how people develop when something or someone interferes with them, like the boy I mentioned in the introductory anecdote? I shall come back to this question later in the chapter.

Another thing about developmental language is that it often suggests that what happens to us when we are young will influence how we 'turn out' when we are older. Contemporary concerns about childhood obesity, youth violence, and drugs and alcohol are all linked to the notion that unless we 'catch them' early, a bleak future for young children awaits — whether this be as an obese adult, a violent parent or a drug addict. Sport is no stranger to the 'catch them quick' notion, either. 'Mastering the basics' is a catchphrase used by many coaches. The notion that children learn to walk before they run, creep before they crawl and float before they swim is an everyday understanding shared by many coaches and instantiated as 'fact' in motor development literature. We do not teach things to children until they are 'ready' because we believe they need the fundamental motor skills *before* they can incorporate these into more complex motor scripts (such as a game). Because we believe that early experiences determine what happens later in life, it is not uncommon to find children as young as 2 years old learning to throw, kick or bat a ball 'in preparation' for their participation in community and/or elite sport. Increasingly, young children are being encouraged to participate in sport not only for the recreational benefits it affords, but also as a way of decreasing the likelihood that those children will grow up to be obese and unhealthy adults (Burrows and Wright 2003).

Because young children are presumed to have 'not yet developed' the cognitive capacity to think sensibly for themselves or to know what they need, parents are often implicated as key facilitators of early experiences in sport and/or physical activity. Indeed, a 'good' parent or caregiver, in middle-class Western terms at least, is often portrayed as one who provides his or her children with early opportunities to participate in sport. When children are enrolled in sports clubs, coaches are charged with taking responsibility for the development of other people's children. In both parenting and coaching roles, the influence of developmental understandings of human change is palpable.

One of the other interesting features of developmental statements is their tendency to imply causal links between development in one sphere and another. In a New Zealand parenting magazine, for example, we read that running, jumping and climbing in the early years set a child up for life. Movement is the key to developing self-esteem, confidence and learning (*First Steps* 1996). In this statement, physical development through movement is explicitly connected to the development of emotional and intellectual capacities. Movement is accorded a primary role in 'setting a child up for life'. Similarly with sport: links are often forged in public and professional discourse between playing a game and becoming a better person – a person with capacities to work in teams, cooperate with others, set and achieve goals, and so on.

None of the above features of developmentalism is necessarily problematic unless we look at who misses out when we think of development like this. As Walkerdine (1984, 1993), Burrows (2002) and Stainton Rogers and Stainton Rogers (1992) suggest, the developmental 'story' of human change is just that: *one* among many possible tales of how people change. The fact that it has so much currency means that other ways of thinking about and practising human development are inevitably marginalized. Furthermore, as Walkerdine (1993) has suggested, developmentalism can actually work to construct the ways in which people recognize themselves and others. In other words, developmentalism *produces* the 'development' we think we observe in ourselves and others. In the next section I use some examples from coaching contexts to illustrate the more pernicious effects of developmentalism.

WHAT DOES DEVELOPMENT DO?

Developmental assumptions shape our view of what people can and cannot do at particular ages. In coaching, they provide a set of lenses through which we observe, monitor and classify children's progress. As I suggested at the beginning of this chapter, we do not consider teaching complex strategic moves to 5-year-olds because we know they will not understand them; it would be developmentally inappropriate. On the other hand, we *do* expect that 16-year-olds will have mastered the basics of throwing and catching and that they can therefore participate in a game of basketball or cricket.

In a general sense, developmental psychologists tell us that children grow larger, taller and more coordinated over time, exhibiting progressively more complex motor skills as they age. Developmental psychologists would also say that because

children's mental structures change as they age, older children are more capable of abstract thought than young ones. The fact that most children *do* seem to be able to run faster, jump further, wield bigger cricket bats and understand game plans better at 12 years than 6 years confers a truth status to these developmental claims. We regard the processes of change that children go through en route to maturity as both natural and to some extent predictable. We 'look' for these kinds of changes in children and worry if we cannot see them. But *whose* development defines 'the norm' against which these children are measured?

Since the 1960s, critical psychologists have been questioning the implied naturalness and universality of developmental 'norms' (Baker 2001; Broughton 1987; Burman 1994; Morss 1996; Walkerdine 1993). Space prohibits a thorough canvassing of this critique, yet what most of this work shares is an understanding that developmental milestones are cultural constructions rather than scientific truths. In other words, 'normal' is what a particular group of people with the power to define what 'counts' say is 'normal'. Commenting on the developmental accounts prevailing in American textbooks, Parker and Shotter (1990: 50) attest that 'what we have here are features of white middle class US society mapped onto models of development which are then treated as universal'. The trouble with developmental 'norms' is that they tend to universalize tendencies and traits that relate to a particular sort of child – a masculine, European one – and stigmatize any child who fails to measure up to that idealized vision (Burman 1991, 1994; Walkerdine 1993). Once standards of 'normal' motor development, for example, are established, those deviating from the 'norm' are inevitably construed as in need of remedial assistance. The following excerpt drawn from a text widely used by physical educators clearly illustrates the evaluative consequences of employing developmental norms:

> Understanding the way people normally develop movement skills throughout the lifespan enables us to diagnose problems in those individuals who may be developing abnormally. . . . Also, because there is a link between all domains of behaviour, improvement in the motor domain may indirectly lead to improvements in intellectual or social development. Activities can, therefore, be devised to assist in the development of movement potential. To accurately create such a movement curricula, we must have a knowledge of normal motor development.
>
> (Payne and Isaacs 1987: 7)

Australian researcher Jan Wright's (1997) critique of the hierarchy of skills development, supported by fundamental motor skills programmes, provides another illustration of the consequences of normalizing particular kinds of development over others. She draws attention to the specificity of the skills included in Fundamental Motor Skills (FMS) assessment batteries widely used in Australia and New Zealand. She shows how skills such as the overhand throw, catch and kick are intimately related to performance in competitive sports played predominantly by men. According to Wright, the lack of emphasis in FMS tests on motor skills that link to activities such as dance or gymnastics contributes 'to the (re) production of gender differences which construct girls and women as deficient, as lacking in comparison to a male standard' (ibid.: 20). I would argue that the standards and norms informing measurement of motor skills marginalize not only girls, but all children whose interests and proclivities lie with skills requiring balance, flexibility or fine motor coordination.

Another problem with developmental claims is their evaluative tone. Because human development is represented as a linear process, people are assumed to be *progressing*, getting *better* at something, improving in an upwards and onwards sort of fashion. But what happens when development does not work like this? What happens when little Johnny stays short instead of developing the towering 6 foot 5 inch frame that was expected at 17 years old? What happens if Mary never learns to 'run'? What happens when 'grown-ups' behave 'like children'? What generally happens is they get labelled as 'developmentally delayed' or 'immature'. These labels acquire their pejorative tone only because a norm or 'ideal' exists, yet as I have suggested, those norms themselves may rest on shaky foundations.

It is not only those who do not fit the 'norm' who are positioned as underdeveloped when age- and stage-related claims and practices are enacted. Caregivers, coaches, teachers – any people who guide young people – also potentially feel the impact of developmental claims. A coach who fields a team of athletes, some of whom have difficulty playing by the rules or respecting the referee, will feel the disapproval of her peers. A parent whose 5-year-old child cannot throw the ball as far as the others in his team will worry. A coach whose teenage athlete fails to develop his 'full potential' under her tutelage will feel that she could have done more. When competency is linked with age, as it is in developmental claims, judgements are inevitable.

Developmentalism also actualizes particular power relations between adult coaches and young athletes. By virtue of being considered 'not yet an adult' (Mayall 1994), children are constituted as 'unknowing' alongside adults who 'know'. It is coaches who decide when their squad will do fitness activities, when they are 'ready' for the game, and for how long and under what conditions they will practise specific skills. In certain circumstances, coaches also involve themselves in planning athletes' nutritional intake, guiding their choice of clothing and controlling their social activities. As Mayall puts it, when children are construed as not yet able to make sensible, informed decisions about their well-being for themselves they become persons 'to whom actions are done' (ibid.: 123). The benchmarks of 'normal development' mapped out in many coaching handbooks provide a set of lenses through which coaches can legitimately 'observe', exercise surveillance on, assess and remediate young athletes 'for their own good'.

Research has repeatedly outlined the multiple ways that childhood has been conceived of in different cultural and historical settings. As Aries (1962) points out, prior to the nineteenth century the notion of 'childhood' itself did not exist. Rather, children were regarded as 'mini-adults' and afforded responsibilities similar to those of grown-ups. In contemporary times the ideal end-point of child

development in some Western communities is an individual, autonomous, rational self. For other cultural groups it is an interdependent adult capable of functioning in, and contributing to, a collective. Some societies expect their young children to be free to play, to 'make believe' and live unencumbered by fiscal responsibilities, while others require their children to participate in the world of work to keep their families afloat. Ideas about who children are, what they can be and how they should behave are inevitably connected to political, economic and cultural investments.

Even if you have difficulty thinking of development as social rather than 'natural', there are bound to be incidents in your experience as a coach that make you question the inevitability of normative ages and stages. At the beginning of this chapter I mentioned the 13-year-old who got an honours degree. There are golfers, runners and swimmers who also do surprising things that are out of step with our developmental expectations (e.g. the 80-year-old who runs the marathon, or the teen golf champion). It is not only the 'exceptional' that alerts us to the problems of assuming age-related competency, though. Athletes of similar chronological age can differ markedly in their skills, aptitudes and behaviours, and the same child can act in different ways in different circumstances (for example, on Monday he was great at goal-kicking but on Thursday he couldn't get one ball between the posts). Precise claims about what children of particular ages can and cannot do simply cannot hold true for all children all of the time.

Despite abundant evidence contradicting the tenets of developmentalism, coaches, parents, officials and children themselves persist in holding expectations of what athletes are like based on their age. Many sports competitions use age as an organizing framework, and children's performances are regularly compared with those of others of the same age. Standards for judging performance and guiding coaching practices are inevitably informed by developmental notions that position some behaviours and skills as immature and others as mature. Children with disabilities, children whose proclivities lie outside the realm of what counts in 'developmental' terms and children for whom accomplishing 'fundamental motor skills' will take a lifetime are just some of those rendered 'underdeveloped' or 'abnormal' when 'development' guides practice. Yet what alternatives are there and do we not need something to help us decide what to do as coaches? It is not my intention to replace one orthodoxy – developmentalism – with another, or to suggest that coaches should have no understanding of what their athletes may need at various points in their life trajectory. Rather, my intent is simply to encourage those working with athletes to think about the consequences of employing developmental assumptions and consider other ways of understanding children's change.

DOING DEVELOPMENT DIFFERENTLY

At one level, doing development differently might simply mean asking ourselves why we categorize athletes the way we do. For example, a starting question might be, is it 'fair' or 'pedagogically correct' to have 9-year-olds of widely varying strength and size playing together in competitive sports? In New Zealand, junior

rugby grades use weight as an organizing framework for allocating athletes to teams. Wrestling and weightlifting clubs adopt a similar practice. In most other sports, however, chronological age continues to function as the means for characterizing children as members of a team or coaching group. Rethinking this mode of classification would be one step towards disrupting the restrictive (short 9-year-olds still have to get the ball in the standard hoop) and often discriminatory connotations (featherweight Johnny being squashed by heavy Karl) of age-related groupings.

A second strategy to disrupt developmental effects is to perpetually adopt a reflective stance towards our own pedagogical choices in terms of both content and delivery. Why do we always do the drills first and then play the game? Why do we presume athletes need to master the basics before moving on to the more complex task of using those fundamentals in a 'real' context? Why do we think we are the only ones with insights about what might make the team work more collaboratively? The authors in this book suggest that practices used in *Game Sense* (Thorpe 1997) are viable pedagogical alternatives to orthodox coaching practice. I suggest these ideas may also form feasible anti-developmental alternatives for coaches. Lave and Wenger (1991), for example, have developed a concept called 'situated learning theory' that offers coaches a different way of regarding their athletes. Rather than assuming that athletes are all at some predefined developmental stage, Lave and Wenger suggest that it is the *differences* of perspective and behaviour among co-participants that yield productive learning. They talk of 'communities of practice' where 'old-timers' with knowledge and skills about something (e.g. attacking the goal) work with newcomers (those who have not played before), each altering the other's way of doing something through the exchanges. This seems like a useful way to think about the coaching context. If age is a non-negotiable classification device, then a promising anti-developmental alternative would seem to be to regard the team as a community comprising co-participants whose capacity to change (e.g. get better at attacking the goal) is located not in the minds and bodies of its individual children, but rather in the culture of the group and the relational possibilities it affords.

Rovegno's (1995) research on skill development in the physical education context may offer another alternative. She suggests that often coaches and teachers ascribe labels such as 'immature' and 'mature' to children in relation to their skill level. Rather than continue to position young people as either advanced or retarded on some normative motor development scale, she emphasizes a holistic approach focusing on the relations between children and their environment. An approach like this means that children do not necessarily find themselves linking their competency to age and finding themselves wanting.

CONCLUDING THOUGHTS

Given what we know about the historical and cultural variability of childhood, why do we continue to use chronological age as a marker to shape our expectations of what children can achieve, think about and do? As Baker (2001) suggests, a grand narrative of child development as progressive, linear and gradual has been entrenched in the thinking and practice of Western peoples for centuries. The idea that children develop through a sequentially organized series of steps towards an ideal is so firmly embedded in both professional and everyday understandings that it seems impossible at times to imagine child development any differently, let alone do it differently. The fact that we have always thought about development this way does not mean it is the best or only framework available for organizing human endeavour.

Age-related norms set up a notion of change over time that regulates, evaluates and excludes many children from positive experiences in sport. Some may argue that this is the nature of the beast; that is, sport is inherently selective, elitist and reliant on the exclusion of many to support the performance outcomes of a few. I would counter that whether you are a participation- or performance-orientated coach (or both), continuing to employ developmentalism as a bedrock for coaching children will always yield consequences, not many of them pleasant, for those at the centre of coaching practice: the athletes.

SUGGESTED READINGS

Burrows, L. and Wright, J. (2003) 'The discursive production of childhood, identity and health', in J. Evans, B. Davies and J. Wright (eds) *Body, Knowledge and Control: Studies in the Sociology of Education and Physical Culture*, London: Routledge.

Morss, J. (1996) *Growing Critical: Alternatives to Developmental Psychology*, London: Routledge.

Rovegno, I. (1995) 'Theoretical perspectives on knowledge and learning and a student teacher's pedagogical content knowledge of dividing and sequencing subject matter', *Journal of Teaching in Physical Education*, 14: 284–304.

Wright, J. (1997) 'Fundamental motor skills testing as problematic practice: A feminist analysis', *ACHPER Healthy Lifestyles Journal*, 44(4): 18–29.

END-OF-CHAPTER TASKS

It is the first day of training for a group of ten 'little nippers' (novice surf life-savers). An assortment of children expectantly hover in the clubhouse. All they have in common is a desire to learn surf skills and their age: they are either 10 or 11 years old.

1 What will you do with this group on their first day?
2 What assumptions about their capacity might you make?
3 How will you tailor a first session to take account of their possibly widely divergent strengths, experience levels and dispositions?
4 What factors other than age will influence what and how you contour this first 'little nippers' session?
5 From where will you get your information about the group?

CHAPTER 7

▼   **UNDERSTANDING ATHLETES' IDENTITIES**

INTRODUCTION

> Coaching is recognising situations, [it's] recognising and responding to
> the people you are working with.
>
> (Steve Harrison, Middlesbrough Football Club,
> in Jones *et al.* 2004: 18)

The above quotation is taken from a book that examines the philosophies and practices of eight top-level coaches who have enjoyed notable successes at both the international and the national levels of sport. In reflecting upon what had made them successful, the coaches highlighted the importance of relating to their athletes as social beings and not just as performing bodies. In this respect, considerable emphasis was placed 'on getting to know them [the athletes] and what makes them tick' (Jones *et al.* 2004: 18) in the quest to optimize sporting performance.

While such inquiry has highlighted the importance of recognizing and appreciating athletes as unique and individual beings, existing coach education schemes have tended to present sports performers as a homogeneous group (Jones 2000). Far from recognizing how an individual athlete is shaped and influenced by his or her gender, race, class and sexuality, the bioscientific view of sports science, which still underpins many coach education programmes, has largely portrayed the athlete as little more than a mechanistic body to be 'serviced' by the coach (Jones 2000; Potrac *et al.* 2000). In commenting upon the technocratic rationality that continues to underpin much coach education provision, Jones (2000) argues that coaches who are driven solely by mechanistic considerations may have difficulty comprehending, and thus adapting to, the complexities of coaching. Indeed, as Jones *et al.* (2004) have suggested, coaching is not only about making connections to different scientific subjects and methods; it is also, and perhaps more importantly, about making connections between other people and life in general. This is not to say that coaches should solely focus on individual athlete needs at the expense of all else. Doing so can easily lead to coaches being accused of inconsistency and even favouritism, and could be difficult to action in a team sport setting. Hence, a coach cannot afford to lavish too much attention (or do so too obviously) on one athlete, even though that athlete may need such concern. Similarly, some athletes prefer not to be highlighted in front of peers in terms of receiving what seems to be a considerable amount of the coach's attention. The trick for coaches, then, is to coach each athlete often *within* the larger group.

Accordingly, the broad aim of this chapter is to explore how athletes' identities may come to bear on the coaching process. In particular, following an introductory discussion of identity, we first explore how notions of disability, gender, sexuality and ethnicity, and their interconnections, may influence how athletes come to view themselves and the impact this has on their sporting performances. Two case studies are subsequently drawn upon to illustrate some of the issues highlighted, namely that of a former elite swimmer, Anne (Jones *et al.* 2005), and that of an Olympic marathon runner, Hussain (Haleem 2005). In keeping with the general ethos of the book, the aim here is not to provide prescriptions as to what coaches should or should not do, but instead to sensitize readers to the critical concerns of culture and social context as they relate to identity and coaching practice.

WHAT IS IDENTITY?

It is useful to recognize that the term 'identity' is a highly complex concept that remains the subject of much debate (Brettschneider and Heim 1997). Brettschneider and Heim (ibid.) suggest that one way identity can be understood is to relate to how a person describes him- or herself to be distinctive or unique. The description could relate to personal or social identity, the latter referring to how we share personal identity within the social environment. Indeed, while people may possess their own individuality, it is not wholly distinct from that of others in society, as through the process of socialization an individual may come to internalize certain values and norms that are associated with a particular identity (Haralambos and Holborn 2000). An important point to consider when discussing identity is that an individual may possess several identities, which may sometimes be contradictory rather than contributing to a single or unified concept of the self (Hall and DuGay 1996; Haralambos and Holborn 2000).

According to Jenkins (in Haralambos and Holborn 2000), individuals are never entirely free to choose the identities they claim. He argues that identity formation is related not just to social interaction, but also to membership of social groups and power relationships. He contends that some groups have the power to assign particular identities to others in addition to claiming certain identities for themselves. In this way we can see how the process of identity creation is heavily immersed in discourse – usually that of the dominant group (Hall 1996). The subsequent creations of identities are, according to Bradley (1997), a critical feature of social life, as our identities shape the way in which we view our worlds. It is perhaps useful to introduce the concept of 'hegemony' here. Hegemony is the sociological concept that refers to the ability of dominant social groups to 'use their power and influence to promote and shape attitudes, values, beliefs, and world-views' that serve to maintain their privileged position in society (Sage 1998: 20). In this respect, Sage (ibid.: 22) states that

> the ways of life and versions of culture and civilisation of the dominant actors are fashioned in a direction that, while perhaps not yielding unquestioned advantage for narrow dominant interests, persuades the masses to embrace a consensus that supports the existing social arrangements.

Hegemony, then, is a practice crucial to the creation of identity and coaching, the influence of which pervades much of the following discussion.

According to Bradley (1997), identities tend to be grounded in social divisions, difference and inequalities (e.g. class, gender, ethnicity, disability and age), although the importance of the divisions for identity can vary from individual to individual, place to place and time to time. Hence, she suggests that it is useful to consider identity as working on three different levels: passive, active and politicized. Passive identities are those that lie dormant but have the potential to become important in terms of how we define ourselves. Active identities are those that an individual is conscious of and that provide a base for his or her actions, while politicized identities are those that provide a constant and consistent base for how an individual thinks about the self. An example of the latter is the work of feminists and gay rights campaigners in politicizing gender and sexual identities. Another framework for understanding identity is provided by Rogoff (1998), who suggests that identity can be understood to operate on three planes: personal, interpersonal and community/institutional. The personal phase refers to an individual enacting a situated identity that is socio-culturally recognized, while the interpersonal involves a relationship that exists between individual participants and the field of participation (Valsiner 1998). Finally, the community or institutional plane focuses on the learning of words that are commonly encountered elsewhere but have a different and specific meaning within the community.

For the purpose of this chapter, we consider identity to relate to our 'understanding of who we are and of who other people are, and reciprocally, other people's

understanding of themselves and others' (Jenkins, in Haralambos and Holborn 2000: 921). Additionally, rather than viewing identity as a set of enduring personality traits that remain with us from childhood onwards, we consider identity to be both fluid and dynamic in nature (Bradley 1997; Tinning *et al.* 2001). Indeed, we believe identity as something that is 'constantly negotiated and performed in relation to changing contexts and circumstances' (Tinning *et al.* 2001: 97). In this respect, it is important to recognize that an individual's identity or identities may be shaped not only by their social engagements with other people, but also through their interactions with what is written, filmed, televised, and photographed (ibid).

DISABILITY AND IDENTITY

> I would probably say that I am an elite athlete running with a disability, for the simple reason that I do the same training as mentioned. You know, I run 100 to 200 miles a week. I do nothing differently from anyone else who is running in the Olympic marathon. I do exactly the same as them. My only difference is that I have a visual impairment.
>
> (Elite marathon runner, in Huang and Brittain 2006: 365)

In broad terms, disability refers to individuals who suffer from a physical, intellectual or emotional impairment or condition. In this regard, people may be born with a disability or acquire a disability during the course of their lifetime (DePauw 2000). Before we examine how this identity may impact upon how an athlete with a disability might make sense of his or her sporting experiences, it is important to explore the discourse surrounding people with a disability in many Western societies.

Traditionally, individuals with disabilities have been subject to disenfranchisement and exclusion in society (Thompson 1998). According to Thompson (ibid.), this state of affairs is largely attributable to the fact that society has traditionally focused on the medical aspects of disability, which emphasizes the limitations that arise for the individual as a result of his or her impairment. Indeed, DePauw (2000: 65) highlights several prominent assumptions surrounding the medical view of disability:

- Disability is located in biology, it is a given.
- Disability is a medical issue, not a social issue.
- Having a disability means needing help and support.
- When a person with a disability has a problem, the assumed cause of the problem is the impairment.
- The person with a disability is a victim.

Thompson (1998) suggests that the dominance of the medical discourse has been so strong that it is often uncritically accepted as *the* way of conceptualizing disability. Indeed, Oliver (1990: 7–8) notes that such 'ideologies are so deeply rooted in social consciousness that they become "facts"; they are naturalised;

hence ideology becomes common sense'. One of the consequences of this discourse is that these individuals have often been portrayed in terms of their 'deficits' and as 'victims' in need of support and protection from their able-bodied counterparts (Ballard 1993; DePauw 2000). Indeed, individuals with a disability are often regarded as 'invalid', or not valid, and, as a consequence, have largely been relegated to peripheral positions and excluded from valued positions in mainstream society (Nixon 1984; Thompson 1998). This sentiment is echoed by Nixon (1984), who argues that it can be attributed to the misplaced sympathy and over-protectiveness of the able-bodied majority, who are reluctant to provide persons with disabilities with access to risky, demanding and valued roles. Such practice can be regarded 'as a form of infantilisation, a patronising approach that over-emphasises the amount of personal care needed and underemphasises the importance of rights and empowerment' (Thompson 1998: 92). Indeed, it is perhaps not surprising that many individuals with a disability experience feelings of anger and frustration in their quest to assume demanding roles and have their abilities and achievements recognized and valued by others (Seymour 1998; Thompson 1998).

De Pauw and Gavron (1995) contend that the performances of elite athletes with disabilities leave no question marks regarding their sporting ability. They note that there are only seconds, or tenths of seconds, of difference between the performances of elite athletes with and without disabilities in sports such as swimming and downhill skiing. They also highlight how disabled athletes have bench-pressed up to 600 pounds (272 kilograms) in competition, while single-leg amputees have high-jumped 6 feet 8 inches (2.03 metres). However, despite such sporting achievements, the available literature exploring how athletes with disabilities experience sport continues to highlight a number of issues for consideration (Huang and Brittain 2006; Seymour 1998). For example, the celebration of the sporting performances of disabled athletes, which often includes the portrayal of their achievements as 'heroic', can contribute to reinforcing their minority status (Nixon 1984; Thompson 1998). This point is well illustrated in the following quotations from disabled athletes, which highlight the feelings of frustration they experience when their achievements are viewed in such a fashion:

> We have done nothing heroic. All we have done is get out there and do what we are supposed to do . . . I am just a normal person who does what he is interested in. I am an athlete, so I have just done what I am supposed to do.
>
> (Huang and Brittain 2006: 366)

> I like to think that I am just an elite athlete, but the circumstances we are in and the treatment we get in many ways makes me feel like I am just a disabled athlete. So how can I expect the public to regard me as an athlete? I think it is very difficult.
>
> (ibid.: 366)

Consequently, it is important to recognize that the social response to an athlete with a disability may be as 'disabling' as the impairment itself, if not more so (Thompson 1998). This point is eloquently highlighted in the following extract from an interview with a world-standard wheelchair basketballer:

> It's just as competitive as any other sport, but you have to deal with the ignorance of people who are not aware of that. People pat you on the back and say 'Good on you boys', and 'Good to see you out of hospital today!'
>
> (Seymour 1998: 115)

In addition to highlighting how their identity is influenced by others' views of their achievements, the research on this topic has highlighted how a disabled athlete's sense of self can also be influenced by his or her interactions with coaches and other able-bodied athletes. For example, Fitzgerald's (2005) and Jackson's (2002) work has outlined how, rather than promoting positive and friendly interactions, the integration of athletes with and without disabilities can also foster tensions. For example:

> The familiar hustle and bustle, murmuring and giggling that follow the instruction 'Get into teams' are always accompanied by the predictable 'Aw Sir, do we have to?' or 'No way are we having him' as the games teacher allocates me to a random team, rather like a spare piece of baggage that no one can be bothered to carry.
>
> (Jackson 2002: 129)

> They don't want you to be there . . . when we're with the rest of the group you can tell some of them, they don't want you there. It's not like I'm the worst. They think I am and that's what it is like all the time.
>
> (Fitzgerald 2005: 51)

These statements are in keeping with the earlier work of Nixon (1984), which suggested that athletes with a disability may experience greater stigmatization and self-denigration as a result of such interactions and experiences. According to Fitzgerald (2005), such feelings can, to some degree, be attributed to the paradigm of normativity that tends to prevail in sport and physical education settings. In this respect, she suggests that the paradigm of normativity is reflected in the dominant conceptualization of sporting ability, which is one that recognizes and values a mesomorphic ideal, masculinity, and high levels of motoric competence.

Given the findings we have highlighted, we believe that coaches who work with athletes with disabilities may benefit from critically interrogating their beliefs and practices. Such reflection could focus on the extent to which their actions, as well as those of any significant others within the coaching environment, serve to provide athletes with a disability with an arena for challenging existing societal stereotypes

(Nixon 1984; Thompson 1998). In order to do this, coaches need to avoid subscribing to inaccurate and oversimplified conceptualizations of these athletes. Such beliefs could lead coaches to develop low expectations for athletes with disabilities in terms of their performance potential, as well as viewing them as victims or alternatively brave heroes (Nixon 1984). Indeed, as with all athletes, coaches should consider the extent to which their respective coaching environments not only allow athletes with a disability to participate in sport in an affirming and open manner, but also strive to optimally stimulate their learning, personal growth and sporting performances (Fitzgerald 2005).

GENDERED IDENTITY

Gender is the sociological concept that refers to 'all the differences between men and women which derive from social expectations about appropriate behaviour, interests, abilities and attitudes for masculine and feminine identity' (Kew 2000: 126). Traditionally, in most Western countries masculinity has been principally associated with notions of independence, decisiveness, aggression, toughness, strength and power. Conversely, femininity has been characterized by qualities such as fragility, sensitivity, and a dependency on men (Coakley 2001; Horne *et al.* 1999; Tinning *et al.* 2001). Although perhaps not as powerful as they once were (Tinning *et al.* 2001), many believe that these particular conceptions and associated discourses still reinforce notions of heterosexuality, nurturing and being supportive among women and those of independence, strong-mindedness and physical strength among men. In this respect, Tinning *et al.* (ibid.) note that the body remains an important source of an individual's identity or identities. In drawing upon the work of Shilling (1993), they suggest that 'the more people attach value to how we look and what we do with our bodies, the greater the likelihood that our self-identities will be tied to them' (Tinning *et al.* 2001: 98). This has obvious implications for anyone who works with people. Indeed, we believe that coaching practitioners should be sensitive to how notions of masculinity and femininity may be intimately linked to an athlete's body. As a consequence, in this section we introduce some discussion of the discourses associated with the male and the female body in contemporary society.

In the context of gender relations, hegemonic masculinity refers to the dominance of one form of masculinity over others (Connell 1995). According to Connell (ibid.), hegemonic masculinity is not fixed in nature across time and place but is, instead, the masculinity that occupies the hegemonic position in a particular social setting. As such, the dominance of a hegemonic masculinity is open to challenge from other masculinities and women (ibid.). In contemporary society the dominant or hegemonic masculinity has tended to be that of white, middle-class males, as opposed to the masculinities of non-whites and homosexuals (Connell 1995; Sage 1998), which are alternatively considered to be 'marginalized' and 'subordinate' masculinities (see Connell 1995). However, this is not to say that non-white and homosexual masculinities are disadvantaged in all social settings (e.g. gay men in the Gay Games). Despite this, the main hegemonic form of masculinity, as mentioned earlier, has tended to emphasize heterosexuality as an important male trait. Failure to comply with this and associated values is not without its consequences. For example, the fear of being labelled a 'poofter' or a 'fag' may cause some males not to participate in what have been traditionally labelled feminine sports and activities despite their interest in and enthusiasm for them (Coakley 2001; Tinning *et al.* 2001). The deterrent effect is well illustrated in the movie *Billy Elliot*, where the main character's decision to pursue a career in ballet is initially met with a mixture of shame, anger and ridicule from his family and significant others.

In terms of coaching practice it is perhaps useful for coaches to understand how sport has provided a particularly fruitful arena for legitimizing and maintaining the hegemonic masculinity while marginalizing or excluding others (Connell 1995; Hickey and Fitzclarence 1997; Kenway and Fitzclarence 1997; Miedzian 1991). For example, the hegemonic 'ideal' male body promoted in magazines, television, films and sports is one that is muscular, strong and powerful (Tinning *et al.* 2001). As a consequence of these images, some male athletes may have concerns about subjecting their bodies to public evaluation in the sporting context for fear of ridicule, especially if they believe their bodies do not conform to social expectations. Hickey and Fitzclarence (1997) thus suggest that coaches need to recognize how sport is a cultural practice, and to acknowledge that what is taught in the name of sport is more than the drills prescribed in the coaching manuals. For example, in the context of Australian Rules football, they note that, through both formal and informal channels, boys learn to adopt a masculinity that is racist, homophobic and patriarchal, in addition to being violent and aggressive (ibid.). They go on to suggest that the cultivation of values such as strength, dominance and aggression in sport is problematic, especially when boys and men are taught to behave in ways that, outside of the sporting environment, would be deemed to be dysfunctional and deviant.

Hickey and Fitzclarence (1997) state that sport has become a space where violence is tolerated, women are marginalized and where abusive behaviour is explained away with the platitude that 'boys will be boys'. In this respect, Coakley (2001) suggests that the record of men's destructive and violent behaviour may be, in part, explained by the hegemonic masculinity that is promoted in the contemporary sports context. Indeed, he notes that

> as boys and men apply this ideology [hegemonic masculinity] to their lives, they learn to view manhood in terms of things that jeopardise the safety and well-being of themselves and others. They may ride the tops of elevators, drive cars at breakneck speeds, play various forms of 'chicken', drink each other under the table, get into fights, use violence in sports as indicators of manhood, use dangerous substances to build muscles, avoid interacting with females as equals, keep sexual scores in heterosexual relationships [or] rough up girlfriends or wives, rape, or kill 'unfaithful' women. Some men learn that size and toughness allow them to get away

with violating norms and that status depends on making others fear or depend on them. If men take this ideology far enough, they may get in the habit of 'forcing their way' on others through physical intimidation or coercion.

(ibid.: 235)

Hickey and Fitzclarence (1997) contend that coaches, through the familiarity, legitimacy and authority they possess, are important agents in the quest to bring about social change in this regard. They suggest that coaches could benefit from an in-depth understanding of young males' interpretation and construction of masculinity within the culture of a particular sport. For example, while the hegemonic practices within rugby, surfing, dance and skateboarding are not the same, they all have 'common-sense' assumptions of what it means to be a male in that specific setting. Despite the differences in what is viewed as 'common sense', the task for coaches is to challenge behaviour that threatens the rights and identities of others. This could include recognizing the way in which power is invested in the hierarchical structures of sports coaching and how this recreates inequalities, reducing the level of covert or overt violence in sports, and assisting boys and men to develop positive relationships between each other and between themselves and women (Connell 1995; Jones 2000; Schempp and Oliver 2000). Consequently, Hickey and Fitzclarence (1997) propose that the following strategies may be useful for coaches who wish to create a climate that enables multiple masculinities to be valued:

- Examine, and prevent the occurrence of, the ways individuals learn to create a 'them' and 'us' mentality by isolating the 'other' in order to assert the authority of the dominant group.
- Do not accept the rationalization of violent behaviour (e.g. 'I just flipped out', 'I have a short fuse', 'boys will be boys'), as such justifications distance the aggressors from taking responsibility for their actions.
- Identify how many of the attitudes and behaviours believed to be 'normal' within the culture of the sport parallel forms of social disharmony and deviance outside of that specific setting.

However, while Hickey and Fitzclarence (1997) believe that new pedagogical strategies and practices are needed to support coaches in their efforts to assist young males explore their masculinity, they warn that this is a far from straight-forward process. Many of the behaviours we may want to change are embedded in traditions, customs, routines and habits, which makes them difficult to recognize and challenge since they do not operate at a rational level.

Coaches may also have to contend with issues similar to those discussed when working with female athletes. In this respect, Bartky (1992) suggests that females in many Western nations are subject to pressures regarding bodily comportment, movements and gestures, the ornamental display of the body, and body size. With regard to the former, she contends that women have less freedom than men in terms of their physical movement and facial expression. For example, she notes that many women have relatively shorter walking strides, take up less space when sitting, make less direct eye contact, and smile more frequently than men. In short, she suggests that 'feminine movement, gesture, and posture must exhibit not only constriction but a certain eroticism restrained by modesty' (ibid.: 107). Furthermore, Bartky argues that, as a group, women are expected to have immaculately coiffed and stylish hair, as well as blemish-free, smooth, soft skin. In this regard, she believes that external appearances can carry extreme importance in terms of how women may be viewed and evaluated in terms of fulfilling the requirements of the hegemonic discourses surrounding femininity. Finally, with regard to body size, she suggests that the fashion for narrow-hipped, taut, small-breasted bodies that border on emaciation has seen many women discipline themselves in terms of their appetite and caloric intake. The result is that many women have become alienated from their bodies as they try to conform to the hegemonic requirements of femininity. Nearly a decade later, Coakley (2001) highlighted how the media promote 'heterosexualised hard bodies' as the most desirable body type for women. Indeed, this image is highly prevalent in magazines, newspapers and television commercials, which emphasize, among other attributes, 'thinness, bust size, lip shape, hairstyles, body hair removal, complexion, [and] allure . . . that "make" the woman' (ibid.: 208).

As a result, female athletes, particularly adolescents, may adopt these discourses as frameworks against which to evaluate their bodies, movements, gestures and appearance. This is a particularly problematic state of affairs, as the body shape promoted is often an image that few women can obtain even if they deprive themselves of food and nourishment (Coakley 2001). Accordingly, the public display of the body (e.g. getting changed in the locker rooms, wearing a team uniform in competition), which is an integral feature of sporting participation, may cause some females not to participate in sport until they are 'thin enough to look "right" and wear the "right" clothes' (ibid.: 210). Furthermore, the pressure to conform to social expectations regarding body shape may manifest itself in the form of eating disorders. For example, Benson and Taub (1993: 360) suggest that 'swimmers may be especially vulnerable to disordered eating due to the display of their bodies in a tight and revealing uniform'. Indeed, the available research (e.g. Jones et al. 2005; Johns 1998; Ryan 1995) on female athletes in general indicates that 'an alarming number of women use laxatives, diet pills, diuretics, self-induced vomiting, binges, and starvation diets in conjunction with their training' (Coakley 2001: 211). Obviously, the consequences of such actions can be extremely painful for the athlete both psychologically and physiologically. As an aside, it is worth noting that eating disorders are not limited solely to females. In this respect, Andersen et al. (2000) suggest that males may be catching up in terms of diagnosed eating disorders and excessive dieting as a consequence of social pressure.

While the media may play an important role in transmitting culturally desirable body shapes, it would be naive to believe that disordered eating and excessive dieting result only from the hegemonic images of the female body provided by them. Indeed, the research of Johns (1998), Jones et al. (2005) and Reel and Gill

(2001), among others, has highlighted that coaches and peers may also have a significant impact upon how a female athlete views her body and, ultimately, herself. More recently, Goodwin (2007) highlighted the role administrators and various significant others play in this regard. Such research has highlighted how the perceived relationship between body fat and performance espoused by significant others may impact upon a female athlete's sense of identity. This is clearly illustrated in the work of Johns (1998), who found that the gymnastic coaches in his study considered 'systematic weight loss' to be crucial to the development of aesthetically pleasing gymnasts. Here, coaches were found to exert great pressure on gymnasts by strictly monitoring the latter's eating habits and frequently measuring their weight, especially in the lead-up to competitions. His findings suggest that coaches tacitly support, and perhaps encourage, gymnasts to achieve rapid weight loss through a severely limited dietary intake. Such pressure has its consequences. Specifically, Johns' (1998) findings revealed how, as a result of the coaches' actions, the gymnasts perceived themselves to be 'fat' regardless of how much weight they lost – a point well illustrated in the following athlete reflections:

> For sure the coaches definitely had a strong influence over what you understood to be the right thing to do, because ultimately you were performing for them, for the sport, and for the country. When it came to the problem about weight they would say, 'Sarah looks a little heavy on the floor, she really should lose some weight, and she'll represent us well'. As a young athlete you automatically become concerned about your weight, and you begin to blow things out of proportion and see yourself as an elephant.
>
> (Johns 1998: 55)

> Another instance really sticks out in my mind, and it was with my team mate and very good friend, [name deleted], who was completely bulimic and was extremely thin. Even though I was healthy and was pretty thin myself, I was being compared to her, but I looked fat and they were saying things like, 'See, [name deleted], she is really looking good, and that is what you have to be like'. Unfortunately, they did not know, or they pretended not to know, that she was barfing her brains up behind closed doors, and then in front of the coaches was the picture of goodness not eating a thing.
>
> (ibid.: 57)

In addition to the coach having the potential to exert a strong influence upon how an athlete may perceive her body (the overwhelming examples here relate to female athletes), comments made by team members, administrators and significant others may also contribute toward this process of self-identity creation (Goodwin 2007; Jones *et al.* 2005; Reel and Gill 2001). This line of inquiry has suggested that through interactions and comparisons with their peers, athletes may arrive at a particular judgement regarding body shape, appearance and physical movements and, ultimately, of themselves. In order to reduce the possibility of athletes developing negative feelings towards their bodies, coaches could adopt a number of strategies. For example, they could avoid group weigh-ins, educate athletes with regard to nutrition and the relationship between body fat and muscle, discourage team members, selectors and administrators from making negative comments to, and about, other athletes, and evaluate their own beliefs regarding femininity and the weight-performance relationship (Johns 1998; Jones *et al.* 2005; Reel and Gill 2001).

SEXUALIZED IDENTITY

Sexuality, in broad terms, refers to the sexual behaviour and characteristics of human beings (Giddens 1997). People can have a wide variety of sexual tastes and inclinations; classified by sexual identity, one finds heterosexuals, lesbian women, gay men, bisexual men, bisexual women, transvestite men, transvestite women, transsexual women and transsexual men. This section, however, will principally focus on the identities and experiences of gay men and lesbian women in sport.

Before we proceed with the exploration of sexual identity as it relates to coaching practice, it is perhaps worth providing some background information relating to homosexuality. While homosexuality exists in all cultures, the notion of a homosexual person is a relatively recent one (Giddens 1997). Here, in drawing upon the work of Weeks (1986), Giddens (1997: 104) indicates that the term 'homosexuality' originates from the 1860s, and was used to describe 'a separate type of people with a particular sexual aberration'. Indeed, homosexuality was, until a few decades ago, not only frowned upon in nearly all societies, but also considered to be a criminal activity. This history of homosexuality might explain why many people are still hostile towards homosexuals (Giddens 1997). In this respect, Town (1999) suggests that the negative reactions to homosexuals may be attributed to the social process of heteronormativity. According to Warner (1993: 21), heteronormativity can be defined as

> the normalising processes which support heterosexuality as the elemental form of human association, as the very model of inter-gender relations, as the indivisible basis of all community, and as the means of reproduction without which society wouldn't exist.

In terms of understanding homophobia in contemporary society, Town (1999) argues that homophobic attitudes may be the consequence of individuals experiencing a range of heteronormative practices from a young age, such as the pathologization of homosexuality, the limited inclusion of homosexuality in school curricula, and religious teachings that classify homosexuality as 'wrong' and 'not natural'.

According to Coakley (2001), gay men and lesbians are often feared, marginalized, ignored or, in some circumstances, subjected to vitriolic criticism, defensive reactions and physical assault. The following extracts, which are taken from the work of Rotella and Murray (1991: 355), give an insight into the views of some parents, coaches, and others involved in sport:

> I don't want my son playing that sport. Most of the guys who play that sport are homosexuals. They are not going to get my son and make him a homosexual. No way. I don't care how much he likes the sport.

> I know she is one of the most talented players in the country but there is no way we are going to recruit her. I hear she is a lesbian and she would just destroy our whole team. Besides, she would kill our recruiting for next year. Other coaches would use it against us.

Given such comments and the stigma surrounding homosexuality, it is perhaps not surprising that many gay and lesbian athletes prefer not to reveal their sexual orientation to their team-mates and coaches. Indeed, the potential and in some cases the actual consequences of 'coming out' in the sporting context include experiencing a sense of isolation, hostility, rejection by coaches and team-mates, exclusion from teams and events, and, for elite athletes, the loss of sponsorship and endorsements (Brackenridge *et al.* 2007; Griffin 1998; Krane and Barber 2003; Pronger 1999; Squires and Sparkes 1996). This is perhaps well illustrated in the following vignette:

> After joining (the campus lesbian and gay student group) I [initially] enjoyed the sense of community I had with other students. I was an anomaly, an out lesbian softball player who wanted to take on the world. I became one of the poster children who were invited to classes or dorms to talk about lifestyles and answer questions. While I was becoming more and more open about who I was, I found myself sitting on the bench more and more. I was there (on the team) as an athlete not a lesbian, but no one in the team could separate the two in their minds and accept me for who I was, so I had a pretty horrible season. On away trips, no one wanted to stay in the same room with me at hotels. Other players preferred sleeping on the floor in other rooms rather than staying in a room with a lesbian. Players shunned me and generally made my life miserable. My coach, who was also rumoured to be a lesbian, was no help. When I was in the health centre with a back injury, no one on the team checked on me.
>
> (Griffin 1998: 98)

Griffin's (1998) work has revealed that there are many myths surrounding lesbian athletes. Among these are that they are sexual predators who prey on their team-mates in order to recruit them to their lifestyle, and that heterosexuals will become lesbians just by associating with lesbian team-mates and opponents. The latter view has tended to present lesbianism as a virus with which a heterosexual athlete can become 'infected' (Fasting 1997). The limited available research exploring the sporting experience for gay male athletes has reported similar findings, with such athletes tending to be feared, mistrusted and stigmatized (Pronger 1999; Woog 1998). In this respect, Coakley (2001) notes that some heterosexual men adopt threatening anti-gay behaviour in the locker room that keeps gay men silent about their sexuality as well as fearful of behaving in a way that could be identified (and could identify them) as 'gay'. According to Messner (1996), such practices have served to generate feelings of shame among men who have strong feelings towards other men, a sentiment well illustrated in the following quotation:

> I could have been a very good major-league player if I was not so emotionally screwed up when I was playing. I was very hard on myself, and I think it all translates back to that feeling of, 'I'm not worthy'. I'm bad because I'm a gay man on the Dodger Stadium field. I don't belong out here. This is wrong. I hate myself . . . I remember walking in the clubhouse every day and feeling that people could see the kiss I gave my lover when I walked out the door. . . . Then you sit down and start talking about strip clubs.
>
> (Wine 2003)

Given such findings, we argue that coaches should attempt to provide an environment that challenges the existing stereotypes regarding gay and lesbian athletes. In doing so, coaches should critically reflect upon their own beliefs on the issue while examining how their current practice may serve to reinforce the dominant homophobic discourse in sport (Schempp and Oliver 2000). For example, by using, or not challenging, the use of language such as 'fag', 'poofter' and 'dyke', coaches may be guilty of reinforcing institutionalized homophobia (Coakley 2001). In addition, coaches may also consider how they provide a coaching environment that actively supports gay and lesbian athletes. This could include dealing with athlete sexuality in a positive, supportive and sensitive manner. Such actions would require some courage on the part of the coach, and might prove to be a far from unproblematic process. However, as Coakley (2001: 238) notes, 'the listener who stands by and says nothing in response to this language perpetuates inequities'.

A further issue for coaches to consider in this context is how the fear of being labelled a lesbian or gay may impact upon female and male athletes. In this regard, it may influence not only the sports that athletes choose to participate in, but also the effort that they expend and their willingness to engage in train-ing programmes. For example, in the context of women's sport, this may be especially so if the result of the training is the development of bodies that differ from the prevailing images of femininity and 'heterosexualised hard bodies' (Bartky 1992; Choi 2000; Coakley 2001; Kew 2000). While coaches are unable to eradicate totally the constraints placed on some women by existing homophobic

discourses, they may be able to create a working environment that promotes the view that developing strength and muscle is a form of personal empowerment for female athletes (Heywood 1998; Schempp and Oliver 2000). Indeed, coaches, through their professional practice, can seek to challenge existing conceptions of femininity. This does not mean that coaches should advocate that females adopt traditionally masculine behaviours, but rather that they can encourage 'girls and women to explore and connect with the power of their bodies' (Coakley 2001: 237).

ETHNIC AND RELIGIOUS IDENTITY

Unlike the concept of race, which has been used to classify people according to physical characteristics, ethnicity refers to 'categories of people who share a common cultural identity and heritage' (Nixon and Frey 1998: 227). In particular, ethnicity is determined by cultural characteristics, such as traditions, values, norms and ideas that constitute a particular way of life (Coakley 2001). In most Western societies, ethnic groups who do not identify with the majority group, which is often white, are often subject to inequality, discrimination and oppression (Thompson 1998; Tinning et al. 2001). This particular state of affairs is mirrored in the sports coaching context. Indeed, while coach education has begun to address the need to cater for athletes with different skill and performance levels, it has largely ignored issues relating to the needs and requirements of different cultural groups (Jones 2000). As a consequence, there has been a proliferation of stereotypes and assumptions among coaches relating to athletes from different cultural backgrounds. For example, Afro-Caribbean athletes are often believed to be physically powerful but lacking in leadership and decision-making skills, while young Muslim males are widely perceived to prefer academic pursuits to any involvement in sport and physical activity (Fleming 1991; Kew 2000; McCarthy et al. 2003). Similarly, Tinning et al. (2001) note that Muslim girls are often considered to be problematic by educators and coaches because of their apparent resistance to sport and physical activity.

In drawing upon the work of Schempp and Oliver (2000), we believe that it is crucial for coaches to develop an understanding of, and sensitivity towards, the ethnic heritage of athletes if they are to provide individuals with positive sporting experiences. For example, in the context of Muslim males' involvement in sport, an appreciation of how religious requirements may constrain sporting involvement could help to dismiss stereotypical beliefs regarding lack of interest. This is illustrated in the following quotation taken from Fleming's (1991: 37) work with Asian schoolboys:

> It's quite difficult for me. I have to pray five times a day. If I have to pray at 12 o'clock and there's a match, I can't play. . . . If it's a matter of 'life and death', you can pray afterwards. But sport doesn't count as a matter of 'life and death'.

Furthermore, Tinning *et al.* (2001) suggest that an understanding of Islamic religious practices and beliefs regarding modesty may help non-Muslims to understand the issues that Muslim females have to contend with in relation to sport. They highlight how Muslim females may, if they expose their bodies and legs to non-Muslims and males, have feelings of guilt and shame. They suggest that rather than Muslim females per se being 'problematic', it is the traditional sporting uniform of skirts or shorts that is a major barrier to their participation. From such a discussion, it is clear that coaches would benefit from a detailed insight into how a Muslim identity may come to bear on an athlete's sporting experience.

In much the same way, many coaches in Aotearoa/New Zealand could benefit from an appreciation of how being a Mäori or Pacific Islander may determine the sense athletes make of their sporting experiences (Salter 2000). For example, an understanding of Mäori beliefs regarding the process of interaction could enable a coach to recognize why a Mäori athlete communicates and responds to team-mates and coaches in the way that he or she does. In this respect, an appreciation of the cultural significance that Mäoridom attaches to *manaakitanga* (the show-ing of kindness, hospitality and respect), *aroha-ki-te-tangata* (love of your fellow man or woman), *whanaungatanga* (familiness), *wairua* (spirituality) and *awhinatanga* (helping, assisting) could be insightful (Bevan-Brown, in Salter 2000). Furthermore, in terms of coach–athlete communication, coaches con-sidering utilizing a questioning-based pedagogy with Mäori athletes need to recognize that such an approach may conflict with the Mäori tradition of not engaging in debate with the *kaumatua* (respected elders) (Thompson *et al.* 2000). Indeed, while there is a paucity of research addressing the sporting experiences of Mäori athletes, the limited findings do provide some initial food for thought. In particular, Wrathall (in Thompson *et al.* 2000) has highlighted a number of issues relating to cultural insensitivity, intolerance and communication between top-level female Mäori athletes and Päkehä coaches and sports administrators. (Päkehä is a term used to describe New Zealanders of European ancestry.) Such issues need to be addressed (or at the very least constructively reflected upon) if such athletes' potentialities are to be realized.

TWO CASE STUDIES: ANNE AND HUSSAIN

This section provides two case studies that highlight many of the previously discussed concepts in action. It thus provides evidence for why coaches should heed not only the factors that create athlete identities and their role in the process, but also the possible consequences of such identities' disruption. The first case details the story of Anne (a pseudonym), a former elite swimmer, who traces her subsequent development of an eating disorder back to a comment made about her weight by her coach (Jones *et al.* 2005). The second recounts the experiences of Hussain, a former Olympic marathon runner whose relationship with his coach became dysfunctional owing to a perceived lack of respect for him as a person as opposed to lack of respect for him as an athlete (Haleem 2005).

Anne

Anne (a pseudonym) is a former top-level swimmer whose career was interrupted and finally terminated by an eating disorder. The case highlights, first, how a strong swimming identity led to vulnerability in terms of an athlete's reaction to perceived body image within a conforming culture of 'slenderness' (Tinning 1991a), and second, the role the coach played in the process of athlete identity creation and disruption. The story starts in earnest when a new coach came to Anne's club. She took an instant liking to his innovations, energy and enthusiasm, which gave her burgeoning athletic identity a substantial boost. She wanted to do well for him as well as for herself. In her own words:

> My new coach promised exciting things and had a lot of new ideas and philosophies. He showed a lot of enthusiasm about my potential, so I took a lot of effort to please him. It was expected that we would eat, live and breathe swimming. Although I felt a bit under stress 'coz he kept putting pressure on us by lowering our [target] times and telling us what we should be eating and stuff, I still really wanted to do well, and was constantly encouraged by him as he seemed to have big plans for me.
>
> (Jones *et al.* 2005: 383)

Soon a strong link was established between Anne and her coach, as she 'bought in' to his ideas, knowledge and methods without question. Her swimming identity became even stronger, as her success became inextricably linked with the person she saw herself as being and becoming. In this respect, Anne's identity as a swimmer and her 'self-esteem within the athletic role became bound ever tighter to her coach's perception of her performance. What he thought and said really mattered' (Jones *et al.* 2005: 383). Then came what Anne termed 'the meeting', where her parents and coach were brought together to discuss progress and future plans.

> I remember it vividly because I respected him so much and I just wanted to be the best. He [the coach] told me that I was doing well, that I was showing progress with my swimming. But then he said 'it would probably be more beneficial if you were lighter and slimmer and could lose a bit of weight and maybe you should look at dieting a bit more'. It just shot me down completely because I never ever thought about it, it just shot everything good that he had to say out of the air. That put doubts in my head about myself and the confidence I had in myself as a swimmer. And I remember feeling so embarrassed, in front of my parents and all. I came away feeling really down; it really affected me. My body was the problem. The focus was on [my body] and I became very conscious of it.
>
> (ibid.: 384)

The identity that Anne had painstakingly built had suddenly been devalued and disrupted by the person who had helped build it. Her coach had encouraged her to train harder and faster, had measured her improvements in terms of time and weight and had promoted her ever-growing investment in a single identity at the expense of others. The process had made her vulnerable, because when such a heavily invested-in persona is disrupted, one that is so closely associated with an essential sense of self, the fall can be great. Brewer *et al.* (1993) neatly refer to it as developing an Achilles' heel as opposed to Hercules' muscles, even though at first glance the opposite may be true. Linking Anne's story to the previous discussion highlights how the overinvestment in her swimming identity exposed her to the potentialities of identity disruption, with the breakage occurring because the coach had judged her through gendered lenses; that is, what the coach thought female swimmers of her level should look like. The value to coaches of considering athletes' identity construction, maintenance and possible disruption comes to the fore, then.

Hussain

Hussain's tale somewhat parallels Anne's story. He too was greatly influenced by a new, foreign coach who seemed to promise much. Taking on board the coach's advice and instructions, Hussain tied himself closely to the coach's methods and philosophies as his running gave him a previously undiscovered focus and purpose in life. As early success further increased his enthusiasm, Hussain's reverence for his coach took the form of zealous overconformity to tough training routines – an attitude that was encouraged and subsequently insisted upon by the coach. Following a better than expected performance at his first major championships, Hussain describes the scene immediately following the race:

> My coach, my mentor, had tears in his eyes. I had never seen him so happy; nor have I since. He came over to me and lifted me off the ground in a bear hug as if I had won. He told me that I had done a great job – the best compliment I ever received from him. All day long he smiled constantly and patted me on my back. He gave me two tracksuits as a reward. He also told me I should train even harder. 'Of course I will,' I replied.
>
> (Haleem 2005: 144)

Soon, however, the relationship became dysfunctional as the coach ignored and increasingly ridiculed Hussain's Muslim faith and the practices he was obliged to undertake. In his own words:

> For him [the coach], the training load for each month should be similar, no exception for Ramadan (a month when Muslims fast during daylight hours). For instance, on the first day of Ramadan (usually the most tiring day of the month) a 5,000 metre time trial would be scheduled. Considering how tired we felt, it would be an unrealistic appraisal of our abilities. We requested that the trials be moved to the following night. He refused to listen. Though we felt fatigued and angry, we ran the time trial.

THE ATHLETES

I had limited energy and felt light-headed, but still managed a decent time. I knew I had done well. Still, Coach was far from satisfied and demanded that we run the entire time trial again following a meagre 15-minute break. A few runners mumbled that they were starting to hate running. Despite feeling disgruntled, I couldn't, I still loved running, but I was starting to have doubts.

(Haleem 2005: 194)

Hussain's identity as a Muslim man was being increasingly ignored and derided, which, allied to the practices of his coach, led to a breakdown in their relationship. Emotionally tired, chronically injured and athletically unfulfilled, Hussain retired from running aged 24. He believes that had his coach taken the time to get to know him as a person, to understand his cultural beliefs and practices, his potential as an athlete would have been better realized.

Comment on the case studies

Although such stories paint coaches in a poor light, the point is not to ascribe sole blame to them. Indeed, it could be argued that both Anne and Hussain willingly entered into the relationships they had with their coaches, and subsequently built their own identities. After all, as Coakley (1992) points out, it would be a mistake to locate social problems at the level of personal failures. Similarly, such relationship breakdowns and their lasting legacies are inevitably multicausal and cannot be traced to a single, linear source. However, as Jones et al. (2005) point out, such a conclusion ignores the 'developmental tunnels' entered into by young 'committing' athletes and the influence coaches, especially when they are revered, have over such charges. Indeed, narrow athlete social perceptions and self-perceptions are often the result when well-intentioned coaches insist on ever greater commitment to sport. Coaches, then, would seem to have a responsibility in relation to protecting and nurturing athletes' various identities. Here, we believe that, in order to avoid the experiences of Anne and Hussain, coaches should respect athletes' existing identities in addition to helping them develop multiple ones. This would ensure that their self-worth is not solely dependent on successfully fulfilling the athlete role. Thus, the aim should be to develop the whole person as opposed to the standardized unthinking athlete (Jones 2000; Jones et al. 2005).

CONCLUDING THOUGHTS

While the concepts of gender, ethnicity, disability and sexuality and how they may influence athlete identity have been discussed separately, they are, in reality, inextricably linked. For that reason, it is in their intersections that the key areas of understanding for coaches lie. Indeed, by recognizing that athletes are social beings rather than mechanistic bodies, coaches stand to gain an important insight into how 'the socio-cultural dynamics which shape identities in the wider society also impinge upon teaching/coaching and learning in sport, and ultimately the ability to perform well' (Jones 2000: 8). In this respect, Jones (2000) believes that an awareness of social prejudices that may cause an athlete self-doubt or similar problems is essential if a coach is to understand the totality of the athlete's performances. Indeed, he concludes that it is only by understanding the social aspects of the coaching process in a thoroughly practical way that coaches can possibly mediate tensions and overcome difficulties.

SUGGESTED READINGS

Brackenridge, C., Rivers, I., Gough, B. and Llewellyn, K. (2007) 'Driving down participation: Homophobic bullying as a deterrent to doing sport', in C. Aitchison (ed.) *Sport and Gender Identities: Masculinities, Femininities, and Sexualities*, London: Routledge.

Fitzgerald, H. (2005) 'Still feeling like a spare piece of luggage? Embodied experiences of (dis)ability in physical education and sport', *Physical Education and Sport Pedagogy*, 10(1): 41–59.

Hargreaves, J. (2007) 'Sport, exercise, and the female Muslim body: Negotiating Islam, politics, and male power', in J. Hargreaves and P. Vertinsky (eds) *Physical Culture, Power, and the Body*, London: Routledge.

Jones, R., Glintmeyer, N. and McKenzie, A. (2005) 'Slim bodies, eating disorders, and the coach-athlete relationship: A tale of identity creation and disruption', *International Review for the Sociology of Sport*, 40: 377–391.

Town, S. (1999) 'Queer(y)ing masculinities in schools: Faggots, fairies and the First XV', in R. Law, H. Campbell and J. Dolan (eds) *Masculinities in Aotearoa/New Zealand*, Palmerston North, NZ: Dunmore Press.

END-OF-CHAPTER TASKS

Prior to answering the questions below, you should read this chapter and at least one of the suggested readings associated with it. Having completed the readings, watch one of the following movies: *Bend It Like Beckham*, *Remember the Titans* or *The Perfect Body*. While watching the movie, make some notes related to the following questions:

1 What are the key issues that the athlete had to contend with both inside and outside of the sporting environment? (Identify specific problems, issues, and scenarios, and their respective impact upon the athlete.)
2 How can the athlete's experiences be understood in relation to the concept of identity? (Make links from what you have seen and read regarding gender, sexuality, disability, ethnicity and athletic identity.)
3 How did the coach or coaches address the issue of athlete identities within the movie? What did you think they did well? Why? What would you have done differently if you had been the coach? Why?

PART THREE
COACHING
CONTENT

CHAPTER 8

▼ **THE DISCOURSES OF COACHING**

INTRODUCTION

This chapter explores the discourse – that is, the language – used to describe and explain coaching. In particular, it considers how that language leads us to think about and perceive coaching and those involved in it in certain ways. Discourses are formed by beliefs, ideologies and power arrangements, and consequently are reflective of those social constructions (Cherryholmes 1988). The study of discourse, then, is an examination of how influence is achieved in and through talk; of what is said and the way it is said (Faulkener and Finlay 2002). It pays attention to the language-in-use and the power that such language has over perception and behaviour (McGannon and Mauws 2000). In addition, this chapter investigates the representation of knowledge through language as it relates to coaching. Here, it examines the discourse used by both coach educators and practising coaches, and the influence this has on athletes. It thus explores the 'discourse of expertise' so apparent in sports coaching, which feeds a dominant rationality-based pedagogy. Within this current arrangement, coaches are viewed as knowledge givers and athletes as receivers who need this knowledge to improve their performances. It is a discourse that legitimizes the power-dominated means of preparing largely unquestioning and compliant athletes (Johns and Johns 2000).

The chapter looks at how both coaches and athletes are situated within this dominant discourse and how their respective locations 'afford and limit how they speak, feel and behave' (McGannon and Mauws 2000: 148). After a discussion on the nature of discourse and the value of studying it within the coaching context, we examine more particularly the discourse of 'coaching science' and its effect on athletes. We then suggest a possible alternative coaching discourse (Johns and Johns 2000), one that is sensitive and considered, and involves athletes in their development to a much greater degree (Tinning *et al.* 1993).

WHAT IS DISCOURSE?

Traditional perspectives of examining language have been defined as representationalist (McGannon and Mauws 2000), where the words we speak are unproblematically considered to represent that to which they refer. Words are thought to be 'merely labels with which we refer to things in the world' (ibid.: 151). However, a differing interpretation of talking, which rejects this assumption as simplistic, comes from the discursive perspective. This focuses not on what words might refer to, but on what can be accomplished by using words in the ways we do (Heritage 1984). Hence, where the primary consideration of the representative perspective is with verbal content, that of the discursive standpoint lies with the outcome of speaking. From the discursive perspective, then, the task is to understand (1) how talk is produced by, and for, its particular audiences; (2) the beliefs and motives that create the talk; and (3) the consequences of such talk (Faulkener and Finlay 2002; Wilkinson 2000).

In delving deeper into its nature, we see that the discursive perspective is interested in the complex ways in which speakers construct and understand conversation, with all utterances being treated as 'meaningful social doings' (Wood and Kroger 2000: 12). Language is therefore considered not only as a tool for communication or description, but as a 'social practice . . . a way of doing things' (ibid.: 12). It is viewed as a 'domain in which our knowledge of the world is actively shaped' (Tonkiss 1998: 246), as it provides the means that allows us to make sense of our own identities and circumstances (McGannon and Mauws 2000). Consequently, any meanings we construct from information given are likely to be greatly affected by the choice of descriptors, metaphors and analogies used by the speaker, as they 'frame' the activity for us. Such 'framing' has been described as having the ability to 'paint pictures in our heads', with all the resultant implications (Sabo and Jensen 1994). Language, thus, should never be viewed as neutral, but rather as a means of communication that is embedded and riddled with 'overt and covert social biases, stereotypes and inequities' (Messner *et al.* 1993: 110). We might say that discourse does ideological work (Kirk 1992), as it both embodies and rationalizes a value-laden structure that allows for the promotion and perpetuation of some interests and practices over and above others (Penney 2000). Discourse, then, according to Ball (1990: 17), is essentially about power; it is about 'who can speak where, when and with what authority'. In this way, it endorses certain possibilities for thought while dismissing others. Hence, it becomes not only about

what is said and heard, but also about what is not, as what is left out in addition to what is included will influence participants' views of 'necessary' knowledge (Penney 2000).

WHY STUDY DISCOURSE IN THE COACHING CONTEXT?

To answer the question of why discourse in the coaching context should be studied, we need only acknowledge the socially constructed nature of language. If we acknowledge that discourse is selective in terms of agenda, interests and values, we accept that it both privileges and legitimizes, and excludes and marginalizes. We need to study it therefore primarily to acknowledge our roles in these processes, thus understanding how our ways of speaking influence our behaviour and the interactions we have with others (McGannon and Mauws 2000). In this respect, knowledge of a discourse's power can help us better manage and frame conversations towards preferred ends. The initial task here is to examine our everyday coaching language-in-use. This allows us to deconstruct the signifiers, behaviours and language of coaches in considering the 'logic' of their privileged positions, and why they come to define both themselves and their athletes in particular ways. It is an 'exercise in vigilance' in relation to 'imagined values' (Bromley 1995: 155), thus treating with considerable suspicion the seductive power of dominant discourses in simplifying, stereotyping and dulling individual experiences (McCarthy *et al.* 2003). Once we understand the micro-workings of language and how these are linked to the cultural macro-effect, we can then recognize our own positions and influence in relation to the discourses that we use, so that we can consider prospects and potential for change. An examination of what we say and how we say it is also significant because our interactions are not characterized by infinite possibility, as 'both what can be said and how it is said are constrained by the characteristics of the discourse within which it occurs' (McGannon and Mauws 2000: 156). We thus need to identify the boundaries of the predominant discourse that we inhabit, as only then can we become aware of different sites within it (ibid.). Such awareness helps us to recognize that the current coaching discourse and the 'knowledge' that sustains it are reflective of vested interests, and of the need to treat the discourse as such. In effect, we need to study discourse so that we can, if desired, 'change our talk' and, because language is reflective of our realities, 'change our practice' (Wood and Kroger 2000).

However, we are very aware that the discourses within which we speak are enabling as well as limiting forces. Consequently, we have no intention of 'throwing the baby out with the bathwater'. Discourses are enabling in that they allow us to speak of things in particular ways, thus increasing our 'sense-making' capabilities. In essence, they allow us 'to understand, to think and [to] make sense' (Kirk 1992: 48). On the other hand, they are limiting in that, as we have outlined, they proscribe definite ways of thinking and speaking, hence restricting 'conditions of possibility' (Foucault 1972). The point in highlighting the workings and influence of language is not to call for an 'objective' neutral substitute within which we can communicate, as such objectivity in a social world is not a credible option. Rather, we acknowledge that we will always live within value-laden discourses, and our interest here is in exploring the freedom to work creatively within the existing framework. In doing so, we can bring to the fore aspects of the current discourse that have previously remained in the background or at the periphery of our practice (Penney 2000). The value of critically examining coaching discourse, then, is multiple. First, through employing a deconstructive strategy to confront the current validity of coaching 'expertise', we can challenge conventional understandings of coaching theories and that which they purport to represent. Hence, we can examine and understand the status quo for what it is, and why it is as it is, before reflecting on other ways to possibly improve it. The least we can do here, according to Kirk (1992), is to question definitions, purposes and current relevance. Second, studying talk allows us to beg the question of what coaches are doing with their words. That is, what is being transmitted and accomplished by their speaking as they do (McGannon and Mauws 2000)? This would enable us to credibly examine the legitimacy of such experts and the knowledges they espouse. Finally, through giving us the ability to uncover what determines actions and thoughts, analysing discourse also gives us the freedom to explore other discursive coaching options, opening the search for ways to 'do it better'. Getting coaches to critically examine their discourse, then, leads to a better understanding of self and one's behaviour, while encouraging them to 'think outside the square' to creatively solve problems. It consequently offers the potential for coaches to be central to, and proactive in, shaping the future of coaching and coach education in particular ways.

THE DOMINANT DISCOURSE OF 'COACHING SCIENCE': PERFORMANCE, RATIONALITY AND A HIERARCHICAL COACH–ATHLETE RELATIONSHIP

According to Johns and Johns (2000), among others, the discourse of modern sport is embedded in a performance pedagogy that is based on scientific functionalism. Here, the body is viewed as a 'machine', one that can be developed and improved through appropriate exercises and training regimes (Prain and Hickey 1995). Similarly, much of the current coaching discourse is also biomedical in nature, which arguably has emanated from coaches and officials whose positions of power depend on its promotion (Cherryholmes 1988; Johns and Johns 2000; Tinning 1991b; Schön 1983). It is a discourse that favours technical description and procedure, with value placed on the specialist 'factual' knowledge of coaches to provide direction and sequence (Prain and Hickey 1995). It is also a discourse which views the athlete's body as a 'biological object to be studied, manipulated and its movements minutely measured' (Wright 2000: 35). For example, witness the topics covered at a conference sponsored by the UK Sports Institute (2002) entitled 'Leadership: World Class Coaching'. They included the biological and rationality dominated 'Optimising trunk muscle recruitment', 'Athens – heat, humidity and pollution', 'The pose method running' and 'The performance enhancement team', among others, leaving delegates in no doubt as to what sort of knowledge 'expert' coaches should have.

Such an approach views coaching as unproblematic, thus assuming the establishment of a clear set of achievable, sequential goals. As a consequence, coaches have been encouraged to 'take charge' and control the coaching process, which includes their athletes, as much as possible (Seaborn et al. 1998). Indeed, the current coach–athlete relationship is characterized by rank and power, with one party perceived as having knowledge, and the other as needing it. This situation has, in turn, reaffirmed the hierarchical discourse often employed in coaching, as it takes for granted the structures of power that exist within the traditional coach–athlete relationship (Slack 2000). In this way, the discourse used tends to bolster the status quo, inclusive of the 'common-sense' assumption that coaches should 'lead from the front'. Athletes, on the other hand, should subordinate themselves to those who can 'help' them achieve their objectives (Slack 2000). It is a presumed top-down structure of leadership, with strategy and expertise necessarily and legitimately viewed as being the domain of the coach. In addition to a subject-specific vocabulary, the discourse has also resulted in what can be described as a coach initiation, athlete response, coach evaluation pattern of interaction (Prain and Hickey 1995). Such a structure can easily degenerate into being automatic 'recitations' (Cazden 1988) rather than opportunities for athletes genuinely to interact with their coaches to develop new understandings (Prain and Hickey 1995). Within such conversations, coaches inevitably control the turn-taking contributions, thus ensuring that a 'desired' agenda is maintained. A basic problem here, which is reflective of the rationality approach in general, is the frequent failure of coaches to account for individual athlete diversity, leaving the athletes, to various degrees, unfulfilled and demotivated. As Alvesson and Willmott (1996) pointed out, in such orthodox manifestations of the coaching role, athletes only really have 'relevance' when the implementation of plans directly depends upon their conscious compliance. The issue for coaches, then, becomes how the support of athletes can be effectively 'engineered', rather than how best to appreciate and address athletes' underlying concerns (Slack 2000). Alvesson and Willmott (1996) refer to such a situation as the use of 'strategy talk'. This works to restrain the involvement of certain groups (such as athletes) in decision-making processes, in that the discourse used by those in positions of power 'frame[s] issues in a way that privileges [their] reason', thus giving them the initiative in any interactions that take place (ibid.: 136). Through using the dominant discourse and identifying with its practices, coaches are able to legitimize their positions and gain influence and credibility, thereby demonstrating the relevance of their role. Additionally, as a consequence of adhering to the dominant discourse, which, more often than not, is heavily supported by formal coach education and related policy initiatives, coaches are well placed to receive both assistance from governing bodies and compliance from athletes, to whom they act as unquestioning authorities in setting workloads and establishing ways of behaving (Johns and Johns 2000).

Not surprisingly, the prevailing rationalistic performance coaching discourse has led to the development of language within the profession which is infused with the driving concepts of productivity, efficiency, prediction and accountability. This has led to binary thinking among coaches, which has profoundly influenced not only the nature of the coach–athlete relationship, but also the subsequent preparation of athletes (Johns and Johns 2000). Consequently, although one can easily assume that athletes are empowered by their own goal orientation and the self-chosen means to achieve it (ibid.), a more critical interrogation of coaches' discourse reveals a power-dominated control mechanism that results in the 'production of docile bodies that monitor, guard and discipline themselves' (Eskes *et al.* 1998: 319). In this way, through continuing to speak and coach in rationalistic terms, coaches can be seen to influence the behaviour of their athletes as well as their own.

THE EFFECT ON ATHLETES OF A POWER-DOMINATED DISCOURSE

A clear example of the current power-dominated coaching discourse in action lies in the increasing emphasis placed on athlete conformity and compliance. Here, any 'conflict' in the coach–athlete relationship is considered dysfunctional – a concept clearly at odds with the messy reality of coaching. It is also a stance that implies that individuality cannot be a force for positive change and progression. The result of the situation is that both coaches and athletes are encouraged to see the 'proper' coaching environment as one that is characterized by cooperation, consensus and conformity (Kirk 1992). It is a view that can lead to social oppression, both physically and cognitively: physically in terms of reproducing an acceptably formed athletic body, and cognitively in relation to inhibiting individual creativity (Apple 1979).

Before examining scenarios of both instances, it is worth noting that the success of this drive for conformity, although instigated by the coach and his or her discourse, is largely achieved through athlete self-regulation. Here, athletes are often seen to rigorously comply with, and strictly adhere to, coach-produced training regimes that include carefully controlled lifestyle and weight management programmes (Johns and Johns 2000). Such apparently voluntary actions have been referred to as the 'technologies of the self' (Foucault 1977), where athletes adopt the means by which they police their own preparation and appearance in line with coaches' expectations. This compliance is often ensured as athletes have limited discourses upon which to draw. Consequently, they 'take their cues' from their coaches in terms of how to think and speak of their preparation, performances and of themselves as athletes. Indeed, this is the crucial point here, that coaches 'frame' the sporting experience for their athletes. They talk in terms of efficiency, productivity and time, hence athletes similarly come to think of themselves in mechanistic terms. In this way, discourse given from positions of power can be considered akin to the 'hidden curriculum' in education (Kirk 1992), which refers to the often subconscious learning of knowledge, attitudes and assumptions as a result of participation in an activity. These learned values become unwritten rules, etched in the mind, and come to influence significantly our behaviours, strategies and the people we become (Kirk 1992). Such readily adopted practices provide clear examples of how power is woven into the fabric of culture (Williams 1977).

The drive for physical conformity and its potential negative consequences have been particularly evident with regard to the female body image, in terms of what it visually means to be an athlete. It appears that the presentation of the sporting body, as viewed in 'subjective' women's sports such as gymnastics, synchronized swimming, figure skating and diving, among others, has increasingly come to rely on the way in which it conforms to social trends and styles, in addition to how it performs athletically (Johns 1998). This has brought the visuality of the body and its preparation within sport, as a site for critical examination, to the fore. Not surprisingly, investigations have revealed paradoxes between the desired body 'look' and weight, and its optimum performance condition (Franklin 1996). They have also revealed a complex set of power and domination structures that normalize in sport many practices that outside might be considered harmful (Birrell and Cole 1994; Chapman 1997).

In many ways, such a situation promotes an ethic of excess (Johns 1998) and is often played out along the thin edge of the body's natural limits (Franklin 1996). It is sustained by the politics of athlete self-surveillance, which in turn is made up of a sense of personal responsibility, obligation to constant practice, and continual self-regulation, and is often manifest through the keeping of training diaries. Such diaries ensure that training workloads become accepted by athletes as 'regimes of truth' (Chapman 1997) over which they have 'control'. Here, athletes are subject to what Foucault (1977: 184–185) has termed a 'normalizing gaze' from coaches (and other athletes) to see whether the training has been adhered to. It is a gaze that makes it 'possible to classify and to punish', and thus further encourages athletes to engage in disciplinary practices. Not surprisingly, such practices can have negative consequences for athletes, as witnessed by two participants from Johns and Johns' (2000) recent study, who recalled how their self-esteem was eroded by similar technologies of power:

> One (gymnastic) coach would weigh us 4 times a day: that was ridiculous. We had to weigh in before each practice and that made us really self conscious. And then she would say 'You're fat, why do you weigh more than you weighed this morning? What did you eat this afternoon?' It was an interrogation and it was terrible.
>
> (Johns and Johns 2000: 228)

> Coaches in rhythmic gymnastics just love to control their athletes. They said I may as well quit coz I wasn't mentally ready to lose weight. It gave me insecurities about my body image and I remember thinking I looked like a whale. I came to realize that it was a question of respect. I don't think a lot of gymnasts are treated with respect, so you end up hating the sport [and] feeling bitter.
>
> (ibid.: 227)

To give another example of how the drive for productivity and conformity can result in negative experiences for athletes, consider a football player who has a tendency and ability to execute creative, individual tasks very well. Hence, she brings an imaginative dimension to team play. On the occasion when, in possession of the ball, she takes the riskier option of penetrating opposing defences, which she is fully capable of doing, she feels a sense of fulfilment, adventure and actualization. If, however, possession is lost as a consequence of the move, she receives criticisms from the coach, and possibly from the other players for losing the ball they worked so hard to gain. Although some of her moves work, her colleagues become loath to support her play as they believe that more often than not, the ball will be lost (that is, her play lacks an 'end product'). Even if the move works, she is often isolated, as her colleagues do not support in enough numbers, through not being confident that possession will be retained. With less support, this becomes a self-fulfilling prophecy as, indeed, the ball is increasingly lost, which in turn leads to more castigation from both colleagues and coach. Subsequently, even when opportunities to be creative present themselves, she begins to experience fear, both of losing the ball and of her team-mates' and coach's reactions if she does lose it. As a result, she ceases to try the difficult and innovative, preferring to adopt a safer, less imaginative passing option, thus sacrificing her talent and the unique contribution she brings to the team. In effect, she conforms to the norm.

This example illustrates the influence that a dominant 'product'-orientated discourse can have over a young athlete's development. The starting point of analysis is the player's position within the discourse – how she is seen by others and how she sees herself as a player (McGannon and Mauws 2000). Here, the individual athlete is constantly positioned as a 'team player', a cog in a larger wheel. Hence, she has functions similar to those of other cogs who must contribute equally to a collective outcome, within an encompassing coach-dominated context. Furthermore, with respect to the socially constructed role of player, the 'good' player is thought of as one who listens to the coach and subsequently carries out instructions without question, trains hard, considers the efforts of team-mates, and puts the team's needs ahead of her own – a concept recently brought to life by Cushion and Jones' (2006) examination of the culture apparent in English professional football. To reinforce such values, players are constantly bombarded with such dressing-room signs and sentiments relating to sacrificing the self for the good of the team (e.g. 'there is no I in team', 'teamwork works', etc.). Consequently, there are a range of expectations, expressed through a particular discourse associated with the term 'player', or more accurately 'good player', that structures how players make sense of their situation and behaviours. The carrying out of these expectations dictates whether the player is regarded as a 'good' one or not, both by others (particularly coaches) and by themselves (McGannon and Mauws 2000).

In our example, the contextual discourse established by the coach becomes too strong for our creative player to resist. To keep her place in the team she will have to conform, thus inhibiting her creative talent and enjoyment of the sport. Indeed, it appears that athletes in general aim for the achievement of an ideal representation of an unwritten subjective standard as set by the coach (Johns and Johns 2000). Furthermore, successful athletes are seen to apply a rigid technology of the

COACHING CONTENT

self to comply with this 'coaches' view of the world', which is strengthened by the perceived constant gaze of coaches, peers and self.

AN ALTERNATIVE COACHING DISCOURSE

The critical analysis embarked upon in this chapter has highlighted the problematic nature of the coach–athlete relationship, particularly within high-performance sport. It is a relationship characterized by one side having knowledge and influence, while the other is defined by a 'need to know', a desire to conform and an inability to risk (Johns and Johns 2000). Realistically, we are very aware that coach and athlete require much self-sacrifice and commitment to be successful in sport. Consequently, compliance and productivity are needed. Indeed, there is no need to reject all notions associated with the current discourse. Alternatively, the point here is to become aware of the relativity of what we hold true and how we express it, and to promote questioning about the consequences of these truths and practices before progressing to examine ways of improving (Wright 2000). Echoing the earlier call by Johns and Johns (2000), therefore, we are not suggesting a total change in the ways of competition preparation and talking about it, but rather that the power arrangements upon which the highly rationalized sport discourse is based be amended somewhat, thus being subject to greater balance.

Johns and Johns (2000) provide an interesting possible reformulation of the current sport performance pedagogy discourse. They reject the current binary coach–athlete structure, and alternatively emphasize a greater respect for athletes through the establishment of more equitable relationships. This would include a discourse that is more 'symmetrical and non-dominated' and not 'distorted by power and ideology' (Cherryholmes 1988: 89). It thus reflects an altered perform-ance pedagogy based on a structured freedom, which emphasizes the importance of the individual within the collective and the social responsibilities of athletes and coaches within the relationship, both to themselves and to each other.

A concrete starting point for developing such a discourse could be to attach greater importance, as a coaching resource, to the personal knowledges of athletes, which in turn are based on individual experiences and practices. Undoubtedly, athletes possess a wealth of knowledge about achievement and, in particular, what 'works' for them, which is not currently being effectively drawn upon in their preparation. The challenge here is to elevate and integrate this knowledge into good practice, as opposed to ignoring or downplaying it. Respecting and building on athletes' knowledge would also alter the lopsided power dynamic in traditional coach–athlete relationships to a more equitable one. Such a change in thinking could then lead to a change in speaking; that is, to an altered coaching discourse characterized less by binary 'us' and 'them' thinking to one more defined by a collective 'we', within which the individual's unique and creative talents are valued. The altered relationships would be non-didactic in nature, with athletes actively contributing to their development through a deeper reflection of their own performances (Cazden 1988). Through such a process, they could experience greater success, pleasure in and understanding of their sporting experience. Alternatively, coaches would be forced to develop flexible discursive practices to continually challenge their athletes at many levels, while allowing more time to better observe, analyse and creatively assess development (Prain and Hickey 1995). This would afford the coach further resources and experiences to develop athletes in more holistic ways, while allowing both coach and athlete new and different means to construct and understand their situations. This type of relationship is needed if athletes are to experience the true value of their commitment. We therefore need to educate coaches to 'gamble' less on the compliance of athletes through claims to expertise, and alternatively to engage in a joint process of knowledge generation involving both parties which could tap into and develop deeper levels of potential.

Discourse and language reflect our beliefs and values, and hence attempts to amend them are often met with some resistance. This is because our utterances serve others, as well as ourselves, in understanding the differing roles each of us plays within the discourse. Consequently, changing our ways of speaking could encounter resistance from others, as 'in addition to repositioning ourselves, [such changes] also serve to reposition those with whom we speak' (McGannon and Mauws 2000: 158). As both coaches and athletes have become socialized into accepting their complementary roles, they are bound to feel uncomfortable and uncertain when the boundaries shift. Thus, a coach could experience resistance from athletes if he or she attempts to change the discourse to one that is unfamiliar. Indeed, evidence suggests this to be the case. Consequently, unless care and sensitivity are exercised, athletes may be unwilling to accept radical new strategies that are alien to them (Jones 2001). Similarly, an athlete who wants to reposition him- or herself within an empowerment discourse may encounter resistance from a coach who is reluctant to view the athlete's behaviours in anything other than the traditional coach-dominated way. Changing the way we talk, then, takes patience, perseverance, effort and understanding. To make a lasting alteration we must be aware of how the conversations we have with others and ourselves affect how we feel, think and behave. This note of caution should not dampen the drive for improved change, however, as to coach is to occupy a very privileged position, one that is accompanied by many social responsibilities (Penney 2000). Therefore, we have a duty to choose our words and our talk carefully, to be aware of their legacies, and to be constantly searching for ways to improve.

CONCLUDING THOUGHTS

The discourse that currently dominates sports coaching can be seen as providing boundaries that define the nature of the coach–athlete relationship and the roles each party plays within it. It is a discourse driven by a scientific, performance pedagogy emanating from a power-dominated hierarchical relationship where the coach is seen as knowledgeable and the athlete not. Although athletes willingly enter the activity, it is a pathway founded on deeply established practice (Johns and Johns 2000). Consequently, athletes generally accept and internalize the discourse present, which is espoused as 'truth' by hierarchically positioned coaches.

COACHING CONTENT

Although some have argued for a radical overhaul of power arrangements in sport to counter the existing discourse (Shogan 1999), a more realistic goal would be to reposition coaching within it. By doing so we could establish an amended coach–athlete relationship based on a more equitable power-sharing relationship. Indeed, athletes in Johns and Johns' (2000) study declared that they were willing to settle for such an amended power structure as long as they understood the reasons for it and their precise place within it. This relates not only to when they could have an impact into their own development, but also to when they could expect guidance and help from coaches. This is not to say that such an amended discourse does not itself require close future scrutiny in the quest for optimal athlete improvement and self-actualization.

In concluding this chapter we would like to echo the words of Penney (2000). She stated that one of the key things to realize in considering issues such as discourse is that 'we are not all going to agree upon what the focus of attention should be, what aims our energies should be directed to, and how these can be best achieved' (ibid.: 62). However, there is a need to be aware of the variety of discourses than can potentially, and perhaps should, find expression in coaching, while recognizing that these will have different implications for the interests of different groups. Before we decide on alternative discourses, then, issues of whom and what coach education and coaches ought to promote and exclude merit consideration (ibid.). Whatever the outcome of such a process, it is worth remembering that the dominance of certain discourses can and should always be contested, and that perhaps the time is now right for such a challenge in coaching.

SUGGESTED READINGS

Cushion, C. and Jones, R.L. (2006) 'Power, discourse and symbolic violence in professional youth soccer: The case of Albion F.C.', *Sociology of Sport Journal*, 23(2): 142–161.

Faulkener, G. and Finlay, S.J. (2002) 'It's not what you say, it's the way you say it! Conversation analysis: A discursive methodology for sport, exercise and physical education', *Quest*, 54: 49–66.

Johns, D.P. and Johns, J. (2000) 'Surveillance, subjectivism and technologies of power: An analysis of the discursive practice of high-performance sport', *International Review for the Sociology of Sport*, 35: 219–234.

McGannon, K.R. and Mauws, M.K. (2000) 'Discursive psychology: An alternative approach for studying adherence to exercise and physical activity', *Quest*, 52: 148–165.

END-OF-CHAPTER TASKS

1   What is discourse and why do we need to study it?
2   Coaching is considered to operate within a performance discourse. What is meant by this?
3   Johns and Johns (2000), among others, believe the performance discourse to be destructive. Do you agree or disagree with this position? Why?
4   How can the prevailing performance discourse be countered?

CHAPTER 9

▼ EXAMINING COACHES' CONTENT KNOWLEDGE

INTRODUCTION

> There is no curriculum that youth sport coaches must adhere to, and they have little or no supervision. Most youth team sport coaches work in isolation and, therefore, have tremendous freedom in the content they select to teach, and the way they structure the training programs.
>
> (Gilbert and Trudel 2001: 17–18)

The freedom coaches have to select the content they use in their practice sessions may be part of the reason why discussions on content have not had a high profile with sports scientists. Yet being aware of some of the educational issues that surround the notion of content knowledge may assist coaches to improve their practice and provide athletes maximum opportunities to learn. Researchers and coaches alike have reported a desire for a greater understanding of content knowledge. For example, Cushion *et al.* (2003: 216) suggest that if the aim is to 'develop imaginative, dynamic, and thoughtful coaches', then it may be useful for coach education programmes to utilize a broader concept of content knowledge, while the participants of the Ladies Professional Golf Association – National Education Program (LPGA-NEP) commented that a strength of their programme was that they 'learned pedagogical knowledge, that is, they learned about *how* to teach (general principles and strategies of instruction), not just what to teach'

(McCullick *et al.* 2005: 129). They further noted that this focus on pedagogical knowledge in coach education was 'novel, yet quite rational' (ibid.: 129). Not surprisingly, the participants in the LPGA-NEP also valued the subject matter content knowledge taught within the programme but recognized that it was not without its problems. These findings support those of Gould *et al.* (1990: 343), who concluded that it would be desirable if coach education programmes included more '"in-depth knowledge" for coaches and emphasize[d] pedagogical knowledge'.

The aim of this chapter is to discuss the complexity of a coach's content knowledge by drawing on the work of Amade-Escot (2006), Shulman (1986) and Metzler (2000). The chapter begins with an introduction to the work of these three scholars. This is followed by a discussion of how Shulman (1986) breaks down the notion of content knowledge into three subsets – subject-matter content knowledge, pedagogical content knowledge and curriculum content knowledge – and how Metzler (2000) subsequently divides these three subsets into three more categories: declarative knowledge, procedural knowledge and conditional knowledge. In keeping with the book's general philosophy, we reflect upon the Shulman–Metzler framework and highlight some of its limitations. We conclude the chapter by questioning the desire many have for 'certainty' and getting things 'right' (Cassidy and Tinning 2004) and what this means for coaches' content knowledge.

CONTENT KNOWLEDGE

A desire to gain a better understanding of content knowledge is not exclusive to the English-speaking world. Content knowledge has also been the focus of those working within the *didactique* tradition of educational research in Europe (Amade-Escot 2006). In the French-speaking educational world the concept of *didactique* is related to '(1) the study of the content and its function in the teaching/learning process; and (2) the way it [content] is embedded in instructional tasks and brought into play during the interactive teaching/learning process' (ibid.: 348). The focus of *didactique* research in the fields of physical education and sports has reflected this mainstream definition. Two English-language reviews of the *didactique* literature in physical education and sport provide a comprehensive insight into this body of work for those who do not speak French (see Amade-Escot 2000; David *et al.* 1999).

A prominent researcher in the area of content knowledge is Lee Shulman. As we have seen, Shulman (1986) described content knowledge as comprising three subsets: subject-matter content knowledge (SMCK), pedagogical content knowledge (PCK) and curriculum content knowledge (CCK). Subject-matter content knowledge is explained as the knowledge a coach has, or has access to, that represents the extent of the activity being coached. To be considered to have adequate SMCK, a coach has to have knowledge of the range of activities that can be included in a session, for example the skills, tactics and strategies that can be adopted by athletes, and the rules of the activity being coached. PCK is the knowledge the coach needs to be able to teach (or communicate) the SMCK to athletes. Drawing on the work of Shulman and Grossman, McCaughtry (2004: 30) described PCK as a 'useful conceptual tool for explaining and analyzing the knowledge teachers use to transform subject matter for student learning'. For example, a coach needs to know when, why and how to adopt particular coaching method(s) and strategies, and how to recognize athletes' learning preferences. Shulman's definition of CCK is premised on a particular understanding of the term 'curriculum', which he views as a set of materials. Consequently, CCK is viewed as the knowledge of resources available to the coach. For example, a basketball coach needs to be able to access the most recent sport-specific coaching information on offer.

While Shulman's (1986) framework is a useful starting point for discussing content knowledge, Metzler (2000) suggested that in order for teachers (and, we would argue, coaches) to become intimate with the content knowledge of their activity, it is useful to break each of Shulman's (1986) subsets into three further categories. The categories identified and described by Metzler (2000) are:

- declarative knowledge (DK) – that which a coach can express verbally and/or in a written form;
- procedural knowledge (PK) – that which a coach can apply before, during and after the coaching session;
- conditional knowledge (CK) – that which informs a coach regarding when and why to make decisions so that they fit a particular moment or context.

According to Metzler (2000), there is a strong relationship between all three types of knowledge, with declarative knowledge being a 'prerequisite' for procedural and conditional knowledge. What this means is that a coach must have a basic knowledge of the sport or activity before she or he can attempt to run a practice session. Once the coach can operationalize the knowledge in one setting or with one group, conditional knowledge enables him or her to adapt the practice sessions to other settings and with other groups.

To some, this discussion of subsets and categories of subsets may sound excessive. But when the subsets (Shulman 1986) and categories (Metzler 2000) are applied to a coaching situation, the process highlights the various forms of content knowledge that can assist coaches to improve their performance, thereby providing athletes with maximum opportunities to learn. The following framework is deliberately designed around a generic, rather than a sport-specific, coach, so it can be applied to a diverse range of activities.

Subject-matter content knowledge:

DK – knowledge of relevant information, e.g. knowledge of rules, biomechanics and psychology;

PK – being able to model and adjudicate the rules of the game in the coaching session;

CK – knowing what tactics to employ against what opposition.

Pedagogical content knowledge:

DK – knowledge of the different methods and strategies that can be adopted;

PK – being able to apply various methods and strategies in the coaching session;

CK – changing the methods and strategies to suit the learning preferences of the athletes.

Curriculum content knowledge:

DK – knowledge of what coaching resources are available;

PK – being able to incorporate the ideas and activities into the coaching session;

CK – using words to explain the drills that suit the context and the type of athletes.

The following vignette illustrates how Georgia, a junior basketball coach, uses the above content knowledge framework to inform what she needs to know for her practices.

VIGNETTE: UTILIZING CONTENT KNOWLEDGE

Georgia is a teacher in a local secondary school. She has played basketball in the metropolitan senior competition for the past eight years and has been a member of the provincial team for five of those years. The school at which Georgia works has a policy that every teacher, regardless of discipline background and on top of a full teaching load, is required to coach, manage or direct a school sport, or a physical or cultural activity. Georgia knew of this policy when she applied for her job and was happy with it, as she was keen to coach basketball. There are five girls' basketball teams at the school, and Georgia is the coach of the 1sts and the 5ths. She finds this works well because often the members of the 1sts are keen to help with coaching, so Georgia harnesses this enthusiasm by having them assist her to coach the 5ths.

When the season begins, Georgia knows that many of the girls in the 5ths will never have played basketball before, so she has to start with some basic rules. For example, she tells the girls about the three-second rule (a player cannot spend more than three consecutive seconds in the opponents' 'key', close to the basket area). Georgia does not spend a lot of time on this but she makes sure that anytime the girls are playing a game in the practice session she, or one of the members of the 1sts, penalizes any infringements of the rule. In an effort to make the practices relevant, Georgia often talks about the up-coming opposition. Over the years, she has come to know which opposition teams play a zone defence and which play one-on-one, so when explaining the simple offensive plays to the girls, Georgia points out that if they are performed correctly against the appropriate opposition then they should not get penalized for being in the 'key hole' for longer than three seconds.

One of the reasons Georgia likes the members of the 1sts assisting her to coach the 5ths is that the former are familiar with the questioning strategy she adopts in her practices. Prior to any practice, Georgia designs various activities for small groups and has a couple of key questions, as well as possible prompts, already identified. By having the questions pretty well set, she can give them to the members of the 1st team who come along to help. She also finds the questions help her to keep focused on the goal of the session. Additionally, Georgia has found that it is useful to write the questions up on the whiteboard so those girls who are not so good at listening can look at the board to be reminded what it is that they are supposed to be focusing on. To get ideas for the practices with the 5ths, Georgia draws on the resources she knows her club and representative coaches use, as well as what she finds on the web and what is produced by the national sporting body. While the resources are good, most of the content in them is far too advanced for the girls in the 5ths. To be able to use these resources, Georgia has to adapt the drills not only to the skill level of the girls, but also to their physical stature.

LIMITATIONS OF THE FRAMEWORK

Subject-matter content knowledge (SMCK) can be somewhat limiting if it focuses only on the knowledge of the activity being coached rather than on the principles informing the knowledge. If the SMCK of a soccer coach incorporates basic movement principles, such as creating space on attack, then the coach has licence to draw on many of the skills, tactics and strategies found in other invasion games such as hockey and basketball to actually deliver the session. To assist teachers and coaches work with generic principles, some scholars have classified games (read sports) into four forms: invasion (e.g. basketball, football and hockey); net/wall (e.g. tennis, volleyball, squash); striking/fielding (e.g. cricket, baseball); and target (e.g. golf, croquet, snooker) (Bunker and Thorpe 1982; Thorpe 1997). By knowing about and utilizing the games classification system, a coach can make coaching sessions more varied and interesting. He or she can do this by selecting activities from different sports within the same category to explore and develop common movement principles. Further, the coach can utilize activities (within the same category) that are not specific to the sport he or she is coaching to develop tactics rather than only focusing on sport-specific techniques (Werner *et al.* 1996). Examples already exist on how a focus on generic invasion game tactics, relating to scoring and preventing scoring, can improve soccer playing performance (see Mitchell 1996), and how a focus on generic net or wall game tactics, such as setting up to attack, can improve volleyball playing performance (see Griffin 1996). Further, it has been documented how top-level coaches such as Wayne Smith (assistant All Black rugby union coach) use basic movement principles at the elite level (Kidman 2001).

It is useful for coaches to remember that the SMCK of any activity or sport is not written in stone. As such, we believe that coaches can question 'why the subject matter is so, on whose authority it is so and under what conditions could this change . . . [and] why one topic is privileged over another' (Rossi and Cassidy 1999: 193). These questions become important ones because knowledge about our world is

increasing exponentially. New so-called experts are being created, which makes it difficult to 'know who and what to believe' and what knowledge, if any, can be considered 'permanent' (Tinning 2002: 384). One consequence of this rapid increase in knowledge is that social practices, such as coaching, are constantly being assessed and revised in light of new information.

Hence, we do not consider Shulman's (1986) conceptualization of content knowledge to be immune from examination and reformation. For example, Cochran *et al.* (1993) refer to PCK as content *knowing* to emphasize the dynamism associated with coming to know. Additionally, Geddis and Wood (1997) contend that the transformation of SMCK into PCK requires recognition of the learner, the context, the place and time. Similarly, Rossi and Cassidy (1999) consider that a weakness in Shulman's (1986) conceptualization of PCK is that it supports a compartmentalized view of the pedagogical act by focusing on teaching at the expense of the learner and the context. An alternative to such a view is the work of Lusted (1986), who views pedagogy as a process rather than an act, thereby recognizing that a dynamic relationship exists between the teacher (read coach), the learner (read athlete) and content. As is mentioned in the introductory chapter, this book is primarily organized around Lusted's notion of the pedagogical process. A similar alternative is to draw on the *didactique* tradition, which is based on the assumption that 'any study of one term of the didactic system (the student, the teacher, the knowledge) cannot have any meaning without taking into account the other two' (Amade-Escot 2006: 349). Another limitation of PCK is that the concept lacks an emotional dimension. It has been suggested that much of the research and theory surrounding PCK has overlooked the role of 'teacher knowledge of student emotion from analyses of how teachers think students learn' (McCaughtry 2004: 33). Indeed, on the basis of empirical research in educational contexts it has become apparent that 'how teachers interpret and respond to student emotion also plays a key role in their pedagogical content knowedge' (2004: 33).

Defining the curriculum is not as straightforward as Shulman's (1986) CCK category may suggest. The reality is that intense debate has surrounded what is meant by the term 'curriculum' (Marsh 1997). Curriculum has been alternatively defined as 'that which is taught in school', 'a set of subjects', 'content', 'a set of materials' and 'a set of performance objectives' (ibid.: 3). Despite uncertainty about the meaning of 'curriculum' in the educational literature, in the coaching context there has been little, if any, debate at all. In coaching, then, curriculum is often published by national sporting organizations as 'sets of materials' (see, for example, Fortanasce *et al.* 2001; Jobson 1998; Readhead 1997). These are distributed to, or purchased by, coaches in an attempt to increase their knowledge and indirectly improve the performances of athletes. This material can be thought of as the overt, formal or official curriculum. However, as a number of researchers have pointed out (see Dodds 1985; Kirk 1992; Marsh 1997), students, and we would also argue athletes, gain knowledge, values and skills not only from the formal, overt or official curriculum, but also from the informal, covert or hidden curriculum.

One of the early physical education researchers in this area was Dodds (1985), who argued for the curriculum to be viewed on four levels: overt, covert, null and hidden. In this section we do not focus on the overt curriculum, which Dodds (ibid.: 93) described as 'those publicly stated and shared items that teachers want students to acquire'. Instead, we examine the other three forms of curricula because Shulman's (1986) framework does not examine them in great depth. The covert curriculum can be considered as those aspects and attributes that a coach has not formally stated in any coaching plans but would like athletes to learn – for example, the value of perseverance, and obeying the referee. Another example of the covert curriculum is well illustrated in a five-minute video entitled *Kick to Kick* (Australian Film Institute n.d.). This video focuses on a back-yard scene with a mother kicking an Australian Rules football to a father and son who challenge each other to catch the ball. Not surprisingly, the father constantly wins the contest. After each catch he provides 'tips' to his son on how to play the game. One 'tip' focused on how to intimidate the opposition. Despite its being illegal in Australian Rules football to push the opposition player in the back, the father points out that if he were to push the opposition in the back early in the game, they would be wary of him in the future. Although the father consciously and intentionally imparts this information, we doubt whether, if he was asked to formally state what it was that he was teaching his son, he would admit to its being a means to intimidate the opposition.

The null curriculum represents those ideas, concepts and values that are knowingly excluded from the formal coaching plan. For example, a junior-level athletics coach may choose not to coach javelin because he or she considers it to be too dangerous for junior athletes (Tinning *et al.* 1993). Another example of the null curriculum is the introduction of Rippa rugby into the junior rugby scene in New Zealand. This is the only form of rugby children under the age of 8 can officially play. The children are not allowed to tackle the opposition players; instead, they have to 'rip' a tag off an opposing player's belt to stop the play. One of the reasons this game was introduced was in response to the increasing concern about the number of children getting injured as a consequence of not tackling correctly.

Finally, the hidden curriculum can be thought of as the learnings of 'attitudes, norms, beliefs, values and assumptions often expressed as rules, rituals and regulations. They are rarely questioned and are just taken for granted' (Marsh 1997: 35). For example, in basketball there is an unspoken assumption that shorter people will not be so successful. Yet whether the hidden curriculum is judged to be negative or positive depends on the perspective of the individual concerned. This can be illustrated in the practices of a basketball coach who focuses on offensive and defensive rebounds. The smaller players on the team may learn from the hidden curriculum that they are not very good at basketball, while the taller players may learn that they are good at the game because they can successfully rebound the ball. This latter group consequently receive positive feedback from the coach and their peers, which in turn increases their social status within the team. However, another basketball coach may value agility, speed and ball dexterity in his or her players

and, as a consequence, the training sessions focus on players running 'plays' up and down the court. Here, the shorter players with greater agility, speed and dexterity may learn via the hidden curriculum that their skills are valued, whereas the taller players, who may not be so agile, learn that they are not so valued.

Hidden messages are portrayed not only by what the coach chooses to do and say, but also by the coach's tone of voice and non-verbal gestural communications. Hence, the routines, dress, body shape, coaching methods adopted and the expectations coaches have of the athletes all carry hidden messages. While we recognize that there will always be unintentionally imparted messages in any social practice, by reflecting on the possible covert, null and hidden curricula, coaches can gain some insight into the way these practices can cause athletes to have pleasant or unpleasant experiences of the coaching process. What is more, by reflecting on the various forms of content it may be possible for coaches to develop practices that increase athletes' opportunities to learn. Some coaches may consider the individual incidents that make up the hidden curriculum to be trite or insignificant, since having one or two negative experiences never damaged anyone for life. We agree; but we also concur with Tinning *et al.* (1993: 108), who stated that there is a powerful cumulative effect of the learnings associated with the hidden curriculum which can be compared to 'the silt in a river bed which eventually hardens to form mudstone'.

(RE)THINKING COACHES' KNOWLEDGE

Viewing the content knowledge of coaches as stable is driven by the modernist desire for certainty and for getting things 'right' (Cassidy and Tinning 2004). In reviewing Daryl Siedentop's engagement with content knowledge in a physical education context, Tinning (2002) highlights the way contemporary knowledge has changed, and goes on to point out that some social analysts even claim that there is no permanent knowledge. What this means for the coaching community is that maybe it is time for coaches and deliverers of coach education to become more sceptical, and modest, in what they claim they can do, and recognize that coaching knowledge is not static. What also may be required is a willingness by coaches to experiment, continually adapt coaching practices, and recognize that the coaching process cannot be controlled completely.

While the above may be good in theory, it is not helpful to view the content knowledge of a coach as separate from his or her identities (for further discussion of identities, see Chapter 7). Much of the knowledge that enables coaches to 'go on' in their coaching life is practical in character, and it is this knowledge that enables them to simply 'do' things while concentrating on other activities that require conscious effort. Associated with this practical knowledge is the way the actions of coaches conform to social conventions, as well as being influenced by their own personality and characteristics (Rossi and Cassidy 1999). For example, when coaches begin to coach, they may choose to teach certain content with which they are very familiar, wear the 'right' gear and adopt an authoritarian approach because they consider these practices to be part of the routines associated with being a good coach, and adopting them goes some way to reducing anxieties associated with coaching. But as is mentioned earlier in the chapter, there are hidden meanings associated with these practices that need to be acknowledged and challenged if the coach is going to progress to become a quality practitioner.

CONCLUDING THOUGHTS

As we have illustrated in this chapter, a coach's content knowledge is multifaceted. Recognition of this enables a coach to move towards developing a comprehensive knowledge of practice. While Shulman's (1986) and Metzler's (2000) frameworks are useful in assisting us to understand the complexity of content knowledge, it is imperative that our exploration does not end there. Rather, we urge coaches to take cognizance of the work that has been conducted in education and physical education. For example, some years ago Kirk (1992) argued that in the physical education teacher education context, the concept of the hidden curriculum had become passé. But as Kirk (ibid.) rightly pointed out, it is a concept that is ignored at one's peril. One alternative way of considering the idea of the hidden curriculum is to utilize the notions of discourse and ideology since these concepts create an opportunity to link learning with wider socio-cultural practices in society (ibid.). (For further discussion of the discourses in sports coaching, see Chapter 8.)

SUGGESTED READINGS

Bunker, D. and Thorpe, R. (1982) 'A model for the teaching of games in secondary schools', *Bulletin of Physical Education*, 18(1): 5–8.

McCaughtry, N. (2004) 'The emotional dimensions of a teacher's pedagogical content knowledge: Influences on content, curriculum, and pedagogy', *Journal of Teaching in Physical Education*, 23: 30–47.

McCullick, B., Belcher, D. and Schempp, P. (2005) 'What works in coaching and sport instructor certification programs? The participants' view', *Physical Education and Sport Pedagogy*, 10(2): 121–137.

Shulman, L. (1986) 'Those who understand: Knowledge growth in teaching', *Educational Researcher*, 15(2): 4–14.

END-OF-CHAPTER TASK

1   Using a context with which you are familiar and the generic Shulman-Metzler framework described in the chapter, provide working examples of the specific types of content knowledge needed to coach your preferred activity in order to provide athletes with maximum opportunities to learn.

CHAPTER 10

▼ ## ASSESSMENT AND ABILITY IN COACHING

INTRODUCTION

Assessment has not been a 'hot topic' among coaches, nor has it had mass appeal among the coaching science research community. According to the bibliography compiled by Gilbert (2002), only 4 per cent of articles in the coaching science literature have focused on assessment, with most of these comprising quantitative measurements of coach behaviour (see, for example, Côté *et al*. 1999; Cunningham *et al*. 2001). However, in the late 1990s some researchers began to use mixed methods, utilizing interviews as well as systematic observation systems or questionnaires to understand the assessment process in coaching (see DeMarco *et al*. 1997; Gilbert *et al*. 1999). On the odd occasion when athletes were the focus of the research, it involved their completing an athlete satisfaction questionnaire (see Riemer and Chelladurai 1998), which again placed the focus on coaches' behaviour. Interestingly, Gilbert (2002) grouped the articles that focused on the *evaluation* of coach education programmes (see, for example, Gilbert and Trudel 1999; MacLean and Zakrajsek 1996) under the *assessment* coaching theme. Conflating the terms evaluation and assessment runs counter to the practice that occurs in the education literature, where a distinction is made between the two (Hay 2006a). Despite this distinction, agreed definitions of both terms remain elusive. This has caused confusion because when we use a term such as assessment, there is an assumption that we all have a common understanding of what it means (Glasby 2006).

We view evaluation as loosely comprising four elements: programme evaluation, curriculum evaluation, evaluation of the opportunities created for learning, and student (or athlete) assessment (Kemmis and Stake 1988). We adopt a rather broad definition of assessment so that we can continue to use it regardless of the purpose for which assessment is being used. Our definition of assessment is a compilation and reads, 'assessment is the purposeful, systematic and ongoing collection of information' (Glasby 2006: 219), which is used to make judgements about athletes learning. Yet the judgement is 'contextualised by the use of that information' (Hay 2006a: 312). This definition rests on certain assumptions. First, it is assumed that if you are purposefully collecting information, then you should 'know why you are assessing what you are assessing' (Glasby 2006: 219). Second, it is assumed that if there is a systematic collection of information, then 'decisions have been made about when and how assessment will be implemented' (ibid.: 219). Third, it is assumed that if the collection of information is ongoing, then 'assessment will occur throughout the learning process and the cumulative evidence of student achievement over time will be the basis of your judgments about the quality of student learning' (ibid.: 219). Finally, it is assumed that the information collected is relevant for the purposes of the assessment (Hay 2006a).

Just as there is no one definition of assessment, so too there is no one purpose of it either. Several scholars (see Broadfoot and Black 2004; Penney *et al.* 2005; Tinning *et al.* 2001) suggest that one way an assessor can be clear on the purpose of the assessment is to ask him- or herself the following questions:

- Who is to be assessed?
- What is to be assessed?
- How is the assessment to occur?
- When is the assessment going to occur?

Once the purpose of assessment is clear, then it becomes easier to decide on the 'types of assessment that will be appropriate and effective' (Penney *et al.* 2005: 58). Clarifying the purpose of assessment is useful not only for those doing the assessing, but also for the ones being assessed, giving everyone involved a common understanding of why the assessment is occurring. The purposes of assessment can be classified into two broad groups: assessment for learning and assessment for accountability (Hay 2006b). Here, we primarily discuss assessment for learning under the heading of educational purposes before discussing the relationship between assessment and ability.

Increasingly, assessment is 'becoming an important point of practice, research and philosophical focus within education discussion' (Hay 2006a: 313). This, however, has not been the case in coaching (Gilbert 2002). We find it surprising there is such a gap, particularly when we consider that one of the principal roles of the coach is to generate athlete learning. But how can such learning be determined if it is not purposefully assessed? One consequence of there being limited discussion of assessment in the coaching literature is that there are few resources available to assist coaches understand the complexities associated with

the practice of assessment. Therefore, the aim of this chapter is to discuss two such complexities associated with the educational purpose of assessment and the relationship between assessment and ability in an effort to contribute to the limited discussion on assessment in coaching.

ASSESSMENT FOR EDUCATIONAL PURPOSES

While there is no consensus on a single definition of assessment, there is an agreement that 'assessment is a vital aspect of learning' (Hay 2006b: 227). An assessment for learning paradigm, which is informed by constructivist perspectives, emerged in response to the perceived limitations of behavioural learning theories and traditional assessment techniques (Hay 2006a). When the aim is to assess for learning, it is useful to be aware of how different types of assessment support the learning process. For this reason, we focus on three types of assessment: formative, summative and authentic assessment.

Formative assessment

Formative assessment has been defined as 'encompassing all those activities undertaken by teachers [read coaches] and/or their students [athletes], which provide information to be used as feedback to modify the teaching and learning activities in which they are engaged' (Black and Wiliam, in Hay 2006a: 316). When assessing formatively, information must be collected *throughout* the learning process rather than at the end of a teaching episode. Since the assessment task is viewed as a learning opportunity that challenges the learner's 'existing knowledge structures and beliefs and fosters the active construction of meaning' (Hay 2006a: 313), the timing of the assessment is crucial. The feedback generated from the assessment is considered to be an important apparatus for monitoring and reflecting upon learning. Drawing on the work of Sadler, Hay (ibid.: 316) goes on to say that while feedback is 'an essential aspect of meaningful and useful formative assessment', it has meaning and use only if the person receiving the feedback knows what to do with the information. It has been suggested that learners could make better use of information they receive if (1) the learning outcomes are explicitly stated, (2) the information relates to the outcomes, and (3) strategies are provided that assist the learners to move towards the desired learning outcomes (ibid.). According to the New Zealand Ministry of Education (1999: 55), a learning outcome is the 'expected learning that occurs as a result of a particular learning activity'.

In Alton-Lee's (2003: 86) *Best Evidence Synthesis*, the literature on assessment for improving learning highlighted that 'when assessment takes the form of effective and formative feedback it is one of the most influential elements of quality teaching'. Such 'interactive' formative assessment is considered 'to be a skilled and complex teacher activity' (ibid.) that requires teachers [and, we would argue, coaches] to have a range of knowledges. These were identified as:

- content knowledge;
- general and specific pedagogical knowledge;
- curriculum knowledge;
- knowledge of the learner;
- knowledge of contexts; and
- knowledge of educational aims (including desired outcomes).

A more detailed discussion of some of these knowledges occurs in Chapter 9, 'Examining coaches' content knowledge'.

Increasingly, cognitive learning theories are informing new educational initiatives in mainstream education, coaching and coach education. This being the case, discussions on formative assessment are set to continue and potentially gather momentum. It is important to remember that while formative assessment can assist the learning process, it can also be used to motivate learners to want to achieve (Siedentop and Tannehill 2000). Yet formative assessment will do so only if the practices are integrated into quality teaching and do not become the focus of the teaching (Alton-Lee 2003).

One example of formative assessment being used in coaching is the collection of game statistics on an athlete throughout the season. For example, at the start of the season a basketball coach and athlete may set the following learning outcome: 'The athlete will be able to extend his or her physical competence by successfully completing 20 defensive rebounds in a competitive game situation.' Over the course of the season, statistics are collected on the number of defensive rebounds the athlete successfully completes each game. After each game the athlete could view the statistics and be able to monitor his or her progress against the learning outcome. If the learning outcome is realistic, the process of being able to track progress can motivate the athlete to want to achieve. Equally, the coach is able to monitor progress and to modify, if necessary, his or her coaching practices to support the athlete reach the learning outcome.

Summative assessment

Summative assessment practices generally occur in controlled settings and at the completion of a sequence of instruction. They are often standardized, contrived, and able to be measured, although not generalizable. An example of this type of assessment is when athletes are required to perform the Beep Test or the Cooper 12-minute run in the process of having their cardiovascular fitness assessed. At the end of the testing the athletes are awarded a number or a level that is then used for comparative or grading purposes (Siedentop and Tannehill 2000; Tinning *et al.* 2001). This example of summative assessment is informed by behavioural perspectives of learning as evidenced by the focus on observable behaviour. But some cognitive learning theories can also inform summative assessment, as seen in the increasingly popular approach of judging an athlete or coach against competencies at the *end* of a unit of work.

An influential event in the competency movement was the Organisation for Economic Co-operation and Development (OECD) Ministers' meeting in Paris on 24 April 2001, the theme of which was 'Investing in competencies for all'. At the meeting it was agreed that for the 2002–2006 period the mandate would be, among other things, the development of 'new and more comparable indicators of competencies and of lifelong learning, with a particular focus on . . . strategies for developing and enhancing competencies' (OECD Directorate for Education n.d.). From this, the DeSeCo (Definition and Selection of Competencies: Theoretical and Conceptual Foundations) competency framework was developed, which is grounded in a version of Lave and Wenger's (1991) situated learning theory (Burrows 2005). Yet there are a number of challenges that need to be recognized and overcome if the summative assessment practices being used to judge competence are to be genuinely informed by cognitive perspectives of learning.

Cognitive learning theories clearly advocate that the learner be involved in the learning process. Therein lies the first challenge. Before any assessment can occur, the content needs to be designed in such a way that it provides opportunities for the learner to work in challenging, complex and authentic situations (Cassidy 2007b). A second challenge is associated with the process of the instructor (i.e. the coach) co-constructing the competences with the learner (i.e. the athlete). Co-construction offers an 'opportunity to clarify concepts in an on-going process of shared meaning-making' (Rutherford 2004: 2) and is consistent with a situated view of learning and learner-centred practices. The process of co-construction increases learners' awareness of the learning process and assists them to set learning goals and criteria for competence (Cassidy 2007b).

Authentic assessment

As we have mentioned, when assessing for learning it is important to adopt assessment practices that support the learning process. One way of doing this is to adopt assessment practices that are authentic and meaningful to the learner. According to Hay (2006a: 313), authentic assessment is that which 'refers to contextually relevant and connected tasks that develop and challenge students' higher-order knowledge and skills that can be transferred beyond the classroom'. Drawing on the work of Wiggins, Hay goes on to suggest that authentic assessment 'should be realistic, replicating the manner in which the knowledge and processes being assessed are utilized in real-life contexts' (ibid.: 316). Some examples of authentic assessment include a golfer handing in a scorecard to illustrate her or his competence, or a 5,000-metre runner using a heart-rate monitor to record the amount of time spent within the training heart-rate zone on a run (Siedentop and Tannehill 2000). For the assessment tasks to be authentic, they should also be structured so that the learners are provided with the opportunities to demonstrate knowledges and skills beyond what they had been taught. If this occurs, then the assessment tasks can 'contribute to an improvement in students' learning and teachers' practice' (Hay 2006a: 316). Authentic assessment in a sports coaching context would require the assessment to be 'based in movement and capture the cognitive and psychomotor processes involved in the competent performance of physical activities' (ibid.: 317). The notion of authenticity is 'closely linked to a need for greater *individualisation* of learning' (Penney *et al.* 2005: 59). Here, Penney *et al.* (ibid.) pointed out that the focus on individualization requires a shift away from traditional assessment practices towards ones that actively involve the learners.

If a coach is to design authentic and meaningful assessment, then it would be advisable to be aware of what he or she, and the athletes, want to achieve. The assessment would then be designed around achieving the co-constructed learning outcomes. Some questions that could stimulate this process are as follows:

- What are the important outcomes? (Remember that the learning outcomes have to be meaningful and authentic, otherwise why will the athletes bother to try to attain them?)
- What must the athletes be able to demonstrate to show that they understand the content?
- What opportunities do the athletes have to demonstrate their skill and knowledge in a way that is unique to them? (Siedentop and Tannehill 2000).

The coach may also wish to consider following some of the principles identified for increasing the involvement of learners in the assessment process. To do so, drawing on the work of Meyer and Nulty, Penney *et al.* suggested that practitioners could:

- explicitly outline the rationale and assessment tasks within the unit of work 'in "*real world terms*", making the "*real life*" relevance explicit to the learners' (2005: 60);
- make connections between what the learner is learning in one context with his or her life in other contexts;
- 'set assessment tasks that are *realistic, inter-linked and cumulative in effect*' (ibid.: 65; italics in original);
- highlight the connections between the various aspects of the unit that will '*produce the desired learning outcomes*' (ibid.: 66; italics in original).

A number of strategies already exist which coaches can draw on to make the assessment tasks authentic and meaningful to their athletes. Some include self-assessment via logs and journals. Journals provide the opportunity for athletes to reflect upon and share their thoughts, feelings and impressions about their performance and/or event. While many coaches may think that journals would be of little or limited use, it is important to remember that the assessment strategies are linked to the learning outcomes. Hence, journals may be appropriate if an outcome is to increase the athletes' ability to think tactically. To help them realize such an aim, a coach may pose some key questions and then request that the athletes write in their journals what they did in response, and why.

Other strategies include peer assessment, observations, open-ended questioning and role-plays. Additionally, more quantifiable, yet still potentially authentic and meaningful, assessment tools are Game Performance Assessment Instrument

(GPAI) (Griffin *et al.* 1997; Oslin *et al.* 1998) and siliconCOACH (see www.silicon coach.com). The evidence gathered by such methods can be displayed in portfolios (Hay 2006a: 318): collections of material that document an athlete's effort, progress and achievement towards a goal or goals. A portfolio is in itself not an assessment strategy until the following requirements have been considered and negotiated:

- An assessment purpose has been determined
- How and what to select for inclusion have been defined
- Decisions on who may select portfolio materials and when they may be selected have been articulated
- Criteria for assessing portfolio have been identified.
                 (Herman *et al.*, in Siedentop and Tannehill 2000: 191)

ASSESSMENT AND ABILITY

If we accept that assessment has educational, social and political purposes, then it is clear that it is not a neutral practice. According to Hay (2005: 42), what we see as the purpose of assessment and how we adopt assessment practices are 'largely mitigated by our understanding of ability'. Yet making judgements as to who has ability, or not, is not a neutral practice either, since how ability is understood 'contributes to differentiating effects for young people in relation to gender, race and social class' (Wright and Burrows 2006: 287). When making an assessment or comment about an athlete's ability, the coach is required to make a judgement. Ideally, the judgement should be transparent since the athletes should be aware of the criteria against which they are being assessed. However, as Hay (2005: 42) pointed out, often our evaluations of abilities 'are based upon far less visible judgments and are much less open to challenge' and scrutiny. He goes on to say that this is potentially problematic because the perceptions of ability may, in turn, shape the judgements that occur during assessment. Because of this, Wright and Burrows (2006: 287) suggest that it is 'imperative to conceptualise "ability" as embedded in social and cultural relations'. At this point, we introduce a vignette in an attempt to demonstrate how 'common-sense' assumptions about ability are actually informed by personal, social and cultural relationships.

VIGNETTE: COACHING THE PROFESSIONALS

Maurice had played for the Tall Blacks (the name of the New Zealand national men's basketball team) for four seasons when he was in his twenties. Not long after he finished playing he took up coaching, embarking on a 25-year career, the last ten of these years being in Europe. Recently, he had returned to New Zealand to coach the franchise team that plays in the Australian National Basketball League (NBL). He was looking forward to the challenge and considered that he was up to it. This was because he was an ex-Tall Black (and that had to count for something), had had some degree of success working in Europe and, while there, had observed the practices of some pretty high-profile coaches. The players in the franchise squad were a diverse bunch with a range of experience and ethnic backgrounds. There were an equal number of athletes identifying as Mäori, Samoan and Päkehä, together with the obligatory African-American imports.

Halfway through the season, Maurice confided in his assistant that he could not work out why some of the players were not practising the drills and skills he had set them. It was not that they were not spending time in the gym or that they were not on task. From Maurice's perspective they just did not seem to have the dedication needed to practise so that desired technique would become ingrained. Maurice often compared the players in his squad to when he trained as a Tall Black. During that period in his life he would spend hours every day shooting from the free-throw line to make sure the shot came almost naturally. He also compared the players in the NBL squad to those he had coached in Europe, whom he perceived as also being more dedicated. While he thought the players in New Zealand had more natural ability, he thought the players in Europe were ultimately more able because they were prepared to practise for hours on end. He could never imagine the players in the NBL franchise squad getting bored, because they were never prepared to stick at a drill long enough. Instead, they always wanted to make up fancy 'plays', and even though he would tell them not to, they were quite prepared to throw the 50:50 pass on the chance that it would work. As far as Maurice was concerned, the players just did not take the practices and games seriously enough.

What Maurice did not know was that some of the players had also confided in the assistant coach. From the players' perspective, Maurice was not allowing them to have any say in the running of the practices and did not appear to appreciate the skill sets the players bought to the team that enabled them to be a little less predictable than some of the other teams. Also, they did not believe Maurice realized that some of the squad had started playing together when they were at school, so they were use to, and enjoyed, playing 'pick-up' whenever they were together, including at team practices. The players knew Maurice saw this as 'fooling around', and could not convince him that they were just being creative, and it was OK to have fun.

Maurice's view of ability appears to be that ability is relatively stable, although it can be changed a little through training regimes – a 'positive eugenic' perspective (Hay 2005: 44). An assumption of this perspective is that any poor achievement in an assessment task reflects the learner's abilities and therefore is an indication of limited talent or lack of motivation and effort (ibid.). Rarely is the assessment instrument considered to be the one that is limited.

RECONCEPTUALIZING ABILITY

One way to challenge the eugenic perspective and disrupt the unproblematic relationship between assessment and ability is to reconceptualize the notion of ability. Evans (2004) draws on the work of social theorist Pierre Bourdieu to do just that. An important concept within Bourdieu's work is that of habitus. Habitus

can be thought of as being 'a person's beliefs, ideals, speech, action and appearance that have been impressed upon them through their interactions with social agents and institutions' (Hay 2005: 46). It is useful to quote at length Evans' (2004) subsequent reinterpretation of ability:

> Evans (2004) proposes that ability may be described as how valued a person's habitus is in a specific field . . . [such as a sports team] and the degree to which the attributes or dispositions that constitute habitus are desirable to the social agents . . . [such as coaches, selectors, administrators] operating within the field. The more symmetry between the characteristics of one's habitus and the defining features of the field, the more an individual is recognised as possessing ability within that field. Differences in ability may be understood as variations in the comparability between the characteristics of an individual's habitus and the field. . . . We might say that the . . . [athletes] considered 'most able' had a habitus that was characterised by the dispositions that . . . [the coach, administrators, selectors] expected, consciously or otherwise, of . . . [an athlete associated with the team and sport code]. . . . [An athlete who was considered less able] perhaps had a habitus that was less reflective of the expectations of the field.
>
> (Hay 2005: 47)

Maurice perceived the players he coached in Europe to be more able than his NBL franchise players. We would suggest that this judgement is based on the habitus displayed by the athletes. That is, the attributes and dispositions of the European-based players such as being prepared to practise drills for hours on end had symmetry with what Maurice expected a professional basketball player to have. Yet it is not only the athletes' habitus that is implicated in the judgements about their ability. Maurice's expectations and perceptions are part of his habitus, which similarly influences his judgements on what constitutes ability. For example, when the expected and desirable characteristics and dispositions are not forthcoming, '[t]hose who work to challenge what is deemed legitimate may be relegated to labels such as "behavioral problems", "lacking effort" or "unable"' (Hay and lisahunter 2006: 309). This was highlighted in the vignette when Maurice described the NBL players as not having 'dedication' and bemoaning the fact that they ignored his request not to throw risky 50:50 passes. Even the players picked up on Maurice's perceptions by saying that they knew he saw their behaviour as 'fooling around'.

The eugenic perspective of ability has also been challenged by Wright and Burrows (2006), who utilize Bourdieu's notion of 'physical capital' in doing so. While Bourdieu usually analysed 'embodied' capital under the heading of cultural capital, Shilling (1991: 654) argued that '"the physical" is too important to be seen merely as a component of cultural capital'. Shilling went on to refer to the production of physical capital as 'the *social formation* of bodies by individuals through sporting, leisure and other activities in ways that express a class location and which are accorded symbolic value' (ibid.: 654; italics in original). Like other forms of capital, physical capital can be converted into economic, cultural or social capital (Bourdieu 1984). Wright and Burrows (2006: 283) pointed out that 'ability as a form of physical capital is profoundly classed'. It is classed because of the 'unequal opportunities to develop ability both through the differential physical and human resources available, and the ways particular cultural and social capital are associated with particular abilities and capacities' (ibid.: 283). In developing this position they drew on the work of Hokowhitu (2003, 2004) to demonstrate the way physical ability has been used to differentiate between ethnicities.

Hokowhitu (2003) mapped the ways Māori have historically been, and continue to be, regarded as achievers in the physical realm yet limited in the academic. For example, in the nineteenth century Māori were constructed as 'physical, unintelligent and savage' by missionaries and European settlers (2003: 193). At the turn of twenty-first century this construction is still apparent in comments about Māori athletes having a 'warrior instinct' or that the athleticism 'is in the blood' or that Māori have 'natural rhythm'. This positioning of Māori and Pacific Islanders as having physical abilities was illustrated by Wright and Burrows (2006: 287), who observed that the

> proliferation of sport 'academies' populated largely by Maori and Polynesian boys, the promotion of professional rugby as a lifestyle choice for Maori and Pacific Islanders, and the deliberate targeting of Maori and Pacific Island young people (with sporting prowess) for recruitment into elite schools, are just a few examples of the ways young people are being encouraged to use the 'physical capital' they are presumed to have 'inherited' by virtue of race.

Hokowhitu (2003: 193) pointed out that 'such "normal" depictions of Māori are undoubtedly tied to a bio-racist history contrived by colonizer privilege'. He went on to say that while some may argue that the above descriptions are complimentary, being 'implicitly linked' to the Cartesian mind–body dualism, they also 'reinforced prevailing stereotypes that Māori lacked the psychology of a white person' (ibid.: 212). The Cartesian dualism is reflected in the view that 'natural physical ability is paralleled by an inherent lack of mental resolve' (ibid.: 212). As is evident in the vignette, Maurice's view on the ability of some of the players in his NBL team reflects this Cartesian dualism. Yet this view not only is held by fictitious coaches such as Maurice, but is also apparent in the views of some leading sporting commentators and coaches in Aotearoa/New Zealand. For example, Murray Deaker, a well-known sports commentator, said:

> I think it is fantastic that we have this wonderfully athletic group of people [Māori and Pacific Islanders] that can help us develop our sport. . . . But I also want the hard, tough white farmer to be part of my All Black side. . . . [The type of player who is] there for 80 minutes in a ruthless uncompromising way.
>
> (Matheson in Hokowhitu 2003: 212–213)

Similarly, ex-All Black turned commentator Grant Fox stated:

> Polynesian players were naturally superior to us [Päkehäs] in talent, but a lot of them aren't there now because they didn't have the discipline for physical conditioning. They lacked the right kind of mental attitude. They'd just turn up and play.
>
> (Hyde in Hokowhitu 2003: 213)

Practices and comments such as these actively construct Mäori and Pacific Islanders as having ability only in the physical realm. One potential consequence of such a construction is that Mäori and Pacific Islanders are disenfranchised from 'resources, both economic and social, that are derived from involvement in the "academic" or "intellectual" world' (Wright and Burrows 2006: 287). Even at the highest professional levels, then, coaching assumptions need to be actively deconstructed, particularly in the fields of ethnicity and culture, if the potential of all athletes is to be maximized.

CONCLUDING THOUGHTS

While assessment may not be a 'hot topic' among coaches or the coaching science research community, it has the potential to be one as it holds the promise to measure whether or not learning has occurred. By neglecting to consider the complexities associated with assessment, coaches are unable to gain an accurate picture of what athletes are learning, nor are they able to recognize how 'common-sense' assumptions of ability influence assessment practices. The work of Evans (2004), Hay (2005, 2006a) and Wright and Burrows (2006) has demonstrated that there are alternative ways to look at ability other than those that have been informed by the traditional eugenic perspective. By not considering these alternative perspectives we potentially place limits around what is possible (Hay 2005) in terms both of what athletes can learn and of the coach's ability to make a positive difference to that learning. Therefore, when one is involved in assessment practices it is important to recognize the habitus of all involved, adopt meaningful and authentic practices, and ask '[q]uestions about what "abilities" count, why, how and with what effects', realizing that the answers 'cannot be considered outside of "culture"' (Wright and Burrows 2006: 287–288).

SUGGESTED READINGS

Hay, P. (2005) 'Making judgements: Student ability and assessment in physical education', *Journal of Physical Education New Zealand*, 38(1): 41–50.

Hay, P. (2006) 'Assessment for learning in physical education', in D. Kirk, D. Macdonald and M. O'Sullivan (eds) *The Handbook of Physical Education*, London: Sage.

Hokowhitu, B. (2003) '"Physical beings": Stereotypes, sport and "physical education" of New Zealand Mäori', *Culture, Sport and Society*, 6(2/3): 192–218.

Wright, J. and Burrows, L. (2006) 'Re-conceiving ability in physical education: A social analysis', *Sport, Education and Society*, 11(3): 275–291.

END-OF-CHAPTER TASKS

1   Using a context with which you are familiar, design a specific learning outcome.

2   In an effort to support the learner achieve the above learning outcome, design:
-   a formative assessment task;
-   criteria against which competence could be judged;
-   an authentic assessment task.

3   Observe the athletes with whom you work or train. Rank them in terms of ability, then reflect on and describe the ways in which your ranking could be informed by assumptions based on gender, race or social class.

COACHING CONTENT

PART FOUR
COACHING
CONTEXT

CHAPTER 11

▼ **COACHING ETHICS**

INTRODUCTION

The notion that sport builds character has been a popular claim for decades, and rests on the taken-for-granted assumption that there is some sort of internal connection between the practice of sport and the development of moral qualities (Carr 1998). Despite its positive overtones, the belief has often led to a culture of non-teaching or coaching in relation to moral values, as it is based on the perception that a coach's task is simply to organize sporting activities for children or athletes, who learn ethical behaviours simply from participating in them. Despite the popularity of the notion of sport being a character builder, it has not been the subject of widespread critical examination. Indeed, it has not garnered anything approaching general consensus, let alone necessary operational definitions. This is particularly so in relation to what is meant by the term 'character', and how the context and/or the coach is meant to develop it (Sheilds and Bredemeier 1995). This lack of clarity has led to inadequate conceptualization of the professional responsibilities associated with the coaching role in terms of coaches' own moral development and that of their athletes (Carr 1998).

Before we enter the discussion related to coaching ethics and coaches' moral behaviour in earnest, it is appropriate that we provide definitions of both ethical and moral actions, lest there should be similar confusion in the ensuing analysis. According to the *Concise Oxford Dictionary* (Oxford 1991: 401), ethics relate to 'moral principles', which are 'concerned with the goodness or badness of human

behaviour or with the distinction between right and wrong'. Hence, a moralist is a 'person who follows a system of ethics' (ibid.: 769–770). The terms are plainly interrelated and therefore, as has been done elsewhere (Kretchmar 1994), will be used interchangeably in this chapter.

In trying to debunk the myth of the character-building qualities of sport, Carr (1998) contends that involvement in it is no more morally or ethically educative than any other pursuit or school subject that involves children learning to work cooperatively with others. The important caveat here is that although it cannot be assumed that ethical behaviour will be learned through mere participation, the sporting environment may well be a place where it can happen. Perhaps the preliminary question to be addressed, then, is whether coaches should be regarded as moral educators.

Echoing earlier work situating the coach as, above all, a social pedagogue (Jones *et al.* 2004, 2006a), and in the light of their often influential positions as 'significant others', we believe that coaches should qualify as agents of moral education. This, however, is a consequence of the particular professional role occupied, not of the peculiar nature of physical activities. The ethical learning context, then, is one that is created and maintained by the coach, and not by virtue of its being defined as 'sport'. To fashion such an environment, coaches must first recognize that the ethical development of the athletes in their charge is a part of their role, and that, like other pedagogic professionals, they are 'employed to teach in a context of wider concerns about how to live and what to value in life' (Carr 1998: 131). They hold important positions (often being *in loco parentis*) with regard to caring for minors, a duty that, like it or not, carries significant ethical obligations and responsibilities. In this respect, a coach's moral responsibilities should extend beyond policing foul play, to the fostering and cultivation of certain virtues that are directly implicated in the realization of the value of sport.

Having declared our stance that a coach should act as a moral guide, the purpose of this chapter is to explore how his or her subsequent behaviour can be representative of such a person. However, the aim is to go further than merely to document circumstances where ethical dilemmas could typically emerge for coaches, or to direct coaches to 'ready-made' moral decisions as manifest in existing codes of conduct. Rather, it is to promote an understanding of the often complex and relative ethical dilemmas in sport, and how to better deal with them. In this respect it builds on the earlier work of Sheilds and Bredemeier (1995) in seeking to extend current theory by discussing a framework useful for understanding, investigating and promoting ethical action in coaching. What informs our approach here is the need to avoid the individual–social dualism, which has so far oversimplified much of the work into coaches' ethical dilemmas, and to emphasize that social interactions and the contexts in which they occur affect the moral behaviour of the individual. Moral dilemmas in coaching, therefore, are often better viewed as 'shades of grey', with the challenges to the fine line of distinction between ethical and unethical behaviour being complex and open to interpretation (Lyle 2002).

COACHING CONTEXT

However, this is not to advocate a totally relativist stance, thus abdicating responsibility for trying to live a life founded on good ethics. Indeed, following a discussion on the purpose of an ethical code and current writings on ethical coaching issues, the work of McNamee (1998) and Fernandez-Balboa (2000) are used to provide a framework whereby coaches' ethical decisions are personalized and made accountable. Here, the case is made for a 'virtues' as opposed to a 'rules-based' code of conduct approach, in order to secure lasting change in the moral climate within which coaching occurs (McNamee 1998). This places the onus firmly on coaches to carefully consider courses of action and their consequences in relation to ethical behaviour. Indeed, it is here, in arguing for the benefits of principled reflection on the nature of coaching practice, that the principal significance of the chapter lies. Finally, the value of the chapter also lies in making the case for coaches to be professionally educated in relation to developing moral sensitivity in their practice while cultivating positive social values among their athletes (Carr 1998).

ETHICAL CODES AND ETHICAL ISSUES IN COACHING

Sport is often thought to mirror society and its prevailing value trends. Additionally, because of its popularity, it is often considered a primary medium through which many young people come to learn about the core values of their culture. Having the potential to convey social values, however, also encompasses the transmission of undesirable as well as desirable ones (Sheilds and Bredemeier 1995). Consequently, some critics have claimed that sport impedes, as opposed to develops, 'good' value learning, and point to the many reports of unethical behaviour related to violence, parental brawls, aggressive nationalism, sexism, racism, homophobia and illegal use of performance-enhancing drugs as evidence of their claim (Reddiford 1998). Such behaviour results both from adopting values that are counter to the norm and from following desired social values too closely. This latter tendency has been termed 'positive deviance', which distorts ideals and leads to twisted value priorities where the ends are seen as justifying the means. Indeed, recent questions about the morality of sport have largely arisen from such deviance, as witnessed in the harsh competitive ethic driven by the huge extrinsic rewards evident at many levels. It is a concern about the emphasis placed on the prize more than the process that tends to blur 'our vision of the human and humane potential of sport' (Sheilds and Bredemeier 1995: 2). According to Kretchmar (1994), it is through such a distorted focus that we develop 'moral callouses', which in turn keep us from engaging with ethical questions of right and wrong at any meaningful level.

Ethical issues, then, are very much a contemporary concern for coaches, with considerable attention having been given over recent years to appropriate and inappropriate coaching behaviour. This has been generated by a seemingly endless array of athletes failing drug tests, allied to several high-profile sexual harassment cases and allegations of child abuse (Lyle 2002). The range of ethical issues likely to concern coaches was recently categorized by Lyle (ibid.) into interpersonal

relationships, power differentials, social role (failure to maintain) and inappropriate goal setting. Consequently, as many coach–athlete relationships are characterized by differences in age, experience, knowledge and gender, as well as close physical contact, psychological dependency and emotional intensity, they are a fruitful context within which unethical behaviour can occur. The resulting tension is heightened in elite sport, where both coaches and athletes constantly stretch the boundaries of permissible action in order to maximize performance (ibid.). Indeed, they are actively encouraged to do so by a performance-driven culture that values the development of an 'edge' over opponents.

Despite the potential for sport to generate unethical behaviour, it can also serve as an important catalyst for moral growth, personal development and social justice. Hence, it can be seen as a moulder, as well as a mirror, of social values, as it is replete with opportunities to encounter, learn and live positive social principles (Sheilds and Bredemeier 1995). Indeed, Sheilds and Bredemeier (ibid.) argued that sport can be a particularly valuable context for moral education, as the 'ground rules' of the game are more generally accepted, assumed and respected as being fairer than those of society. Consequently, in providing a platform for the further development of ethical behaviour, the 'fair play' assumption associated with participating in sport could work in its favour.

As a consequence of the potential to break the rules, and in response to those who have done so, many sport-specific and generic ethical codes of conduct have been established. For example, in 1979 Martens and Seefeldt proclaimed the Bill of Rights for Young Athletes, while in 1992 the Council of Europe created the European Sports Charter, both of which arose from unease regarding issues of overcompetitiveness in youth sport. These were followed, in 1998, by the Brighton Declaration on Women and Sport in response to concerns over gender equity, and in 1996 by the National Coaching Foundation's wide-ranging guide to ethical practice (Kidd and Donnelly 2000). Their value has been justified by the premise that by giving an outline of what is permissible and what is not, they demonstrate to everyone concerned what behaviours can be expected from professionals (Lyle 2002).

Such codes are considered to be 'issues-led', with general concerns related to cheating, drug taking and child abuse dominating the agenda. Additionally, despite their potential for developing positive virtuous practice, they have traditionally been presented in negative terms. That is, such codes have focused on apparently inappropriate behaviour. Thus, they remind us of the social rules by which we should live, of what 'ought to be', by emphasizing what we should not do. Similarly, the rationales for writing such codes have been couched in negative terms; for example, 'to avoid arbitrariness', 'to highlight impermissible conduct', 'to impose clarity and simplicity in a confusing world', 'to set out standards and criteria by illustrating the need for them' and 'to provide a framework for resolving conflict' by confirming what is not allowable (McNamee 1998). It is a common-sense view of morality, expressed as a set of rules that are designed to stop people from acting unfairly in the pursuit of their own interests to the detriment of others.

PROBLEMATIZING ETHICS: MOVING TOWARDS VIRTUES-BASED CONDUCT (McNamee 1998)

Despite the fact that existing codes of professional practice are generally accepted to be necessary documents, some scholars have questioned whether they are entirely relevant (Carr 1998; McNamee 1998; Reddiford 1998). The concerns relate not to the aims of such codes, but to their inadequacy in dealing with the ethically complex coaching environment, and to their view of morality as a set of clear regulations to be unproblematically followed. The absolutist lines they draw have been criticized for leading us to 'right-wrong' binary thinking, and to the false belief that we are successfully addressing moral difficulties when we are not (McNamee 1998). Consequently, although their clarity is often unquestioned in terms of outlining 'proper' human relationships in the coaching environment, such codes have been accused of inviting us to think of ethical life in terms of a series of rigid obligations. McNamee (1998: 148) views them as being reflective of moral conservatism, 'a flight back to the language of moral certainty, of duties, and rules', and to a 'culture of blame and punishment for perceived wrongdoing' (ibid.: 151). Such regulations maintain that rule adherence is at the heart of ethical conduct, and imply that if coaches follow rules, then they must have a sense of moral maturity. Although such codes have been useful in identifying those who are unethical in their practice, thus enabling punishment, needless to say we believe there is more to the development of moral maturity than that. Indeed, Reddiford (1998) considered such codes as having had little, if any, effect on the moral motivation of those who seek to make unjust gains, and felt that their existence merely leads to more sophisticated ways of cheating. McNamee also questioned the need for rules that outline obvious wrongdoings. For example, he asks:

> Why do we need a rule concerning sexual harassment in a code of conduct? Is it not clear that such actions are wrong, so why do we need a code to tell us this? We can no more sexually harass our colleagues or athletes than any other person in the street. The rule tells us nothing new.
>
> (1998: 158)

Alternatively, he believes that the psychology of the situation that produces such unacceptable behaviour needs to be understood in order to ensure (as best we can) that it does not happen. To secure such adherence, we should work towards a climate of conduct that precludes such actions because we sincerely believe them to be inherently wrong and not just because a rule-book tells us they are. Finally, McNamee (1998) criticizes the rule-based approach as being, by its very nature, underdetermined. That is, he questions how a set of regulations can anticipate or describe all the actions that may be considered unethical, or tell everyone what to do and what not to do in all circumstances. Plainly, it cannot. Such codes appear to leave many questions unanswered as they are simply unable to write out the particularity of quandary (ibid.) or to assist coaches in addressing the infinite variety of moral issues they constantly face once they have avoided obvious wrongdoings. Even when attempts have been made to achieve absolute rule clarity

and precision in terms of a certain act, judgement is often still needed in interpreting a possible unethical behaviour as fitting a given category (Reddiford 1998). Such codes, then, are regarded as being too simplified to have much impact on behaviour, while being inadequate in preparing coaches to answer the morally fundamental recurring question of 'what will I do here in the light of what I consider myself to be?' (McNamee 1998).

To further illustrate the problematic nature of ethical decision making in coaching, consider the following scenario, which has been adapted from the work of McNamee (1998). I am the coach of a middle-distance 16-year-old athlete, Rhys, who shows great promise. His parents are keen and supportive, both of his involvement in sport and of me as a coach. They want him to be pushed to fulfil his potential. However, at present he is struggling with his interval training and just cannot reach the agreed targets set ('agreed' in terms of me suggesting a training schedule, and him just nodding!). In all probability this is because he has not kept to the strict training regime laid out for him. This afternoon, he is tired after the morning run and looks distinctly unenthusiastic about the session ahead. How should I react, what should I do? A multitude of questions run through my mind. Should I make him run more intervals on the track? Is he too tired to do them properly? Is he self-motivated enough to do them properly? Have I done enough to prepare him for the forthcoming championships? Has he achieved the 'agreed' goals? Were they really agreed goals? Have I pushed him too hard? Do I have to toughen him up? These are everyday ethically tinged questions for a coach that fall well outside the rule-governed jurisdiction of proclaimed codes of conduct. There are no rules to guide me here. After a minute's consideration, I decide that the only way to get Rhys to succeed is to push him harder; after all, that is what his parents want. I warn him that if the next set of sprints is not completed within a certain time, 'we'll be here all night till they are'. I tell him to 'harden up' and to 'tough it out'. In response, through great effort, he completes the set satisfactorily. I feel vindicated. I have proved to him what he's capable of if he is only prepared to work hard enough. I chastise him for his lack of will-power and remind him of others' sacrifices that allow him this opportunity to explore and exploit his talent. Rhys walks away in an angry sulk, his animosity towards me obvious. To a degree, I understand his reaction. However, I am comforted in the knowledge that I have simply complied with the wishes of his parents, while demonstrating to him what he is capable of. I have engaged in no obvious wrongdoing, and merely kept to the agreed training schedule.

Although no rules as enshrined in a code of conduct were broken in the scenario described, it could be argued that the trust between the athlete and the coach has been violated, or at the very least placed under considerable strain. On the other hand, perhaps it was exactly what Rhys needed to make him value his talent. Such dilemmas highlight the complexity of the ethical dimension in coaching and the inadequacy of rules-based codes of conduct in helping coaches to deal with it. As there are no rules here, such an issue as how hard young athletes should be pushed must be left to the discretion of the coach. In short, we just have to trust the coach

COACHING CONTEXT

to make the right decisions. To help coaches in this regard, coach education programmes should include a personal ethical component grounded in such real issues as described above. For McNamee (1998), the main consideration within such a situation should be not 'whether I have broken any rules', but 'what I should do in the light of what's best for my athlete and the claims I make for myself as a good person'. The immediate issue for coaches, then, becomes how to distinguish right from wrong; that is, 'What do I believe qualifies as ethical behaviour and what does not?' and 'What is this decision based on?'

In relation to the wider issue of what qualifies as ethical behaviour, a common view in Western culture is to believe that moral perspectives are strictly a matter of preference (Sheilds and Bredemeier 1995). Although we acknowledge the role of context in deciding the most appropriate course of action, as is stated in the introduction to the chapter, to abandon the debate to total relativity would leave coaches with no pilot or rudder by which to navigate rough and dangerous seas. The perspective of the cognitivists, on the other hand, appears a little more convincing in providing assistance (Sheilds and Bredemeier 1995). They consider that behaviour is ethical only if it is motivated, at least in part, by such reasons. For example, if a coach passes on some knowledge to another coach because he or she thinks that doing so will give him or her an emotional edge that can later be exploited, while a second coach does the same thing for purely altruistic reasons (i.e. just to help the other coach), we would say that only the second coach acted morally. Such a stance echoes the classic work of Rokeach (1973) in psychology, who equated morality with altruism or 'other-regard' (i.e. regard to the 'other'), considering selfishness a threat to it. Although this might provide a good guide to moral action, to parcel and leave it so neatly is unrealistic, as such a stance can be countered by the argument that often a concern of the moral agent is to cultivate his or her own morality by virtue of acting morally. This inevitably involves a focus on the self and can be termed selfish. Others meanwhile have disagreed with the altruistic thesis from the viewpoint that 'what is required to be fair and just is not self-denial but a balancing or coordination of self interest with the interests of others' (Sheilds and Bredemeier 1995: 19).

Similarly, when searching for the meaning of morality, the philosopher Habermas attempted to explain ethical action in terms of its relationship to the general 'norm' (Sheilds and Bredemeier 1995). Consequently, 'truth' was defined as the consensus reached through dialogue. Critics, however, have contended that not every such agreement leads to good ethical actions – for example, witness the positively deviant yet accepted subculture of many sports, which often lead to brutalizing training regimes. Additionally, within contests there frequently appears to be a shared limited appreciation of the 'spirit of the rules', as there is general agreement on pursuing every advantage possible to secure on-field victories (Reddiford 1998). Such a sentiment was even expressed by that model of traditional English sporting excellence and sportsmanship C.B. Fry, who believed that 'if both sides agree to cheat, then cheating is fair' (Reddiford 1998: 225). Indeed, many actions carried out under the guise of sport would be considered unacceptable in wider society but

are tolerated in context by all concerned, as they are considered 'part of the game'. Defining moral actions in the sporting context, then, is elusive in itself. Despite the seemingly problematic and often contextual nature of ethical actions, however, we do believe that some moral principles should be virtually unassailable. These include concepts such as respect, integrity, equity and fairness. The difficulty, of course, comes in interpreting and implementing them, in a social environment that is forever changing, so that they are consistently upheld. Perhaps a way forward in this regard is to accept that while such principles form the core of ethical action, they can and should remain flexible. Rokeach's (1968) work on values can help our understanding here, as he believed there were different kinds of values which could be classified by what he termed the 'regions of the person'. The metaphoric language was used to highlight that some beliefs are more critical and more central to self-identity than others. This is a view supported by Blasi and Oresick, who concluded that

> not all beliefs have the same value and the same effects. Some are only peripherally related to our identity. If one acts against such beliefs, one is inconsistent, but only in a weak sense. On the other hand, certain beliefs are so central to one's identity that one is compelled to act in accordance with them by psychological necessity; if one fails to do so, one is inconsistent in a strong sense.

> (1987: 72)

Consequently, it appears that we are able to have principles and to treat them flexibly, particularly the more weakly held ones, without being considered inconsistent. In this way, we can be adaptable while constantly upholding certain moral standards (this is similar to the discussion in Chapter 4 on the development of functional coaching philosophies). Sheilds and Bredemeier (1995: 13) liken it to a 'belief tree', where the roots equate to core beliefs, the branches are the intermediate beliefs, while the 'peripheral beliefs, like leaves, drop off easily in response to the shifting winds of life'.

The ethical flexibility implied in the metaphorical 'belief tree' was recently found in the behaviour of expert coaches (Jones *et al.* 2004; Saury and Durand 1998). It also falls broadly in line with the call of McNamee (1998) to educate coaches through a 'virtues' as opposed to a rule-based approach, thus ensuring that contextual decision making takes place, as opposed to rigid rule adherence. For him, ethics and ethical conduct cannot simply be reduced to the idea of rule responsibility, hence what is important is to develop coaches who genuinely follow the spirit of the rules and not those whose behaviour merely equates to rule observance, where this means the avoidance of rule-breaking actions (ibid.). Such a stance builds on the work of Kohen (1994), who believed that the professional must be given discretion, grounded in a highly internalized sense of responsibility, in order to effect context-sensitive ethical action. This sense of responsibility is crucial to answer the earlier-cited recurring internal questions of 'In what do we ground our interpretations of what is right?' and 'What makes us confident of the rightness of our decisions?'

According to McNamee (1998), the answer lies in developing a deeper moral code to live by, one based on personal virtue. Such a code seems particularly applicable to the sporting domain, where coaches' goals, and the accompanying decisions they take, are both relative and absolutist, and almost always complex. Unavoidably, then, owing to the inability of rules-based codes of conduct to cover all eventualities, the coach becomes someone in whom an element of trust and discretion is invested. The least athletes and parents can expect is that decisions affecting them are taken within a good ethical framework of responsibility to performer, self and sport (ibid.). Hence, we need to develop coaches who respect the rules to ensure that the contest is a fair and enjoyable one, as opposed to not breaking them from a fear of being caught and punished (ibid.). We need coaches who adhere to the spirit of the game and do not bend the rules as much as possible, who do not substitute codes of conduct in place of their own virtuous development, or who fear creatively engaging with the range of options open to them over and above the rules laid out. In trying to give flesh to such considerations, C.R. Jones *et al.* (under review) proposed the question of 'What kind of person should such a coach be?'

In answer, and in line with a virtues-based approach, we believe that coaches should be individuals who, at their core, conduct their lives consciously as moral agents. Such a holistic account differs somewhat from the 'professionalized' view of coaching as a time-bounded activity having a clear start and finish, as reflected in formal coaching settings. Although we realize that in practice there are (or should be) temporal and spatial boundaries to coaching practice, in terms of personhood (i.e. one's moral behaviour) the job of coaching really allows for no 'time off task' (C.R. Jones *et al.* under review). Consequently, although social circumstances change, core qualities of character and behaviour should remain the same. This may mean that coaches need to understand that how they behave and what they say outside immediate coaching contexts may be just as influential as technical and tactical information imparted during a coaching session (ibid.). Though we are not advocating that at all times coaches need to be overly sensitive and self-conscious of how their behaviour impacts others, coaches do need to recognize that the impact they may have on athletes extends in a multitude of ways through a range of situations. Thus, the coach will need to consider not only those purposeful actions intended to have a transforming effect, but, importantly, also those behaviours that have unintended consequences (ibid.). The next section outlines a suggested strategy for how such moral character can be achieved.

PERSONALIZING COACHES' ETHICAL BEHAVIOUR

Despite much having been written about morality (or the lack of it) in sport and the widespread production of rules-based codes, most coach education programmes continue to devote minimal or very superficial attention to ethical issues (Fernandez-Balboa 2000). Consequently, the coaches who pass through such programmes are unaware of the complexity or even of the existence of much unethical behaviour, nor are they mindful of how to deal with it. What is more,

because they are not encouraged to think critically about such issues, many do not see the relevance of doing so when asked. Fernandez-Balboa neatly encapsulates the prevailing attitude in this regard:

> Spending a lot of time on ethics does not really apply to me. You see, I am (or am going to be) a coach, and my role is to teach physical skills to help athletes improve. I will help many people this way, and that is a good thing, isn't it? Besides, I think I am a pretty good person. I get on well with people and some of my friends are from different ethnic backgrounds.
>
> (ibid.: 134)

He goes on to say that such a line of argument denotes great naivety with regard to unethical behaviour and its damaging consequences. While we may think ourselves to be basically good and try to do what we consider to be the right thing, unless we critically examine our beliefs and actions we could be teaching and practising unethical behaviours without being aware of it (Dodds 1993). This is because coaching exists not in an interpersonal vacuum, but in 'socio-cultural systems which have inherent discriminations and values attached to them' (Fernandez-Balboa 2000: 135). It is through the subsequent process of socialization that we acquire certain beliefs about others and ourselves and what is considered appropriate behaviour. It is also a process from which we invariably learn concepts such as 'us' and 'them' – that is, a dichotomous (i.e. either/or) way of thinking – and how to manifest such notions in actions of acceptance or rejection (Eckert 1989). The resulting behaviour often leads to stereotyping, stigmatization and the humiliation of others (Fernandez-Balboa 2000). Despite good intentions, then, unless we critically reflect upon knowledges and actions, we always run the risk of perpetuating what is damaging and degrading (Fernandez-Balboa 2000; Jones 2000). This is precisely why it is not enough to simply list ethical issues and consider the work of morally educating coaches to be done. Rather, we must critically engage with such issues at the personal level, so that we can deal with them as they appear in practice. It is through such engagement that we can aspire to base our coaching on virtuous, good ethical practice which we sincerely believe to be right, as opposed to given rules.

Despite ample evidence that the traditional coaching model does little to develop the moral characteristics of participants, there continues to be a disproportionate emphasis placed within it on physical development as opposed to the ethical and social aspects of the person. Hence, the enhancement of skills appear more important than matters of bigotry, discrimination and abuse (Fernandez-Balboa 2000). This is evident in both coach education programmes and coaching practice. For example, how often in coach education programmes do we encourage coaches to critique and deconstruct the assumptions that they live by in their coaching? How often do we ask them to question the myths that surround sport (e.g. 'participation builds character') with regard to the unethical behaviours that such assumptions could engender? Indeed, do not the traits that appear so valued in competitive

sport (e.g. prowess, dominance, aggressiveness) go against much moral reasoning and social responsibility? Similarly, does not the presumed meritocratic nature of sport encourage coaches to treat their athletes as convenient commodities that can easily be disposed of once they no longer fulfil their purpose? To address such issues, we need to examine and question our logic and recognize that even when it is well intentioned, uncritical coaching has problematic and dangerous implications (ibid.). This is precisely why it is important to consider our actions in the light of what we deem to be virtuous behaviour. Such behaviour should be based on the well-being and development of the 'other', in balance with a degree of self-respect and a strong awareness of the consequences that actions bring. The reflection that takes place is important, as it keeps us vigilant in relation to our sentiments and practices, and encourages us to constantly ask whether what we do denies the rights, choices and potentialities of others in any way (Dodds 1993).

According to Fernandez-Balboa (2000), a direct way to address the potential that we have to act unethically, and thus to develop a more virtuous approach, is to follow the systematic steps devised by Johnson (1996). These involve:

- admitting the possibility that we have prejudices;
- making honest attempts to identify what they are;
- identifying specific actions that reflect those prejudices;
- seeking support from others who may be able to help us in overcoming them.

Such a process is aimed at making us realize the limitations of our thinking and helping us recognize that our view of 'truth' is only one such version where many exist. To contextualize the process into the coaching context, the questions that we should ask ourselves relate to those ethical issues that are important to us. For example:

- Do I give athletes a real range of choices that are agreeable to them?
- Are my comments and actions considerate of others' beliefs and life experiences?
- Do the athletes I work with fear me? Why?
- Do they respect me? Why?
- How well do I actually know the athletes I work with as people? What evidence do I have on which to base that belief?
- What is my first reaction when an athlete makes a mistake?
- Do I include athletes in the decision-making process? If so, how? If not, should I?
- Do I take the time to learn the perspectives of others?
- 'Does my physical presence confer dominance?' (Fernandez-Balboa 2000: 140).
- How much power do I have over the athletes I work with?

By critically engaging with such questions we can expose some of the 'common-sense', everyday actions of normal life that can lead to unethical behaviour, and so aspire to develop a virtues-based framework through which more moral coaching

can occur. The above list is by no means definitive; coaches should expand on it in ways they deem appropriate to their context and circumstance.

CONCLUDING THOUGHTS

In relation to fighting unethical issues in coaching, we agree with Fernandez-Balboa (2000), who concluded that the battle can never be considered over. This is because not only is there a great deal to confront in the outside world, but much also remains embedded and embodied in ourselves. Consequently, it is a process that is both private and public. As coaches, we have numerous opportunities to deal with many and varied ethical issues on a daily basis. Therefore, it is important that we learn to recognize such issues both in others and within ourselves, and be able to deal with them. If we accept that unethical behaviours are not natural but learned and can permeate many areas of our lives, we can accept that, through critical vigilance and reflection, there are ways to break the cycle and the 'traps of our own reasoning and conditioning' (Fernandez-Balboa 2000: 142). Through such engagement we can better aspire to a virtues-based as opposed to rule-based coaching, thus better ensuring sincere ethical behaviour in our practice.

SUGGESTED READINGS

Carr, D. (1998) 'What moral educational significance has physical education? A question in need of disambiguation', in M. McNamee and J. Parry (eds) *Ethics and Sport*, London: E & FN Spon.

Fernandez-Balboa, J.-M. (2000) 'Discrimination: What do we know and what can we do about it?', in R.L. Jones and K.M. Armour (eds) *Sociology of Sport: Theory and Practice*, London: Longman.

McNamee, M. (1998) 'Celebrating trust: Virtues and rules in the ethical conduct of sport coaches', in M. McNamee and J. Parry (eds) *Ethics and Sport*, London: E & FN Spon.

Sheilds, D. and Bredemeier, B. (1995) *Character Development in Physical Activity*, Champaign, IL: Human Kinetics.

END-OF-CHAPTER TASKS

1   Do you think coaches should be good ethical role models for athletes (more than other professionals)? Justify your answer.
2   Discuss McNamee's argument for a virtues-based approach. Do you agree with it? Why (not)?
3   Consider the scenario presented on p. 154 of the chapter. As coach, how would you react? Why?
4   Try to develop your own ethical code of behaviour through engaging with Fernandez-Balboa's reflective questioning (see p. 159 of this chapter).

COACHING CONTEXT

CHAPTER 12

▼   ## THEORY, PRACTICE AND
PROFESSIONALISM IN
COACHING

INTRODUCTION

In recent years there has been increasing debate surrounding the profes-
sionalization of coaching (Lyle 2002). Lyle (ibid.) suggests that this can be
primarily attributed to two factors: the accountability of coaches for their actions
in contemporary society, and the desire among many practitioners and educators
for coaching to be regarded as a *bona fide* profession. In seeking to contribute to
this ongoing discussion, the aim of this chapter is twofold. First, in drawing upon
the work of Thompson (2003) we seek not only to examine the issue surrounding
the integration of theory and practice in the human services, but also to consider
the implications of his work for coaches in terms of professionalizing their practice.
Second, we propose some definitive principles and subsequent pedagogical
strategies through which the goals of developing a professional approach to
coaching practice can be realized. Such means reflect our belief that coach
education, be it introductory certification or continuing professional development
provision, should be located in, or replicate as nearly as possible, Schön's 'swampy
lowland of practice' (1987: 3), as only there can it be tailored to address the
thorny questions that equate to coaching's holistic complex reality. The strategies
discussed include critical tasks, narratives, problem-based learning scenarios
(PBL) and negotiating mutual engagement within coaches' communities of
practice.

THEORY, PRACTICE AND PROFESSIONALISM

> The fact that many workers do not explicitly apply theory to practice does not mean that they are not relying on a theory base. What it does mean is that they are drawing on ideas in an implicit, indirect, and unsystematic way. At worst, therefore, 'I prefer to stick to practice' can mean 'I prefer to act without thinking' or 'I prefer not to question the basis of my practice'. Clearly, this is not an attitude conducive to professional development, nor does it provide any safeguards against bad practice. Needless to say, this attitude is, therefore, a very dangerous one.
>
> (Thompson and Bates, in Thompson 2003: 33)

The use of formal or academic knowledge as a part of a process of maximizing personal and collective effectiveness has in recent years been increasingly recognized as an integral feature of professionalism (Thompson 2003). Indeed, Thompson (ibid.) suggested that the application of this form of knowledge is essential to the achievement of high standards in practice. This sentiment regarding the relationship between formal knowledge and professional practice is well illustrated by the importance that organizations responsible for the training and education of practitioners in the human services (such as nursing and social work) place on relating theory to practice as a significant element of professional credibility (ibid.). Similarly, Thompson (ibid.) suggested that as the provision of human services often involves considerable public expenditure and can have significant implications for people's quality of life, there is a need for practitioners to be able to justify their actions. Hence, responses such as 'it seemed a good idea at the time' are unlikely to be afforded much store. Instead, he suggested that such accounts need to be grounded in an explanatory framework which:

- clarifies the basis of the intervention and the objective set;
- explains the actions taken to meet the objectives and the reasons for doing so; and
- evaluates the intervention.

(ibid.: 35)

Simply put, he advocated that actions need to be founded on theory. We agree, as approaching coaching practice in this manner would undoubtedly serve to raise the standards of professionalism in practice. Thompson (ibid.) also argued that such an approach may help reduce the number of inappropriate responses to clients, issues and situations as well as providing a number of possible options that could be productively utilized to deal with everyday issues. While he recognized that an 'explicitly theory-based approach by no means guarantees an appropriate response' (ibid.: 9), he suggested that it often provides a useful fall-back position for practitioners when they feel stuck or are in times of difficulty. Indeed, he stated that theory provides 'useful "reserves" to back up the routine use of implicit knowledge' (Thompson 1991: 29). We similarly believe that such a view of practice is important not only for coaches in the field, but also for those responsible for the

education and ongoing development of coaches, especially if they are to assist the former in providing athletes with high-quality sporting experiences.

Thompson's (2003) work highlights a number of issues that coaches and coach educators may benefit from considering in the quest to enhance professionalism through the integration of theory and practice. These relate to helping coaches develop an understanding of the different types of theory that might underpin practice and become cognizant with their respective strengths and limitations. In this regard, he argues that practitioners need to become aware of the differences between 'theories of practice' and 'practice theories'. The former term relates to the formal or 'book' theories that are recorded in the academic literature, while the latter are not officially recognized or codified. Practice theories, then, are defined as the assumptions and informal knowledge that are built up through experience and are often culturally transmitted to new recruits entering specific fields (Thompson 1992, 2003). Examples of this cultural transmission of knowledge have been highlighted in the coaching literature (Cushion *et al.* 2003; Sage 1989). For example, Sage (1989) pointed out how neophyte coaches become inculcated with, or learn, the dominant culture in a particular sport from more senior coaches. Here he documented how the novice coaches learned 'what matters' in terms of coaching in a particular sport and 'how one should' act in the coaching environment.

Thompson's (2003) work also outlines the strengths and limitations of each type of theory. For example, he suggested that because theories of practice are once removed from practice, they are explicit and, as such, are open to challenge and are refined through analysis, debate and empirical investigation. In contrast, practice theories are closely linked to the realities and concerns of everyday action, making them less open to challenge because of their status as received wisdom. Importantly, Thompson (2003) noted that both types of theory have a role to play in terms of developing professionalism, as theories of practice can inform practice theories and vice versa. However, he cautioned against an over-reliance on one at the expense of the other.

In developing this point with regard to practice theories, he suggested that some human service workers may unknowingly be guilty of reflecting the 'fallacy of theoryless practice' (Thompson 1992). This could occur when practitioners inappropriately assume that complex actions can be separated from thought. Underpinning this fallacy is the belief that the only theory that exists is the formal 'book' theory and that informal theories, or practice theories, do not matter. The issue for practitioners (coaches) to become aware of here is that if theories of practice do not underpin their actions, then they need to become aware of the values and ideological frameworks that influence how they act. Indeed, failure to recognize the practice theories that guide their actions can lead practitioners to dogmatism, which ultimately deters reflection and the ability to review, adapt and abandon ideas in the light of changing circumstances (Thompson 2003). Additionally, failure to consider the theory that underpins action could also lead to 'dangerous practice', as, in addition to failing to be effective, misguided behaviours could well serve to make situations worse (ibid.).

A related issue that Thompson (2003) raised here was the need for practitioners to question the extent to which their practice is informed by 'common sense'. He suggested that 'common sense' is 'to a large extent a shorthand for dominant cultural values, the ideology – or sets of ideologies – into which we are socialised from an early age' (ibid.: 97). While Thompson (ibid.) recognized that 'common sense' is not necessarily wrong, he suggested that such beliefs are often unquestioned in that they are based on assumption as opposed to any critical analysis or assessment. He also highlighted that 'common sense' is ideological in terms not just of the nature of its content, but also of how it can be used as a tactic for closing debates, rather than opening them. Specifically, he noted that 'to argue that a particular point of view is "just common sense" is a powerful way of discouraging people from challenging that point of view. Many people will not be prepared to risk being seen to go against common sense' (ibid.: 97). Given this situation, he unsurprisingly stated that a reliance on 'common sense' can act as a hindrance in terms of optimally integrating theory and practice. We would certainly echo this sentiment in the context of coaching.

With regard to his critique of theories of practice, Thompson (2003) highlighted how the false belief that theory can provide 'off-the-peg' solutions to all the issues and scenarios that practitioners face is also problematic. In this respect, and in keeping with the literature in sports coaching (e.g., Jones 2000; Jones and Wallace 2005; Jones and Turner 2006), he argued that practice

> takes place in a context of complexity, conflict, uncertainty and change. It is, therefore, characterised by 'messiness' and does not fit neatly into theoretical schemata based on technical rationality. . . . Theory needs to fit practice, rather than practice being distorted to fit a particular theory.
> (Thompson 2003: 142)

Indeed, in the context of coaching and coach education, such a viewpoint would warn against seeing athletes as a homogeneous group or as automatons who respond in a uniform manner to the same stimuli. As is argued in the preceding chapters, such a stance only serves to ultimately deskill coaches in terms of the cognitive abilities required to successfully provide athletes with situationally relevant and meaningful sporting experiences (Jones 2000).

In order to redress the issues discussed above, Thompson (2003) suggested that practitioners should strive towards achieving research minded practice. This would provide a helpful midpoint between the total rejection of research findings at one extreme and their uncritical acceptance at the other (ibid.). In drawing upon Thompson's (2003) work, we believe it is important to develop a mindset whereby coaches recognize not only the value of theory in terms of providing general guidelines and predispositions that can point them in productive directions, but also

COACHING CONTEXT

the importance for them to critically reflect upon and adapt theory to meet the specific needs of the athlete or athletes in their charge. Professional practice can thus be seen to consist of a blend of both rigour and creativity (ibid.). The remaining sections of this chapter focus on some practical strategies to help coaches explore and develop this blend of theoretical rigour and practical creativity in their coaching.

COACH EDUCATION AND THE DEVELOPMENT OF PROFESSIONALISM IN COACHING PRACTICE

So, how then might we best assist coaches to integrate theory and practice? How can we help coaches explore the assumptions that underpin what they do? What approaches and methods might we use to achieve this goal in coach education programmes and continuing professional development provision? A good place to start, as with most curriculum development exercises, is with the aims and desired learning outcomes. We therefore need to ask the basic questions of what knowledges and attributes we would like coaches to possess so that they can work in a professional manner and, more importantly, how it is possible to develop them. Similar to the argument posited by Culpan (2000) in a physical education context, we believe that, in addition to information related to physiology, psychology, human movement and the technical and tactical specifics of particular sports, coaches should also be required to learn about the socio-pedagogical factors associated with those sports. This is particularly so in terms of (1) athletes' self-actualization (which refers to the identity and personal worth of athletes within the socio-cultural context), (2) athletes' learning processes (which equate to how individual athletes learn and prefer to learn), and (3) social competencies (which focus on coaches' abilities to develop socially responsible behaviours towards the self and others).

The next question to be addressed is how we can integrate and teach such knowledge in coach education programmes. The emphasis here should be on balance, critical examination and what Burbules (1995) terms 'reasonableness', which in turn possesses three interrelated aspects. The first of these is avoiding distorting tendencies by learning to deconstruct socially imposed patterns, allowing informed reason to take their place (Fernandez-Balboa 2000). The second is that of pragmatism. This differs from practicality in that where the latter often contributes to choosing the easier, more comfortable path, pragmatism 'forces us to be sensitive, to deal with uncertainty, to acknowledge our limitations and to be flexible' (ibid.: 139). The third aspect is that of judiciousness, which equates to a capacity for moderation, 'even in the exercise of reasonableness itself' (Burbules 1995: 96). Judiciousness is considered crucial, as it makes the others accountable (Fernandez-Balboa 2000). It also enables us to consider evidence and consequences, and to deal better with paradoxes and contradictions while remaining principled. In other words, it gives us the ability to make judgements 'about whether a given state of affairs is just or not' (Evans and Davies 1993: 23).

Through engaging with coaching knowledge in this way we can better approximate developing the cognitive 'quality of mind' essential for success in a dynamic environment (Jones 2000; Potrac *et al.* 2000). 'Quality of mind' here equates to certain well-honed 'mind traits', as identified by Fernandez-Balboa (2000). These include:

- Intellectual humility, which relates to engaging with such self-addressed questions as 'Do I understand why I believe in what I do?', 'How do I bring a holistic perspective to what and how I coach?', 'How do I acknowledge that my views are limited?' and 'How are my views limited?'
- Intellectual courage, where further self-confrontational questions could include 'How can I be more open-minded?', 'How do I react when confronted with opposing points of view?', 'How often do I explore ideas with which I usually do not conform?' and 'Why do I choose to engage with some new ideas and not with others?'
- Intellectual integrity, where we may wonder 'Do I know what my principles are?', 'How are my actions congruent with my declared moral principles?' and 'How might my principles and hence my coaching methods be ill-conceived or inadequately informed?'
- Intellectual perseverance, where we may ask 'How much time do I invest in reflecting on this aspect of my practice and deciding on what is the right thing to do?' and 'Once I discover a potential danger, how do I follow it through to ensure my athletes' safety?'
- Intellectual caution, which refers to the ability to discern false paths and premises. Here, possible self-questions could be 'Why do I coach as I do?', 'Which of my methods are just the result of habit?' and 'How can I devise more empowering, holistic methods of coaching?'

Before it can be placed within a coach education programme, this process of personal and cognitive development needs to be encased within more definitive coaching scenarios for it to have contextual relevance. Furthermore, it needs to be delivered in an integrated, as opposed to a compartmentalized, manner. This may be realized through the use of critical tasks, narratives and problem-based learning (PBL), and by understanding coaches' communities of practice (CCoPs). It is to an examination of these that we now turn.

Critical task-based approach

As presented here, a critical task-based approach has been adapted from the work of Kirk (2000). Central to it is the notion of caring for, and about, the needs of athletes, with the term signalling an attempt to actively engage coaches in their learning. Learning is also viewed as being situated and multidimensional in that 'individuals typically learn more than one thing at a time' (ibid.: 204). The coach educator's role within the task-based approach is that of facilitator. His or her principal duty is to structure the learning environment in ways that encourage and assist coaches to acquire the needed information, skills and understanding. This can be done in a number of ways, including conducting a situation analysis, continuously setting progressively challenging and interesting tasks, using and

COACHING CONTEXT

discussing a range of pedagogical styles, providing a positive and supportive learning environment, and giving timely, detailed and appropriate feedback on student progress (ibid.). For example, coaches can be given written tasks that require them to extract information from a range of relevant sources, including video, written texts or tutor explanations, thus acknowledging that individuals learn in different ways. In common with the other strategies to be discussed, the approach is informed by the belief that students (in this case coaches) will develop a better understanding of concepts and information if they seek out the materials for themselves, as opposed to being given them (ibid.). It also allows learners to work at their own pace, acknowledging that on any given course there will be a range of capability levels. Further, it recognizes experience as a resource to be used to make sense of new information (ibid.). While a degree of discomfort among student coaches is inevitable and perhaps desirable when using a task-based approach, a function of the facilitator is not to allow the discomfort to degenerate into defensive or dismissive responses (ibid.).

A possible topic for a task could relate to the nature of power within coaching. With regard to the structure of the exercise, coaches would initially be required to read a number of texts both supporting and opposing a power-dominated leadership style and to note the key issues raised. This is intended to act as a 'primer' (Kirk 2000) for discussing such questions as 'Should the coach–athlete relationship inherently be a power-dominated one? Justify your answer.' Coaches would be encouraged to respond and to rationalize their answers in the light of the texts and of their experiences, noting the nature of the discussion and the points made. They could then view two contrasting video clips depicting how top team-sport coaches address players before and after games. One coach chastises, yells and verbally abuses his or her players, while the other talks in a calm and measured manner. Students would be asked to consider the merits and drawbacks of each approach, and of their effects on the players and the ongoing coach–athlete relationship. The discussion could be given direction through the posing of key focus questions; for example:

- To what extent is the hierarchical nature of the coach–athlete relationship problematical?
- Where does the power lie in this relationship?
- How is the power exercised and what are the consequences (for both parties) of using it?
- How do such behaviours influence the creation of a learning environment?

The video clips and questions are aimed at challenging student coaches' personal perceptions of such issues as leadership, communication, philosophy, appropriate behaviour, coaching knowledge, pedagogy and the nature of the coach–athlete relationship. Hence, they are expected to draw together many aspects of practice into an integrated and holistic examination of the coaching role. The assessment could be based on either a verbal presentation or a piece of written work (or both) depending on the stated learning outcomes. Finally, an opportunity to follow up and discuss adopted initiatives could be built into subsequent sessions.

Narrative approach

Narrative is a pervasive mode of organizing human experience that draws upon a variety of data sources to understand the individual (Connelly and Clandinin 1990). Hence, it would appear a very appropriate strategy to develop and represent holistic knowledge. It can be looked upon as a 'universal form of knowing the world' (Langley 1997: 149), as narrative 'tales' not only resonate with contextual lived experience and inner sense-making, but also facilitate reader understanding and engagement (Denison and Rinehart 2000). Such stories, then, have the potential to capture, perhaps more than scientific formulae ever can, the richness and imprecision of the coaching experience, and our understanding of what coaching is (Anderson 1997; Carter 1993; Jones *et al.* 2003, 2004). They are able to do so as they are very often typified by a framework that includes a set of characters, a situational dilemma or struggle, events that attempt to resolve the conflict, and the temporal relationship between them (Langley 1997). Through such a framework, experience and how to deal with complex problems (as frequently witnessed in coaching) are organized into a coherent whole. Consequently, the narrative approach is able to link the personal to much wider cultural and social issues through getting coaches to reflect on what they know, why they know it and how they use that knowledge in practical settings to achieve desired ends. This potential to develop connections between knowledge and action is a particularly useful quality (Anderson 1997; Langley 1997). The learning that takes place, then, is both personal and holistic, as it takes account of individuals' complex, unique yet social circumstances.

Regarding the use of narratives on coach education programmes, coaches could first write and then deconstruct their own narratives in relation to particular issues, for example the nature of the coach–athlete relationship. Such a process would highlight the interconnected and holistic nature of the coaching process, focusing on the many factors that influence the relationship and how coaches try to best manage them. These could include the use of power and empowerment, inter-personal skills, leadership, organization, pedagogy, motivation, cohesion and athlete expectations, among others. Focus questions around which such narratives could be constructed include:

- Which issues in the coach–athlete relationship do you consider significant, and how do you think they are connected, if at all?
- How has your personal biography influenced the way you coach and why?
- What are the contextual constraints on coaching practice, and how do they affect the way that you coach?
- What knowledges are vital for a coach to have, and why? Where do you get these knowledges?

The coaches could then be given a set of readings related to contextual influences on practice, and asked to further identify, through the production of a second written piece, with the issues raised. This would solidify the relationship between the social and the personal in getting coaches to better reflect upon and understand why they coach as they do. Once limitations have been identified, options on 'how

to do it better' could be examined. Indeed, recent evidence suggests that coaches are beginning to engage with narratives in an attempt to reflect insightfully on their actions (Jones 2006c, in press; Purdy *et al.* in press). Within such self-stories, issues of 'face', caring, power and social norms are considered to better identify and clarify the often invisible aspects of everyday coaching practice. As with critical tasks, the role of the coach educator is one of facilitator, to assist coaches to explore and express, both orally and through the written word, their subjective realities in a structured manner. It is also to highlight the multi- and inter-dimensionality of coaching, and to suggest ways of how eventual declarations and insights can be directly useful to practice.

Problem-based learning (PBL) strategy

Within a PBL framework, the 'curriculum' would be constructed around a set of carefully designed coaching issues or scenarios. The aim is to develop an integrated and holistic knowledge base in coaches founded on real-life problems that are typically cluttered and multidimensional. This would demand that coaches construct personal solutions drawn from a variety of sources. The strategy also requires them to take an active part in planning, organizing and conducting their own learning. Once the problem is set, coaches would typically engage with the knowledge they need to solve it, before applying a solution. Consequently, a PBL strategy aims to encourage and develop coaches' creativity and problem-solving cognitive skills by engaging them in challenging learning activities.

Within the wider PBL concept there are many possible approaches or methods that could be adopted, ranging from the more prescriptive to the facilitative (Barrows 1986). A starting point, as suggested in relation to all these strategies, could be to decide on the objectives in terms of what coach educators want coaches to learn. For example, and borrowing from the work of Bridges and Hallinger (1996) in leadership, if it is believed that the essence of coaching has much to do with 'improving performance through realizing the potential of others', the objectives would derive from this. Hence, they could emphasize the development of skills related to facilitating group problem solving, communicating ideas, dealing with conflict, implementing solutions to identified problems and motivating the individual within the collective. More specifically, it is the precise problem or written scenario that drives choices in relation to the content investigated towards its proposed solution. Such problems could involve a forthright and disruptive group of parents; inheriting a team created by, and still loyal to, a sacked predecessor; coaching a team with opinionated veteran players; and dealing with discipline and relationship breakdown – to name but a few. The problems could be presented in a number of forms, including highly contextualized written cases, via videotape or role play (ibid.). However, they should always be bound by a time frame and have an end product (e.g. a written declaration or document about how the problem could be tackled). This provides a focus for the problem's solution and how to reach it, both of which should relate to the learning aims. Additionally, a number of unannounced interruptions that demand immediate attention can be built into the larger problem, to be solved within a given time limit of their own. This combination of general set problems, allied to on-the-spot surprises, mirrors several characteristics of coaching practice; that is, 'unpredictability, ambiguity and working on several problems at once' (ibid.: 56).

The knowledge needed to address each PBL scenario would be drawn from relevant disciplines and the individual craft knowledge of the coaches, upon which they are encouraged to reflect. It can be gathered through a number of means, for example set readings, class discussions and personal reflections. The content unearthed is meant to provide insight into the problem and its solution. For example, as coaches work through the conflict resolution issue with parents, they learn about the legal aspects of such disputes and the extent to which they can discipline athletes, the need to develop and appropriately publicize a functional coaching philosophy, the theory of how to 'diffuse' a potentially difficult situation, and current research related to constructively channelling aggression and (re)integrating the individual into the team. This interdisciplinary approach mirrors the way that knowledge application occurs in the workplace, thus highlighting the relevance of PBL in the creation of a reality-based holistic coach education programme.

With regard to the teaching process, it can be done in a number of ways. For instance, coaches could be arranged into groups, within which they organize themselves into the separate but rotating roles of leader, recorder, researcher, and so on. Initial reading lists could be provided, but only as guides, thus encouraging the coaches to research independently and creatively for solutions. The unannounced interruptions would take place when all the coaches are together, and would be required to be addressed immediately within a given time frame of, for example, 30 minutes. Discussion, reflection upon experience, and researched knowledge provide the basis for the reasoning here. Similar to the earlier examples discussed, the role of the tutor is that of initial organizer and facilitator, with his or her behaviour being driven by the objective of allowing the coaches to manage as much of the problem-solving process as possible.

While the merits of a PBL approach to coach education have been highlighted, there has been little in the way of empirical inquiry exploring this approach in action. However, Jones and Turner (2006) provide an insightful example. Their study explored student perceptions of a problem-based learning course focusing on the issue of holistic coaching practice. The findings were encouraging in revealing that the approach provided an explicit opportunity for student coaches to use theoretical knowledge in a really practical manner while leading many of them to better appreciate the inherent complexity and integrated nature of coaching knowledge.

Coaching communities of practice

The final strategy to be discussed in this chapter is negotiating mutual engagement within what Culver and Trudel (2006) refer to as coaches' communities of practice (CCoPs). According to Culver and Trudel (ibid.: 98), a coaching community of

practice can be defined as a 'group of people [coaches] who share a common concern, set of problems, or a passion about a topic, and who deepen their knowledge and expertise in this area by interacting on an ongoing basis'. They suggest that the coaching staff of a team, club or organization have the possibility of forming a CCoP, but only if the participants are prepared to use their interactions as a learning resource. Here, coaches should not restrict their discussions to purely organizational issues when they meet, but should also take the opportunity to further develop their knowledge and expertise. Indeed, they argued that the hallmark of a CCoP is a genuine desire among coaches to work closely with one another and with a sense of purpose in order to accomplish something together. We would add that the learning for coaches within CCoPs can be enhanced when those leading or facilitating practices can integrate appropriate theoretical concepts to guide and inform the discussions of the 'real-world' issues that coaches have to contend with in the field. This point is discussed later in this section when we use the case study of the CoDe programme (Cassidy et al. 2006a) to illustrate the point.

In drawing upon the work of Wenger (1998), Culver and Trudel (2006) claim that the interactions that take place within a CCoP will be influenced by the elements of mutual engagement, joint enterprise and shared repertoire (see Chapter 5, 'Learning and development', for a further discussion on this). With regard to the former, they consider that coaches in a CCoP will be mutually engaged in negotiating the meanings of their interactions. This does not mean that those who participate will do so identically, as it is important to recognize that engagement in such practice is individual, making tensions and challenges common elements of involvement. For example, they suggested that 'coaches' meetings to discuss how to prepare for the season, which exercises to include in training sessions and which strategies to use during competition, are examples of contexts where coaches negotiate their practice' (ibid.: 100). The element of joint enterprise refers to the CCoP as cooperative not because all the participating coaches agree on all things but because the discussion embarked upon and the subsequent 'solutions' generated are collectively negotiated. In this respect, Culver and Trudel (ibid.) claim that the outcomes of participating in a CCoP will never be fully determined by prescription, an outside mandate, or by any individual coach. Finally, the development of a shared repertoire can be understood as referring to a sense of community coherence. Here, Culver and Trudel (ibid.) stated that the repertoire of a community allows for the negotiation of meaning because it reflects the CCoP's history of shared engagement, while remaining ambiguous. They suggest that this can be illustrated in terms of the specific ways to do things (routines) and the materials and resources that participants develop as a consequence of the collaborative engagement.

The use of CCoPs has attracted increasing attention in the coaching literature in recent years (e.g. Cassidy et al. 2006a; Culver and Trudel 2006). For example, the work of Cassidy et al. (2006a) highlights how a coach education programme (CoDe) designed along these lines was understood by the participating coaches. The authors were requested to design and implement a programme that was informed by sociological and pedagogical concepts for rugby coaches operating at the representative level. Rather than creating a didactic, tutor-led course, however, Cassidy *et al*. (2006a) developed a framework that aimed to introduce not only relevant theoretical content, but also reflection, discussion and coach ownership over how to implement such content in context.

The data revealed some interesting findings with regard to the coaches' mutual engagement with the theoretical principles that were introduced within the CCoP setting. Significantly, the coaches highlighted how the discussion of, and reflection upon, a number of concepts related to athlete learning and the coaching process had varying impacts. Indeed, all the participant coaches considered such inter-actions to have not only made a useful contribution to their knowledge develop-ment, but also provided them with a number of practical strategies to consider in relation to their coaching practice, albeit in different ways. For example, some of the respondents noted how their involvement in the CCoP that had developed around the CoDe programme had served to give them greater confidence in their coaching practice, as the discussions served to reinforce their existing beliefs regarding quality coaching practice and athlete learning. This point was well illustrated by Simon, one of the coaches, who as a consequence of his career as an educator had developed a range of educational media to support players' learning. In this respect, he noted that he enjoyed the discussions on athlete learning within the CCoP as it served to reinforce his belief that 'coaching is really about working with people and understanding how they learn' (Cassidy *et al*. 2006a: 149). In contrast, Brendan, another coach, discussed how he had 'instinctively' used 'quite a lot of different learning styles' in his coaching without realizing why he was doing it or why it 'worked' (ibid.: 149). The discussions within the CCoP provided Brendan with the knowledge to use such strategies in an insightful and considered manner rather than relying on trial and error. For others, the debates led them to reflect critically upon their practice and to make changes to how they coached. Indeed, a further coach, Jake, noted that the discussions around learning had 'been a real revelation to me . . . that's been huge and it has changed my way [of taking] people through new moves' (ibid.: 148).

The findings also revealed that all the coaches agreed that even if participating in the CoDe programme had achieved nothing else, having the opportunity to talk to other coaches was very beneficial. While most of the coaches knew each other from the local premier rugby competition, they had never previously had any formalized opportunities to talk to each other about their practice, or coaching in general. For Brendan, this was particularly rewarding. In his own words:

> That was the thing I probably looked forward to most of all about the meetings. I was keen to see what you guys were going to come up with this week, and what we were going to be talking about. It was as much about the melding of ideas and stuff . . . to have that sort of forum where you could just talk and even argue, even disagree with guys . . . was really good.
> (Cassidy *et al*. 2006a: 151)

Other coaches also enjoyed the sharing of ideas that occurred. The positive responses were attributed to the fact that the conversations were often grounded in the everyday realities of coaching and, as such, were more focused on practical solutions to professional problems (Jones *et al.* 2003). Some participants, however, were more circumspect in their comments. In particular, while they saw considerable merit in a pedagogy that provided them with the opportunity to talk with the other coaches about the coaching process, they believed that just providing a forum to talk to each other was not enough in itself. Rather, the group needed to be mediated so that participation for all coaches was meaningful.

As is mentioned in Chapter 5, the above finding is in keeping with the work of Culver and Trudel (2006), which also highlighted how the participants in a CCoP voiced the need for the facilitators to exert some control over the direction and length of the discussions if they were to be of optimal value. The facilitators responsible for such groups, then, need to keep to an agreed structure in line with the objectives of the exercise, in terms of contextualizing the content while allowing adequate turn taking and voice among the participants. As we alluded to earlier in this section, we would suggest that engaging with others in a CCoP can enhance the professionalism of coaching practice, especially when those facilitating the engagement use academic theories and concepts as a base for stimulating discussion and reflection upon the practical issues that coaches have to contend with in the field.

CONCLUDING THOUGHTS

The argument for professionalism in practice presented here is based on the premise that we should coach with the contextual totality of humans in mind if athletic potential is to be fully realized (Rothig 1985). Towards this end, the strategies presented in this chapter are underpinned by the belief that it would be useful for coaches to consider and synthesize all their knowledge sources and to rationalize their actions, to help them to 'see beyond the obvious' and to think critically about their practice. The aim is to get coaches to think cognitively and creatively about alternative ways to coach, thus pushing back the boundaries of both coaching theory and coaching practice. It is important to note that these comprise only a limited number of ways in which professionalism in practice could be delivered, none of which is without its unique contradictions and problems. Despite their shortcomings, however, we believe that getting coaches to think about their practice in terms of professionalism holds the key for future excellence in coaching.

SUGGESTED READINGS

Anderson, A. (1997) 'Using personal histories to explore theories about the teaching/ learning process in physical education', *Avante*, 3(1): 71–82.
Culver, D. and Trudel, P. (2006) 'Cultivating coaches' communities of practice: Developing the potential for learning through interaction', in R.L. Jones (ed.) *The Sports Coach as Educator: Re-conceptualising Sports Coaching*, London: Routledge.

Jones, R.L. and Turner, P. (2006) 'Teaching coaches to coach holistically: Can Problem-Based Learning (PBL) help?', *Physical Education and Sport Pedagogy*, 11(2): 181–202.

Kirk, D. (2000) 'A task-based approach to critical pedagogy in sport and physical education', in R.L. Jones and K.M. Armour (eds) *Sociology of Sport: Theory and Practice*, London: Addison Wesley Longman.

Thompson, N. (2003) *Theory and Practice in Human Services*, Maidenhead, UK: Open University Press.

END-OF-CHAPTER TASKS

1   Consider and discuss Thompson's (2003) notions of 'theories of practice' and 'practice theories'. Which have been most important in developing your knowledge bases? Why? How can they inform your developing knowledge?

2   Discuss the traits identified by Fernandez-Balboa (2000) as necessary to develop a 'quality of mind'. Try to address those associated with 'Intellectual courage' (see p. 166 of this chapter).

3   Address some or all of the components of the critical task related to 'the nature of power in the coach–athlete relationship' presented on p. 167 of this chapter.

4   Establishing a coaches' community of practice is the best way to develop professionalism within coaching. Discuss.

CHAPTER 13

▼ **POWER AND THE COACH–ATHLETE RELATIONSHIP**

INTRODUCTION

> Football players will test you. When you go to a new club . . . they will test what you know . . . and if I can't say what I want done and why I want it done that way, then I've got trouble. You can't afford to lose players. If they have no respect for your coaching ability then you've had it, you've lost respect and your coaching sessions become very difficult.
>
> (Potrac *et al.* 2002: 192)

While the issue of power within interpersonal relationships has taken firm root in disciplines such as sociology and organizational, industrial and social psychology (Bruins 1999), its role within coaching, with a few notable exceptions, has largely been ignored (e.g. Shogan 1999; Johns and Johns 2000). The above quotation from a top-level professional football coach, however, is indicative of recent research, which has begun to examine the power evident in the coach–athlete relationship from the perspectives of both coaches (e.g. Jones *et al.* 2004; Cushion and Jones 2006) and athletes (e.g. Johns and Johns 2000; Purdy *et al.* in press).

Power has typically been viewed as 'the ability to get others to do what you want them to do' or 'to get them to do something they otherwise would not do' (Hardy 1995: xiii). In taking a broader view of its nature, Tomlinson (1998: 235) described power as a 'central dynamic of human societies'. Indeed, it has been suggested that power is an omnipresent feature of social life, one that impacts upon not only our thoughts and ambitions, but also our interactions with others (Lee Chai and Bargh

2001; Lukes 1993; Tomlinson 1998). In this respect, Kipnis (2001) contends that as individuals are dependent upon others to fulfil their needs and desires, whether these are material goods, information or to dominate, they are subsequently impelled to exercise power and influence on a daily basis. Similarly, Foucault saw power as diffuse, permeating every aspect of social life in ways that could be productive as well as repressive (Danaher *et al.* 2003). It is also important to recognize that power is not merely imposed from above, but involves the active consent of subordinate groups and the taming of resistance through accommodation (McDonald and Birrell 1999). Power, then, in some instances can be seen as given to the more powerful, while resistance can be understood as an expression of power itself. Indeed, it has been argued that as long as a participant in a social encounter has a function and a value, then that participant is not completely powerless (Dunning 1986; Jones *et al.* 2002; Purdy *et al.* in press). In this respect, Layder (1996) highlights how subordinates always have some resources at their disposal that they can draw upon in an attempt to alter the balance of the power relationship. For example, he notes that even 'prisoners can engage in "dirty protests" or hunger strikes to put pressure on the authorities' (ibid.: 137).

The aim of this chapter is to build on the existing work by further highlighting the importance of power within the coach–athlete relationship and, in so doing, somewhat reconceptualizing it as a power relationship. In terms of structure, following this introduction we discuss a number of established theoretical frameworks of power. As power is very much a social construct, such theories are, not surprisingly, rooted in the field of sociology and include the work of Bourdieu, Foucault, French and Raven, and Giddens. We do not claim to provide a complete and detailed overview of each theorist's work here; rather, the intention is to provide a brief introduction into how each of these scholars has examined power and the applicability of related concepts to the coaching context. In conclusion, we discuss the key points related to the interactional nature of power, before summarizing the benefits to coaches of taking account of such considerations when dealing with athletes.

POWER AND THE COACH–ATHLETE RELATIONSHIP

French and Raven's bases of social power

The first framework to be examined is the 'bases of social power' developed by French and Raven (1959) and further refined by Raven (1992). The focus lies in examining the different sources or bases that an individual uses to get others to follow his or her bidding. Within the perspective, power is classified into six 'types': legitimate, expert, informational, reward, coercive and referent. Like all typologies, it should be treated with caution, as the 'types' are rarely as easily divided in reality as they are in theory. However, the framework does have considerable value in illuminating some of the different dimensions of the multilayered, multifaceted and complex nature of power (Jones *et al.* 2003). To date, French and Raven's typology has been utilized by Jones *et al.* (2004) and Potrac *et al.*

(2002), who respectively studied the coaching practices and philosophies of a number of top-level coaches in various sports. Hence, it is from their work that the examples of French and Raven's power bases in action will be drawn.

According to French and Raven (1959), legitimate power, also known as positional power, is the power that derives from a person's position within a particular social structure or organization, rather than because of any special qualities that a person may possess. It can be suggested, then, that simply occupying the role of coach affords the incumbent a degree of legitimate power. However, reliance on this form of power is insufficient for an individual to maintain the confidence, trust and respect of subordinates as, although a new coach may initially enjoy considerable legitimate power over athletes, it is the coach's future actions that decide whether such power is eroded or enhanced. In this respect, the power a coach subsequently exercises over his or her athletes is not a fixed quantity but is instead determined by the choices he or she makes (Jones *et al.* 2003, 2004; Thompson 1998).

According to French and Raven, one way an individual can maintain and enhance the power afforded to him or her by others is through the demonstration of expert power. Expert power is defined as the power that accrues to a person because of the special knowledge or skills that he or she possesses (Slack 1997). Expert power could be gained (or lost) by a coach's knowledge, demonstrations of techniques, qualifications, reputation, and record of success (Potrac *et al.* 2002). Perhaps the key point for coaches to consider here is that expert power is based on athletes' perceptions of such factors. This is well illustrated in the work of Johns and Johns (2000), who highlighted how athletes' perceptions of their coach's expertise led them to comply with the latter's regime. Coaches thus may wish to consider how they demonstrate their expertise within the sporting environment through their interactions with athletes. Indeed, the coaches studied by Jones *et al.* (2004) and Potrac *et al.* (2002) considered the projection of a knowledgeable and credible coaching persona as an essential ingredient for coaching effectiveness. In order to achieve this goal, the coaches utilized a number of strategies, including actively demonstrating cutting-edge technical and tactical appreciation of their particular sport. Interestingly, these coaches also highlighted how they took measures to ensure that they avoided situations which could dilute their expertise in the eyes of athletes. For example, because of self-confessed limited physical ability, they avoided performing demonstrations if they thought that poor execution would result in a loss of respect. Furthermore, the coaches in these studies also avoided an overly pompous or dictatorial manner, as they considered that it could result in barriers arising between themselves and the athletes. Their belief here is in keeping with the work of Benfarri *et al.* (1986: 14), who concluded that expertise demonstrated in 'an authoritarian manner [could well] be seen as a put down' by its recipients.

Closely allied to the concept of expert power is informational power. According to Raven (1992), this power base is demonstrated by the strength of an argument or the quality of information that an individual can present to others. In the context of coaching, informational power is subtly different from expert power (Jones *et al.* 2004) as, unlike expert power, where an athlete's thinking might be 'I don't really understand why but the coach knows this topic so he (or she) must be right', the strength of informational power lies in the athlete's recognition that 'I listened carefully to coach and I can see that this is clearly the best way to deal with this particular situation' (Erchul and Raven 1997; Jones *et al.* 2004). All the top-level coaches studied by Jones *et al.* (2004) and Potrac *et al.* (2002) reinforced the need to demonstrate informational power if they were to persuade athletes to fully 'buy into' their respective coaching programmes. In this respect, they strongly emphasized the need to make sure not only that the learning which takes place in training sessions is directly transferable to competitive situations, but, crucially, that the athletes are fully aware of how the tasks, activities and roles that they are asked to perform actually contribute towards enhancing their performances. For example, netball coach Lois Muir was critical of 'warm and fuzzy drills' and strongly advocated that 'no-one should do an activity [in practice] not knowing how they can use it on the court' (Jones *et al.* 2004: 156).

A further component of power that coaches have at their disposal is reward power (French and Raven 1959; Raven 1992). This can be understood as the power that results from one person's control over another's rewards (Slack 1997). It should be noted that such power is not limited to tangible incentives, but also includes what Raven (1992) describes as the personal form of reward power, for example personal approval from someone we like. Echoing this point, football coach Steve Harrison believed that players are more likely to respond to coaches 'who tell them positive things' (Jones *et al.* 2004: 157), while the coach in Potrac *et al.*'s (2002) study also considered praise to be a valuable strategy for persuading players to believe in their individual and collective abilities.

In keeping with our discussion of expert and informational power, the effectiveness of reward power is determined by the value and meanings that recipients attach to it (Benfarri *et al.* 1986). In this respect, Tauber (1985: 5) argues that 'the key to the effective use of reward power is to be able to tell how much of which reward, delivered how frequently and for how long is best for each student'. For example, while some athletes may respond to high levels of praise, others may not. Here, Cushion and Jones (2001) suggest that if athletes perceive praise to be given too cheaply by the coach or to be unwarranted, then it may become devalued and meaningless to them. Such a perspective could be useful in terms of helping us to understand how and why coaches create climates of incentives within the coaching environment, what impact they may have on the coach–athlete relationship, and why they are sometimes successful or unsuccessful.

The penultimate power base in French and Raven's (1959) typology is coercive power. This derives from the ability of one person to punish another or others (Slack 1997). While coercive power is generally perceived to be 'dysfunctional because it alienates people and builds up resentment' (ibid.: 181), it nevertheless remains at the disposal of coaches. While the coaches in Jones *et al.*'s (2004) and Potrac *et al.*'s (2002) studies acknowledged that it was occasionally necessary to

give an athlete 'a kick up the arse from time to time' (Potrac *et al*. 2002: 196), the practice of publicly berating players for poor performance was seen as wholly unproductive. In particular, they argued that an over-reliance on punishment more often than not resulted in a loss of respect for the coach and, significantly, a decline in the receptiveness of the players to the coach's instruction and advice. For example, football coach Steve Harrison noted that 'if you hit people with negatives all the time, they'll think, "bollocks to you"', leading to a breakdown in the coach–athlete relationship. He questioned the value of such an approach, considering it to be counter-productive ('why damage your relationship with a player when you're going to need him [or her] tomorrow?' (Jones *et al*. 2004: 157)). However, this does not mean that coaches should never utilize coercive power; rather, they should carefully consider its impact and its legacy for future interactions. Indeed, Shetty (1978: 177) suggests that 'the judicious use of reward power and coercive power can increase the effectiveness of legitimate power; inappropriate use, however, will decrease the effectiveness of legitimate power'.

The final component of French and Raven's (1959) typology of power is that of referent power. According to Tauber (1985), referent power is founded on an individual's identification with another person and his or her desire to be like that person. In contrast to legitimate power, which is based on title, referent power is based on respect for the person. In everyday parlance, this type of power is often referred to as charisma – an elusive quality that only a lucky few seem to possess (Jones *et al*. 2004). However, the coaches in Jones *et al*.'s study (ibid.) suggested that this is something which coaches can develop and plan for. In this respect, they highlighted how demonstrating an ethic of social care for athletes was the most important strategy employed to maintain and develop their respective referent power bases. For example, rugby union coach Bob Dwyer suggested that it was essential for coaches to convince athletes that they care about the athletes' well-being as people and not just their development as performers. Such care was demonstrated through remembering the birthdays of athletes and their families, welcoming new performers and their families to the club, and being willing to offer support to all concerned during times of need (ibid.). According to football coach Graham Taylor, such gestures serve to reinforce athletes' respect for a coach as a person, as opposed to their just regarding him or her as a competent and knowledgeable professional. In his words: 'You're actually showing them [the players] that you care, and whilst you show them that you think about them and the other side of life, you stand to gain a great deal in terms of your working relationship with them' (ibid.: 158). With such reverence, however, also comes responsibility. A recent study by Jones *et al*. (2005) highlighted how reverence for a coach can result in total compliance, leading to athlete vulnerability. As outlined in Chapter 7, 'Understanding athletes' identities', the coach's powerful position obligates him or her to tread carefully during interaction with athletes, as careless actions can lead to far-reaching, often unintended, consequences related to athletes' physical and mental well-being.

Bourdieu and capital

The work of sociologist Pierre Bourdieu provides the second conceptual framework of power to be discussed. Central to Bourdieu's thinking was the notion of capital. According to Tomlinson (2004), capital refers to the capacity of an individual or a group to have an impact upon, change or control situations. The amount of capital available to a person, then, will determine the degree to which he or she can control not only the person's own destiny, but also that of other people (Tomlinson 2004). Capital is not distributed on an equitable basis, and Bourdieu asserts that social life is characterized by individuals constantly engaged in the process of striving to accumulate their capital and therefore their ability to influence others (Calhoun 1995).

Bourdieu identifies three broad types of capital: economic, cultural and social. Economic capital refers to control over economic resources such as money and assets, while cultural capital relates to forms of education, knowledge and experience that give an individual an advantage in society. Finally, social capital refers to the resources an individual may have that are based on membership of a particular group or groups (Calhoun 1995). While these forms of capital can be identified separately from a theoretical viewpoint, in the context of everyday life they interact in a fluid manner to influence social behaviours and practices (Tomlinson 2004). In this respect, Wacquant (1995) suggests that the position of an individual within a particular organization or group can be charted by two coordinates. These are the overall volume and the composition of the capital the individual possesses, both of which can vary over time. Similarly, it has been argued that an appreciation of the forms and workings of capital can help us understand how an individual has moved through social space to reach the position he or she currently occupies (ibid.).

There has been a paucity of research utilizing Bourdieu's concept of capital to critically analyse the nature of the power relations that exist between coach and athlete. However, the work of Cushion and Jones (2006) in top-level English youth football provides us with some fascinating insights into how Bourdieu's work could be applied to enhance our understanding of this context. Their ethnographic study revealed how the young players at Albion FC (a pseudonym) willingly subscribed to a coaching regime that was almost exclusively coach led, and was frequently harsh and belligerent in nature. The authors highlight how this authoritarian behaviour manifested itself in the form of abusive language, direct castigation, and threats of physical exercise as a form of punishment. This is well illustrated in the following extract:

> A coaching session is just starting in the sports hall. The players have begun to pass the ball amongst themselves in a circle. Greg [the coach] arrives and formalises the practice by nominating two players to act as defenders in the circle with those on the outside expected to keep possession of the ball. The players who make the circle's rim frequently misplace passes.

Greg stops the practice, 'Circle shit, 5 minute warm up shit. . . . No, shit's too kind. . . . Game Saturday against United, if we start like this against them, then fuckin' god help us.'

Greg then organises a passing practice where the ball is passed via the four corners of the hall. One of the players controls the ball badly, loses possession, and then jokes about it with another player.

Greg stops the practice, 'E, if you want to fuck about, get into the car park, I couldn't give a shit. Go on, fuck off, out'.

E says nothing and trudges, head down, out of the sports hall. The rest of the players get press-ups and 'shuttle' sprints as punishment for 'their' mistakes.

(Cushion and Jones 2006: 149–150)

So what made the players comply with such a regime? While the authors highlight several interacting concepts, of particular importance was the role of capital. Here, Cushion and Jones (2006) suggest that the players were willing to forgo a critique of their position for two key reasons. The first was related to the respect that the players afforded to the coaches' previous professional playing and coaching experiences in football. Much as in French and Raven's work on expert power, the coaches were considered by the players to know not only the social field of professional football, but also how to negotiate it successfully. For example, the players noted:

J: I quite like Pete, because of where he's been and what he's done really. He's been there and done it.

N: Yeah, he's someone who's played before, who knows what it's like. I respect that.

R: Yup. He's got to be someone who knows what he's talking about, worth listening to. He's someone who can do what he's saying.

(ibid.: 156)

Hence, the cultural capital (in terms of previous professional playing and coaching experience) afforded by the players to the coaches led the players to comply with the coaches' regime. Even the abusive discourse was viewed by the players as a legitimate part of the culture of professional football and, as such, was something they were unwilling to criticize.

The second reason why the players appeared to willingly accept their status and station centred on their recognition that the coaches acted as 'gatekeepers' to the world of professional football. They were fully aware of the fact that it would be the coaches who would decide who would be awarded a professional contract and who would be 'released' (required to leave the club). It is therefore perhaps unsurprising that the players chose not to question openly or critique the coaches' regime as such actions could result in their (the players) being labelled as having a 'bad attitude' and thus excluded from receiving a professional playing contract. Instead, as Cushion and Jones (2006) point out, the players were more concerned with manoeuvring so as to improve their status (or capital) in relation to each other. Here the players' ability and their willingness to demonstrate a good attitude were forms of cultural capital that could be converted into economic capital if and when they received a professional contract. Given that professional contracts were in short supply, the players were more interested in ensuring that they as individuals did not get 'off-side' with the coaches than in questioning the belligerent and oppressive nature of the environment. The players' need for greater capital, then, dictated their actions in terms of how they related to their coaches and the context.

Foucault and disciplinary power

The work of sociologist and philosopher Michel Foucault informs the discussion in this penultimate framework of power. For Foucault, power is something that is not possessed by particular individuals (Chapman 1997; Markula and Pringle 2006), but involves 'both a complex flow and a set of relationships between different groups and areas of society which changes with circumstances and time' (Danaher *et al*. 2003: xiv). Like Bourdieu, Foucault argues that power relationships are not set in stone but can alter very quickly depending on changing alliances and the nature and dynamics of particular circumstances (Danaher *et al*. 2003). In addition, Foucault argues that power is not just repressive or negative; it can also be highly productive (Chapman 1997; Danaher *et al*. 2003; Markula and Pringle 2006).

Of particular importance to Foucault was the relationship between power and knowledge. He was interested in illuminating the ways in which knowledge is something that makes us its subjects (Danaher *et al*. 2003; Markula and Pringle 2006). His work in this area challenged the conventionally held belief that the acquisition and development of knowledge is always 'good' for people. Specifically, he proposed that knowledge may instead play a 'disciplining' role and lead to the production of docile, healthy bodies that can be regulated in terms of time and space (Danaher *et al*. 2003). By way of an example, Danaher *et al*. (ibid.: 50) provide an interesting insight into how Foucault's thinking could be applied to school and university students:

> For instance, to be a student at school or university we must enter into different academic disciplines, and gain certificates and degrees that provide credentials which will help make us suitable for various jobs. But to be a student is also to make ourselves known to the school system, so that it can monitor our progress, pass judgements upon us, and mould our behaviours in various ways. In these ways, discipline and knowledge make us certain kinds of people.

Of particular interest here is Foucault's suggestion that we often willingly submit ourselves to such processes rather than having them imposed upon us (Danaher *et*

COACHING CONTEXT

al. 2003). Illustrating this point, the young footballers discussed in the preceding section were only too happy to conform to a harsh and belligerent coaching regime. In this respect, they became, and affirmed their roles, as docile and obedient bodies (Cushion and Jones 2006). So how did Foucault suggest such docile, regulated individuals are created? And what relevance does Foucault's work have for our understanding of the coach–athlete relationship?

According to Foucault, docile bodies are created as a result of disciplinary power. Disciplinary power refers to a form of power that focuses on the control and discipline of bodies, and is predominantly exercised through the regulation of the body in time and space, and the process of surveillance (Denison 2007; Foucault 1979). With regard to the former, Danaher *et al.* (2003) highlight how work patterns are often regulated by timetables, so that people move from one set of skills to another throughout the day. For example, in a factory the workers are often organized according to the tasks that they perform, which require specific skills. In addition, individuals are also often assigned a specific rank within the hierarchy (e.g. floor manager, head machinist, bolt cutter). The staff can be moved from one place to another depending on the needs of the institution and the performances of the people themselves. With each move a person's position in the literal and metaphorical space of the institution changes. Such ranking enables institutions to regulate both the movement of people throughout its space and the progress that they can make (ibid.). As we have already mentioned, Foucault illustrates how such discipline is imposed not simply from above, but also by people imposing discipline upon themselves. Hence, discipline can work through a process of gratification and punishment (ibid.).

The production of disciplined bodies sees the regulation of the body in time and space accompanied by surveillance, which Foucault refers to as the panopticon (Danaher *et al.* 2003). To illustrate the power of the panopticon, Foucault utilizes Jeremy Bentham's eighteenth-century design for prisons. Bentham's model of the panopticon was a tower placed in a central position within the prison. From this tower, the prison guards would be able to observe every cell and see the prisoners inside them. However, the tower was designed in such a way that the prisoners would never know whether they were being observed by the guards or not (ibid.). Thus, the prisoners were the potential targets of authority's gaze at every moment of the day. Given this situation, it was envisaged that the prisoners would adjust their behaviour to conform with the prescribed set of acceptable behaviours in order to avoid being punished (ibid.). In contemporary society we can see how surveillance operates in a similar way in other institutional spaces. For example, Danaher *et al.* (ibid.: 54) state that 'school teachers use this authoritative gaze as they move about a classroom, and so do security cameras in shopping malls and night clubs. Surveillance techniques have become a fundamental part of life in modern western societies'.

Interestingly, the authoritative gaze is not just something that is only directed at us by others. It can also become part of how we look at our own behaviours (Danaher *et al.* 2003). Danaher *et al.* (ibid.) suggest that our socialization experiences influence us to make ourselves the subject of our own gaze, and so we can become engaged in a process of constantly monitoring our own bodies, actions and feelings. For example, in order to become desirable to the male gaze, some women may monitor their own bodies and engage in activities such as 'plucking out facial hairs, exercising grimly in aerobics classes, pouring hot wax upon themselves and so on' (ibid.: 55). Such women, then, often choose to engage in 'punishing' practices in the quest to ensure that they conform to the societal expectations learned regarding desirable body shapes and appearance.

In the context of coaching, Foucault's notion of disciplinary power has been utilized to provide us with some fascinating insights into the coach–athlete relationship (Denison 2007; Johns 1998; Johns and Johns 2000; Jones *et al.* 2005). Indeed, the case study of Anne in a preceding chapter (Chapter 7) on athlete identities highlights how disciplinary power may contribute to eating disorders in female athletes (Jones *et al.* 2005). More recently, Denison (2007) has provided a rich illustration of how he utilized Foucault's work to make sense of why Brian, a cross-country runner whom he was coaching, performed below expectation. Denison describes how he initially blamed Brian for lacking the mental toughness needed to succeed in this event. He noted how he considered the 'problem' to be firmly located within Brian and hence ignored how his own coaching practice may have been a contributing factor to the athlete's poor performance.

However, Denison (2007) describes how his exposure to Foucault's work on disciplinary power and, in particular, how disciplining techniques can gain hold of individuals' attitudes, movements, gestures and rapidity led him to construct an alternative explanation for Brian's performance. Denison suggests that what he considered to be Brian's apathetic response during and after the event could instead be understood as a form of docility that was the enduring effect of the control that he, as a coach, exercised over the training environment. Indeed, while he notes that his relationship with Brian was communicative and open, Denison begins to reflect upon how it was always he who decided what was considered to be legitimate for Brian to do within the training undertaken. He goes on to describe how he controlled selecting the spaces where Brian's training would take place. This not only included the route, but also the surface, be it the athletic track, the road or cross-country. Denison suggests that his control over the athlete's location for training had, in the long term, the unintended impact of restricting Brian's flexibility and freedom. Here, he argues that

> a track, a gym, a forest or a field could, if a coach was not careful, bear the characteristics of a tightly controlled and regimented disciplinary space that could produce in athletes this discomfort or apathy that I witnessed in Brian.

(Denison 2007: 375)

He noted how he determined Brian's timetable in terms of how often Brian trained, when he trained, and how much time and effort would be required for

each session. Drawing upon the work of Halas and Hanson (2001), Denison (2007: 376) believes that such coaching practice may have contributed to rendering Brian docile, as in his role as coach he became an 'agent of normalisation'. It is thus suggested that the organization and restriction of training into specific sites and times for Brian could have been a contributing factor to his performance, as it may have impacted upon how he felt about and experienced his running. In particular, Denison suggests that the discipline and control he imposed upon the training environment may have resulted in the removal of Brian's sense of self from the act of being a runner.

Finally, in drawing upon the work of Shogan (1999), Denison (2007: 378) discusses how his repeated attempts to teach Brian effective race tactics may also have had a significant disciplinary effect. His conversations with Brian in this regard often became a way for him to control how Brian raced and may also have further contributed to removing Brian's self from his athletic endeavours. This is eloquently illustrated in the following passage:

> [I]t is apparent to me now that getting Brian to talk about his tactical awareness, and specifically his tactical weaknesses became a way for me – the expert assigned to interpret his confession – to control his race: the more he confessed what he did or did not know about tactics the easier it was for me to prescribe techniques – interventions – to mould him into my vision of a productive competitor. It was in this way, accordingly, that I might have stripped Brian of his athletic identity such that he entered his race with little or no sense of why he was running or who he was running for.
>
> (Denison 2007: 378)

While Denison does not claim that coaches should totally abandon the leadership practices discussed, he does suggest that coaches may wish to consider how such activities impact upon the ways in which athletes think, feel and generally experience their sporting activity. For example, this Foucauldian reading of his coaching practice has led Denison to consider carefully how he talks to athletes about tactics and what might be the unintended consequences of doing so in particular ways. In his own words:

> [N]ow that I am aware of a possible unintended consequence of talking tactics with an athlete – it can turn into an act of confession not an act of learning – I would need to be more careful in the future with how I helped an athlete devise a race plan – how I used my knowledge and power as a coach in forming a relationship with my athlete around the topic of tactics. For instance, instead of talking about tactics as if they were rules, or in a way that removed the option for an athlete to make his or her own tactical decisions, I might speak about tactics through a series of scenarios and then allow the athlete to come up with a response. Moreover, I would

need to remember that athletes are free to decide their own response and ultimately whether they will follow any tactical advice I might offer.

(Denison 2007: 378–379)

Finally, and importantly, he suggests that what might be considered to be controlling and manipulative actions are often not enacted by coaches in forceful or even conscious ways. Instead, they 'occur subtly over time through numerous unquestioned everyday coaching practices' (Denison 2007: 375). Indeed, Denison believes that it was the cumulative effect of his everyday actions that led to Brian's docility, rather than his desire as a coach to be omnipotent. Denison's study, then, provides an evocative example of how Foucault's work could provide coaches with a range of insights for critically reflecting upon their practice.

Giddens and the dialectic of control

According to Giddens (1984), power refers to the capacity of individuals to transform (to some extent) their social worlds. Rather than viewing power as being an unlimited capacity that one person wields over another individual or others, Giddens believes that subordinate individuals or groups have some power at their disposal. Indeed, he argues that while all human action involves the use of power in some way, people are not completely free or unfettered in the things they can transform or achieve (ibid.). Giddens thus argues that power is relational, as it is influenced by the resources that an individual has at his or her disposal at a particular point in time and space on the social landscape. There are two types of resources that individuals may draw upon to effect change in their social circumstances: allocative and authoritative (Layder 1996). The former refers to material objects and economic resources that help get things done, while the latter refers to non-material features (political factors such as status, position, etc.) that enable an individual to exert control or command over another or others (Horne and Jary 2004; Layder 1996)

For Giddens, then, the dialectic of control refers to the changes in the balance of power that occur over time and from situation to situation which are brought about by the attempts of subordinate individuals and groups to use the resources at their disposal. This dialectic of control is seen as operating at both an individual (e.g. a person going on strike) and a collective level (e.g. collective strike action). In illustrating Giddens' thinking here, Layder (1996: 137) provides the following example:

My power over you is to some extent dependent upon the power that you wield over me – and this means that the wider social context has to be taken into account. I might have more formal authority over you and this requires you to obey my commands (as in the armed forces, or a hierarchical work organisation). In other circumstances you may control my behaviour because you have a loaded gun pointed at my head.

COACHING CONTEXT

In a similar vein to the work of Bourdieu and Foucault, perhaps the key point for us to consider here is Giddens' belief that 'people are never simply the helpless playthings of social forces completely beyond their control' (Layder 1996: 138).

Giddens' theorizing has scarcely been used to analyse coaching. However, Purdy's recent work in the area of elite rowing is illustrative of the potential application of Giddens' work in this context (Purdy 2005; Purdy et al. in press). For example, her autoethography of the coach–athlete relationship in subelite rowing (Purdy et al. in press) charts the various and constantly changing measures of athlete compliance, cooperation and resistance to a particular coaching programme. Indeed, this work, which describes the creation of an ultimately dysfunctional coach–athlete relationship, serves to illustrate how athletes are not entirely powerless and are far from 'inert and inept' actors within the coaching process (Giddens 1993: 4). Purdy's (2005) narrative begins by discussing how she and other crew members initially bought into their new coach's training philosophy and methods. The relationship was initially positive, as the athletes were impressed by the new coach's enthusiastic nature, record of success, qualifications and expertise. In measuring her new coach against previous experiences, Purdy believed that the coach looked and acted like a coach should. In this respect, Purdy et al. (in press) suggest that athletes are willing to forgo an element of power as long as a coach's behaviour is in keeping with what Giddens (1998) termed the accepted social rules and routines of everyday life. In this respect, Giddens suggests that such confidence in the practice of others develops from, and further develops an increase in, one's ontological security, which can generally be understood as the security of being (Giddens 1984, 1991).

Despite the positive start, the relationship that existed between the coach and crew began to deteriorate just a few months later. According to Purdy et al. (in press), this deterioration was caused not by any perceived deficiency in the coach's expertise or knowledge, but by her increasingly authoritarian behaviour, curt responses and patronizing comments. Furthermore, Purdy et al. suggest that the shared power relationship which the coach had promised the athletes at the start of her tenure was taken away without explanation in what was a considered a deceitful and disrespectful way – events that led the crew to frequently experience feelings of anxiety and anomie.

Ultimately, the feelings of dissatisfaction and frustration led the crew to engage in acts of resistance in order to regain their 'ontological security'. The resistance manifested itself in a variety of forms as the crew sought to utilize the resources at their disposal to change their social circumstances. For example:

Journal Entry: February 15.

I have to admit that I was being deliberately awkward at practice this morning. When coxing the eight she [the coach] asked me to switch from the drill I was doing to another. I was still mad at her for telling me I'd have to trial for my seat, but there was something about her tone that put me off. She was barking orders but she has hardly been coaching us all week. Why should we suddenly listen to her? . . . I kept going, ignoring her request. After a few strokes she yelled at me again to switch drills. I stared at Matt, who was stroking the boat. He gave me a knowing grin, I nodded my head, and counted five more strokes before I switched the drill. And for those five strokes there was nothing she could do. She could yell until she was going blue in the face, I wasn't going to give in and, from Matt's grin, I knew the crew would support me. . . . Today, I wanted control. I wanted to show her that she couldn't run everything. It was our showdown and for five short strokes I felt I had won.

(Purdy et al. in press)

The crew also challenged the coach's authority by referring to her among themselves as 'the Seagull', because she spent much of her time screaming incomprehensibly. Willis (1977) suggests that humour, banter and aggressive sarcasm can be used to directly question authority by subverting the language in which it is normally expressed. In a similar vein, Nyberg (1981: 53) suggests that one of the ways that subordinates can withdraw power from those in authority is through laughter, as 'authority fears no more threat than the laughter that comes from scorn'. In the context of this study, the repeated use of the 'Seagull' nickname and other acts of resistance had a significant effect on the crew's attitude towards the coach and the training programme. Indeed, the coach's tenure was ultimately short-lived as she failed to maintain the trust, respect and confidence of the athletes in her charge.

Purdy *et al.*'s (in press) study serves to illustrate Giddens' contention that power is always a mix of authority and dependence, as even the powerful depend on the less powerful to carry out certain practices (Cohen 1998; Light 1999). Dependence, then, can be exploited by subordinates to lever concessions or to openly resist perceived oppression. Accordingly, we believe that coaches may benefit from carefully considering, and not underestimating, the power that athletes may potentially exert in and over the coaching environment.

Empowerment

The final conceptualization of power to be discussed is that of empowerment (Kidman 2001) or 'nutrient power' (May 1972). The term 'empowerment' derives from sociological theory and is generally regarded as the process by which individuals acquire greater control over the decisions that affect their lives (Thompson 1998). In the context of coaching, an empowered athlete is one who is actively engaged in shaping and directing what happens in his or her sporting life (Arai 1997; Kidman 2001). For example, in implementing an empowering approach, a coach could involve athletes in challenging an agreed game plan or playing style in the interest of improving it and their wider knowledge of the sport (Jones *et al.* 2004). If athletes are provided with opportunities to share the

leadership and decision making, it is believed that they will take greater ownership and responsibility for their performances. Indeed, it has been suggested that such an approach could result not only in an increased retention of tactical and technical aspects of performance on the athletes' behalf, but also in higher levels of commitment from them because they are investing a greater amount of their selves in their sporting endeavours (Gagne *et al.* 2003; Hollembeak and Amorose 2005; Kidman 2001).

Undoubtedly the notion of sharing leadership and power is attractive, particularly to more humanistic thinkers and practitioners. Indeed, it expresses an idea that few would quarrel with; that is, that all concerned can get a collective grip, allowing athletes greater equity after years of being dominated and silenced in hierarchical coaching relationships. Hence, as rhetoric, it promises groups and/or individuals access to a higher degree of power than they previously had through the delegation of authority to influence policies, plans and processes. Little wonder, then, that its popularity has expanded (Jones *et al.* 2006).

However, although there have been many generalist statements regarding the advantages and benefits of a more athlete-centred approach to coaching, there has been little in the way of any in-depth examination of its implementation (Jones and Standage 2006). The value of utilizing an empowering philosophy was voiced by several of the elite coaches in Jones *et al.*'s (2004) study. In particular, the coaches from individual sports such as track and field athletics and swimming highlighted how this was beneficial owing to the nature of these particular sports; that is, athletes of such sports often have to compete without the coach being present, while the rules of competition may also forbid the coach from advising athletes once the event has begun. Consequently, assisting athletes to take ownership over their performances and to develop their respective problem-solving abilities was highlighted as desirable.

Alternatively, while the team sport coaches interviewed by Jones *et al.* (2004) also emphasized the need to 'grow players' for on-field responsibility and decision making, they raised some interesting concerns regarding inviting such players to share in the leadership of the coaching programme (ibid.). The coaches highlighted how they provided their athletes with what could be considered 'an illusion of empowerment'. Indeed, rather than allowing the athletes to have a 'full and free' input into the decision-making process, the coaches described how they controlled the agenda items upon which athlete input was requested. In this way they were able to exert considerable influence over the environment by confining the agenda to 'safe items', while the athletes simultaneously considered their lot to be a satisfactory one (Bachrach and Baratz 1963, 1970). Indeed, the emphasis here was on inviting input in a way that led the athletes to 'buy into' the coach's agenda and programme.

Interestingly, all the coaches interviewed by Jones *et al.* (2004) appreciated the benefits of empowering athletes but considered that it was still necessary for them to be seen by athletes as someone with, and in, authority. Indeed, they believed that the coach had to be seen to be more than just another source of advice or information that athletes can accept or reject at will (Jones and Standage 2006). Such coaches framed empowerment in terms of setting the boundaries within which athletes were allowed to take part in the decision-making process – a structure that allowed for different behaviours within established zonal boundaries, as opposed to giving athletes total control over decision-making processes (Gronn 2000; Jones and Standage 2006). Indeed, the latter was seen as likely to be detrimental to athlete development and sporting performance, as the coaching environment could become characterized by indecision, uncertainty and role confusion.

Such insights cast doubt on a view of empowerment as a straightforward approach upon which to base coaching practice. In this respect, Jones and Standage (2006) critiqued the unproblematic implementation of shared leadership and empowerment in coaching situations by pointing out a number of contextual considerations that appear to have been overlooked. For example, there may well be avenues of resistance against it from those being empowered. Some athletes may not wish to become involved in the decision-making processes, but instead expect the coach to deploy his or her expertise to help them best advance as a performer. Given that many athletes may have experienced sporting success from prescriptive coaching environments, it is perhaps unsurprising that they may expect and desire this type of leadership behaviour from coaches. Additionally, a sporting culture, though open to change, is not directly manipulable through coach activity (Jones and Standage 2006; Nias et al. 1989). Coaches just do not hold such unfettered freedom as to implement a policy so cleanly. Similarly, a culture often contains incompatible elements as manifest in contradictory beliefs and values coexisting in a tension, while any attempt to alter an existing culture may lead to change in unforeseen and undesired directions (Jones and Standage 2006; Jones and Wallace 2005; Wallace 1996). A further stumbling block to the unproblematic acceptance of empowerment in the coaching context relates to overcoming the current authoritarian culture within the profession. This has been manifest in coaches' desire to take charge of each and every situation. Not only has this resulted in coaches being caught in a particular philosophy of leadership which few are willing to forgo, but the perceived risky nature of sharing power precludes engagement with it at anything more than the most superficial of levels (Jones et al. 2004; Jones and Standage 2006). It is a culture that also casts athletes firmly in the role of followers, who in turn are often reluctant to accept such responsibility while believing the coach not to be doing his or her job properly if more inclusive strategies are followed, as the coach has stepped outside the athletes' perception of the coaching role (Jones et al. 2004; Jones and Standage 2006). Here there appears to be an uneasy coexistence between actors believing they want more power or not, and actors wanting to devolve powers or not. It reflects part of the complex social and political conflict between change and tradition. Hence, in addition to the usual difficulties inherent in sharing power, the coaching context and culture appear to have added inbuilt deterrents against the smooth implementation of such sharing (Jones and Standage 2006).

COACHING CONTEXT

Consequently, while the traditional arguments presented for the principle of shared leadership in coaching are persuasive as far as they go, they fail to take into account the realities of coaching. Similarly, the approach has not addressed the unique coaching context in terms of coaches' hierarchy of accountability whereby they often have to answer for everything that goes wrong. Hence, we believe that any prescriptions for shared leadership should, wherever possible, be informed by evidence and rest on principles that are context sensitive. According to Jones and Standage (2006: 76), while this 'is a less romantic conceptualization of shared leadership', it is one 'which places it within the everyday complexity of coaching'.

CONCLUDING THOUGHTS

The aim of this chapter was to provide an insight into the complex and power-dominated nature of the coach–athlete relationship. Through the introduction of a variety of theories of power we have tried to illustrate the importance of the need to be sensitive to, and never take for granted, the various forms of power inherent within the coaching context. In this respect it is important for coaches to recognize that the control they exert over athletes is always variable and limited, as coaching is too problematic and complex to allow anything else (Jones and Wallace 2005). Given this situation, we believe that coaches may wish to carefully consider and reflect upon the ways in which they present themselves to, and interact with, athletes in their desire to hold sway and influence. It would appear that such an approach is needed if coaches are to be successful in obtaining the trust, respect and confidence of athletes and ultimately develop positive learning environments (Jones *et al.* 2004).

SUGGESTED READINGS

Cushion, C. and Jones, R. (2006) 'Power, discourse, and symbolic violence in professional youth soccer: The case of Albion Football Club', *Sociology of Sport Journal*, 23(2): 142–161.

Denison, J. (2007) 'Social theory for coaches: A Foucauldian reading of one athlete's poor performance', *International Journal of Sport Science and Coaching*, 2(4): 369–383.

Jones, R.L., Armour, K.A. and Potrac, P.A. (2004) *Sports Coaching Cultures: From Practice to Theory*, London: Routledge.

Jones, R.L. and Standage, M. (2006) 'First among equals: Shared leadership in the coaching context', in R.L. Jones (ed.) *The Sports Coach as Educator: Re-conceptualising Sports Coaching*, London: Routledge.

Potrac, P., Jones, R.L. and Armour, K.M. (2002) 'It's about getting respect: The coaching behaviours of a top-level English football coach', *Sport, Education and Society*, 7(2):183–202.

Purdy, L., Potrac, P. and Jones, R. (in press) 'Power, consent and resistance: An autoethnography of competitive rowing'. *Sport, Education, and Society*.

END-OF-CHAPTER TASKS

Watch and compare two movies in which two coaches use contrasting styles (for example, see *Blue Chips* and *Living with Lions*). Having watched them, reflect upon, and develop a written response to, the following questions:

1 Who has power in the coach–athlete relationship?
2 To what extent is the coach–athlete relationship a dynamic and fluid power-based one? Provide examples to support your answer.
3 How do coaches get athletes to do their bidding?
4 How could coaches realistically employ an empowering approach in their practice?

COACHING CONTEXT

▼ BIBLIOGRAPHY

Abbott, A. and Collins, D. (2004) 'Eliminating the dichotomy between theory and practice in talent identification and development: Considering the role of psychology', *Journal of Sports Sciences*, 22: 395–408.

Adams, R., Turns, J. and Atman, C. (2003) 'Educating effective engineering designers: the role of reflective practice', *Design Studies*, 24(3): 275–294.

Alleman, E., Cochran, J., Doverspike, J. and Newman, I. (1984) 'Enriching mentoring relationships', *Personnel and Guidance Journal*, 62: 329–332.

Alton-Lee, A. (2003) *Quality Teaching for Diverse Students in Schooling: Best Evidence Synthesis*, Wellington: Ministry of Education.

Alvesson, M. and Willmott, H. (1996) *Making Sense of Management: A Critical Analysis*, London: Sage.

Amade-Escot, C. (2000) 'The contribution of two research programs on teaching content: PCK and didactics of physical education', *Journal of Teaching in Physical Education*, 20: 78–101.

Amade-Escot, C. (2006) 'Student learning within the *didactique* tradition', in D. Kirk, D. Macdonald and M. O'Sullivan (eds) *The Handbook of Physical Education*, London: Sage.

Anderson, A. (1994) 'How constructivism and behaviourism can complement each other in the preparation of physical education professionals', *CAHPERD Journal*, 60(3): 13–18.

Anderson, A. (1997) 'Using personal histories to explore theories about the teaching/learning process in physical education', *Avante*, 3(1): 71–82.

Andersen, A., Cohn, L. and Holbrook, T. (2000) *Making Weight*, Carlsbad, CA: Gurze Books.

Apple, M.W. (1979) *Ideology and Curriculum*, London: Routledge & Kegan Paul.

Arai, S. (1997) 'Empowerment: From the theoretical to the personal', *Journal of Leisurability*, 23(1): 3–11.

Aries, P. (1962) *Centuries of Childhood: A Social History of Family Life*, London: Jonathan Cape.

Armour, K.M. and Jones, R.L. (2000) 'The practical heart within: The value of sociology of sport', in R.L. Jones and K.M. Armour (eds) *The Sociology of Sport: Theory and Practice*, London: Addison Wesley Longman.

Australian Film Institute Distribution Ltd (n.d.) *Kick to Kick* (video recording), Melbourne.

Bachrach, P. and Baratz, M.S. (1963) 'Decisions and non-decisions: An analytical framework', *American Political Science Review*, 57: 641–651.

Bachrach, P. and Baratz, M. (1970) *Power and Poverty*, London: Oxford University Press.

Baker, B. (2001) 'Moving on (part 2): Power and the child in curriculum history', *Journal of Curriculum Studies*, 33: 277–302.

Bale, J. and Sang, J. (1996) *Kenyan Running: Movement Culture, Geography and Global Change*, London: Frank Cass.

Ball, S.J. (1990) *Politics and Policy-Making in Education: Explorations in Policy Sociology*, London: Routledge.

Ballard, K. (1993) 'A socio-political perspective on disability: Research and institutional disabilism', *New Zealand Journal of Educational Studies*, 28: 89–104.

Bandura, A. (1971) 'Analysis of modeling processes', in A. Bandura (ed.) *Psychological Modeling: Conflicting theories*, London: Transaction Publishers.

Barrows, H.S. (1986) 'A taxonomy of problem-based learning methods', *Medical Education*, 20: 481–486.

Bartky, S. (1992) 'Foucault, femininity and the modernization of patriarchal power', in J.A. Kourany, J.P. Serba and R. Tong (eds) *Feminist Philosophies*, Englewood Cliffs, NJ: Prentice-Hall.

Bean, D. (1976) 'Coaching grid: A simple way to increase effectiveness in teaching games', *HPECR Runner*, 14(3): 16–20.

Benfarri, R., Wilkinson, H. and Orth, C. (1986) 'The effective use of power', *Business Horizons*, 29: 12–16.

Bengtsson, J. (1995) 'What is reflection? On reflection in the teaching profession and teacher education', *Teachers and Teaching: Theory and Practice*, 1(1): 23–32.

Benson, R. and Taub, D. (1993) 'Using the PRECEDE model for causal analysis of bulimic tendencies among elite women swimmers', *Journal of Health Education*, 24(6): 360–368.

Bergmann Drewe, S. (2000) 'An examination of the relationship between coaching and teaching', *Quest*, 52: 79–88.

Birrell, S. and Cole, C. (1994) *Women, Sport and Culture*, Champaign, IL: Human Kinetics.

Blasi, A. and Oresick, R. (1987) 'Self-inconsistency and the development of self', in P. Young-Eisdendrath and J. Hall (eds) *The Book of the Self: Person, Pretext, and Process*, New York: University Press.

Bloom, G.A., Salmela, J.H. and Schinke, R.J. (1995) 'Expert coaches' views on the training of developing coaches', in R. Vanfraechem-Raway and Y. Vanden Auweele (eds) *Proceedings of the Ninth European Congress on Sport Psychology*, Brussels: Free University of Brussels.

Bloom, G.A., Durand-Bush, N., Schinke, R.J. and Salmela, J.H. (1998) 'The importance of mentoring in the development of coaches and athletes', *International Journal of Sport Psychology*, 29: 267–281.

Borrie, A. (1998) 'Coaching: art or science?', *Insight*, 1(1): 5.

Bourdieu, P. (1977) *Outline of a Theory of Practice*, Cambridge: Cambridge University Press.

Bourdieu, P. (1984) *Distinction: A Social Critique of the Judgement of Taste*, London: Routledge.

Bourdieu, P. and Wacquant, L. (1992) *An Invitation to Reflexive Sociology*, Cambridge: Polity Press.

Bowes, I. and Jones, R.L. (2006) 'Working at the edge of chaos: understanding coaching as a complex, interpersonal system', *The Sport Psychologist*, 20(2): 235–245.

Brackenridge, C., Rivers, I., Gough, B. and Llewellyn, K. (2007) 'Driving down participation: Homophobic bullying as a deterrent to doing sport', in C. Aitchison (ed.) *Sport and Gender Identities: Masculinities, Femininities, and Sexualities*, London: Routledge.

Bradley, H. (1997) *Fractured Identities: Changing Patterns of Inequality*, Cambridge: Polity Press.

Brettschneider, W.-D. and Heim, R. (1997) 'Identity, sport, and youth development', in K.R. Fox (ed.) *The Physical Self: From Motivation to Well-Being*, Champaign, IL: Human Kinetics.

Brewer, B., Van Raalte, J. and Linder, D. (1993) 'Athletic identity: Hercules' muscles or Achilles' heel?', *International Journal of Sport Psychology*, 24: 237–254.

Brewer, C.J. and Jones, R.L. (2002) 'A five-stage process for establishing contextually valid systematic observation instruments: The case of rugby union', *The Sport Psychologist*, 16(2): 139–161.

Bridges, E.M. and Hallinger, P. (1996) 'Problem-based learning in leadership education', in L. Wilkerson and W.H. Gijselaers (eds) *Bringing Problem-based Learning to Higher Education Theory and Practice*, San Francisco: Jossey-Bass.

Broadfoot, P. and Black, P. (2004) 'Redefining assessment? The first 10 years of assessment in education', *Assessment in Education*, 11(1): 7–27.

Bromley, R. (1995) 'Richard Hoggart: The real world of people: Illustrations from popular art – Peg's paper', in J. Munns and G. Rajan (eds) *A Cultural Studies Reader: History, Theory and Practice*, London: Longman.

Broughton, J. (ed.) (1987) *Critical Theories of Psychological Development*, New York: Plenum.

Bruins, J. (1999) 'Social power and influence tactics: a theoretical introduction', *Journal of Social Issues*, 55(1): 7–14.

Brustad, R.J. and Weiss, M.R. (1992) 'Psychological dimensions of children's physical activity: theoretical and measurement issues', paper presented at the meeting of the Association for the Advancement of Applied Sport Psychology, Colorado Springs, CO.

Bump, L. (1987) *Coaching Young Athletes* (video recording), Champaign, IL: Human Kinetics.

Bunker, D. and Thorpe, R. (1982) 'A model for the teaching of games in secondary schools', *Bulletin of Physical Education*, 18(1): 5–8.

Burbules, N.C. (1995) 'Reasonable doubt: Toward a post-modern defence of reason as an educational aim', in W. Kholi (ed.) *Critical Conversations in Philosophy of Education*, New York: Routledge.

Burman, E. (1991) 'Power, gender and developmental psychology', *Feminism and Psychology*, 1: 141–153.

Burman, E. (1994) *Deconstructing Developmental Psychology*, London: Routledge.

Burrows, L. (2002) 'Constructing the child: Developmental discourses in school physical education', *New Zealand Journal of Educational Studies*, 37(2): 127–140.

Burrows, L. (2005) 'Proposed key competencies and health and physical education in the New Zealand curriculum', paper prepared for New Zealand Ministry of Education New Zealand Curriculum/Marautanga Project. Available at http://www.nzcurriculum.tki.org.nz/references (accessed 14 June 2005).

Burrows, L. and Wright, J. (2003) 'The discursive production of childhood, identity and health', in J. Evans, B. Davies and J. Wright (eds) *Body, Knowledge and Control: Studies in the Sociology of Education and Physical Culture*, London: Routledge.

Burt, J.J. (1998) 'The role of kinesiology in elevating modern society', *Quest*, 50: 80–95.

Busen, N.H. and Engebretson, J. (1999) 'Mentoring in advanced practice nursing: The use of metaphor in concept exploration', *The Internet Journal of Advanced Nursing Practice*, 2(2). Retrieved from http://www.ispub.com/ostia/index.php?xmlFilePath=journals/ijanp/vol2n2/mentoring.xml.

Bush, G. (2006) 'Learning about learning: From theories to trends', *Teacher Librarian*, 34(2): 14–18.

Butler, J. (1997) 'How would Socrates teach games? A constructivist approach', *JOPERD*, 68(9): 42–47.

Calhoun, C. (1995) 'Habitus, field and capital: The question of historical specificity', in C. Calhoun, E. LiPuma and M. Postone (eds) *Bourdieu: Critical Perspectives*, Oxford: Blackwell.

Carlson, N. and Buskist, W. (1997) *Psychology: The Science of Behavior*, London: Allyn & Bacon.

Carr, D. (1998) 'What moral educational significance has physical education? A question in need of disambiguation', in M. McNamee and J. Parry (eds) *Ethics and Sport*, London: E & FN Spon.

Carr, W. (ed.) (1989) *Quality in Teaching: Arguments for a Reflective Profession*, London: Falmer Press.

Carter, K. (1993) 'The place of story in the study of teaching and teacher education', *Educational Researcher*, 22: 5–12, 18.

Cassidy, T. (2000) 'Investigating the pedagogical process in physical education teacher education', unpublished doctoral dissertation, Deakin University, Australia.

Cassidy, T. (2007a) '"Generation Y" or "Generation Why?": Learning about the physical', paper presented at the Physical Education New Zealand conference Kristin College, Auckland, July.

Cassidy, T. (2007b) 'Framing the discussion of competencies in coach education', paper presented at the International Council for Coach Education Global Coach conference, Beijing Sport University, Beijing, September.

Cassidy, T. and Rossi, T. (2006) 'Situating learning: (Re)examining the notion of apprenticeship in coach education', *International Journal of Sports Science and Coaching*, 1(3): 235–246.

Cassidy, T. and Tinning, R. (2004) '"Slippage" is not a dirty word: Considering the usefulness of Giddens' notion of knowledgeability in understanding the possibilities for teacher education', *Journal of Teaching Education*, 15(2): 175–188.

Cassidy, T., Jones, R. and Potrac, P. (2004) *Understanding Sports Coaching: The Social, Cultural and Pedagogical Foundations of Coaching Practice*, London: Routledge.

Cassidy, T., Potrac, P. and McKenzie, A. (2006a) 'Evaluating and reflecting upon a coach education initiative: The CoDe of rugby', *The Sports Psychologist*, 20(2): 145–161.

Cassidy, T., Stanley, S. and Bartlett, R. (2006b) 'Reflecting on video feedback as a tool for learning skilled movement', *International Journal of Sports Science and Coaching*, 1(3), 279–288.

Cassidy, T., Potrac, P. and Allen, J. (2006c) 'Examining the developmental experiences of elite athletes using a social theory of learning', paper presented at the Association Internationale des Ecoles Supérieures d'Education Physique (AIESEP) conference, Jyväskylä, Finland, July.

Cazden, C. (1988) *Classroom Discourse: The Language of Teaching and Learning*, Portsmouth, NH: Heinemann.

Chapman, G.E. (1997) 'Making weight: Lightweight rowing, technologies of power and technologies of the self', *Sociology of Sport Journal*, 14: 205–223.

Cheffers, J. (1997) 'No man is an island', *AIESEP Conference Proceedings*, Singapore, p. 4.

Chen, A. (2001) 'A theoretical conceptualization for motivation research in physical education: An integrated perspective', *Quest*, 53(1): 35–58.

Chen, W. and Rovegno, I. (2000) 'Examination of expert and novice teachers' constructivist oriented teaching practices using a movement approach to elementary physical education', *Research Quarterly of Exercise and Sport*, 71(4): 357–372.

Cherryholmes, C. (1988) *Power and Criticism: Post-structural Investigations in Education*, New York: Teachers College Press.

Choi, P. (2000) *Femininity and the Physically Active Woman*, London: Routledge.

Christina, R. and Corcos, D. (1988) *Coaches' Guide to Teaching Sport Skills*, Champaign, IL: Human Kinetics.

Chu, D. (1984) 'Teacher/coach orientation and role socialization: A description and explanation', *Journal of Teaching in Physical Education*, 3(2): 308.

Coakley, J. (1992) 'Burnout among adolescent athletes: A personal failure or social problem?', *Sociology of Sport Journal*, 9: 271–285.

Coakley, J. (2001) *Sport in Society: Issues and Controversies*, 7th edn, Dubuque, IA: McGraw-Hill.

Cochran, K.F., DeRuiter, J.A. and King, R.A. (1993) 'Pedagogical content knowing: An integrated model for teacher preparation', *Journal of Teacher Education*, 44(4): 263–272.

Cohen, I.J. (1998) 'Anthony Giddens', in R. Stones (ed.) *Key Sociological Thinkers*, Basingstoke, UK: Macmillan.

Cole, C. (1998) 'Addiction, exercise and cyborgs: Technologies of deviant bodies', in G. Rail (ed.) *Sport and Post-modern Times*, Albany, NY: State University of New York Press.

Collins (1992) *Concise English Dictionary*, London: HarperCollins.

Collins (2003) *Pocket Dictionary and Thesaurus*, London: HarperCollins.

Communities of Practice (n.d.) retrieved 20 April 2007 from http://www.infed.org/biblio/communities_or_practice.html.

Connell, R. (1985) *Teachers' Work*, London: Allen & Unwin.

Connell, R. (1995) *Masculinities*, Sydney: Allen & Unwin.

Connelly, M. and Clandinin, D. (1990) 'Stories of experience and narrative inquiry', *Educational Researcher*, 19: 2–14.

Côté, J., Salmela, J., Trudel, P., Baria, A. and Russell, S. (1995) 'The coaching model: A grounded assessment of expert gymnastic coaches' knowledge', *Journal of Sport and Exercise Psychology*, 17(1): 1–17.

Côté, J., Yardley, J., Hay, J., Sedgwick, W. and Baker, J. (1999) 'An exploratory examination of the coaching behaviour scale for sport', *Avante*, 5(2): 82–92.

Cross, N. and Lyle, J. (eds) (1999) *The Coaching Process: Principles and Practice for Sport*, Oxford: Butterworth-Heinemann.

Crum, B. (1995) 'The urgent need for reflective teaching in physical education', in C. Pare (ed.) *Training of Teachers in Reflective Practice of Physical Education*, Trois-Rivières, Quebec: Université du Québec à Trois-Rivières.

Culpan, I. (2000) 'Getting what you got: Harnessing the potential', *Journal of Physical Education New Zealand*, 33: 22–36.

Culver, D. and Trudel, P. (2006) 'Cultivating coaches' communities of practice: Developing the potential for learning through interactions', in R. Jones (ed.) *The Sports Coach as Educator: Re-conceptualising Sports Coaching*, London: Routledge.

Cunningham, G., Keiper, P., Sagas, M. and Ashley, F. (2001) 'Initial reliability of the coaching isomorphism questionnaire for NCCA coaches', *Psychological Reports*, 88(2): 332–334.

Cushion, C. (2001) 'The coaching process in professional youth football: An ethnography of practice', unpublished doctoral thesis, Brunel University, UK.

Cushion, C. and Jones, R. (2001) 'A systematic observation of professional top-level youth soccer coaches', *Journal of Sport Behavior*, 24(4): 354–376.

Cushion, C. and Jones, R.L. (2006) 'Power, discourse and symbolic violence in professional youth soccer: The case of Albion F.C.', *Sociology of Sport Journal*, 23(2): 142–161.

Cushion, C., Armour, K.M. and Jones, R.L. (2003) 'Coach education and continuing professional development: Experience and learning to coach', *Quest*, 55: 215–230.

David, B., Bouthier, D., Marsenach, J. and Durey, A. (1999) 'French research into the didactics and technology of physical activities and sports: An expanding new field', *Instructional Science*, 27: 147–163.

Danaher, G., Schirato, T. and Webb, J. (2003) *Understanding Foucault*, London: Sage.

Daniels, H. (2001) *Vygotsky and Pedagogy*, London: RoutledgeFalmer.

DeMarco, G., Mancini, V. and West, D. (1993) 'Self-assessment and modification of coaching behaviour', paper presented at the meeting of the International University Sports Federation, Buffalo, NY.

DeMarco, G., Mancini, V. and West, D. (1997) 'Reflections on change: A qualitative analysis of a baseball coach's behavior', *Journal of Sport Behavior*, 20(2): 135–163.

Denison, J. (2007) 'Social theory for coaches: A Foucauldian reading of one athlete's poor performance', *International Journal of Sport Science and Coaching*, 2(4): 369–383.

Denison, J. and Rinehart, R. (2000) 'Introduction: Imagining sociological narratives', *Sociology of Sport Journal*, 17: 1–4.

DePauw, K. (2000) 'Social-cultural context of disability: Implications for scientific inquiry and professional preparation', *Quest*, 52: 358–368.

DePauw, K. and Gavron, S. (1995) *Disability and Sport*, Champaign, IL: Human Kinetics.

Dewey, J. (1910) *How We Think*, Boston: Heath.

Dewey, J. (1916) *Democracy and Education: An Introduction to the Philosophy of Education*, New York: Macmillan.

Dewey, J. (1966) *Selected Educational Writings*, London: Heinemann.

Dodds, P. (1985) 'Are hunters of the functional curriculum seeking quarks or snarks?', *Journal of Teaching in Physical Education*, 4: 91–99.

Dodds, P. (1993) 'Removing the ugly "isms" in your gym: Thoughts for teachers on equity', in J. Evans (ed.) *Equality, Education and Physical Education*, London: Falmer Press.

Douge, B. and Hastie, P. (1993) 'Coach effectiveness', *Sport Science Review*, 2: 14–29.

Drewery, W. and Bird, L. (2004) *Human Development in Aotearoa: A Journey through Life*, 2nd edn, Sydney: McGraw-Hill.

Driscoll, M. (2005) *Psychology of Learning for Instruction*, 3rd edn, London: Pearson.

Duda, J. (1993) 'Goals: A study of social-cognitive approaches to the study of achievement motivation in sport', in R. Singer, M. Murphy and L. Tennant (eds) *Handbook of Research on Sport Psychology*, New York: Macmillan.

Dunning, E. (1986) 'The sociology of sport in Europe and the United States: Critical observations from an "Eliasian" perspective', in R. Rees and A. Miracle (eds) *Sport and Social Theory*, Champaign, IL: Human Kinetics.

Dunphy, B. and Dunphy, S. (2003) 'Assisted performance and the zone of proximal development: A potential framework for providing surgical education', *Australian Journal of Educational and Developmental Psychology*, 3: 48–58.

Durie, M. (1998) *Whaiora: Mäori Health Development*, Oxford: Oxford University Press.

Eby, L.T. and Lockwood, A. (2005) 'Protégés' and mentors' reactions to participating in formal mentoring programs: A qualitative investigation', *Journal of Vocational Behaviour*, 67(3): 441–458.

Eckert, P. (1989) *Jocks and Burnouts: Social Categories and Identity in the High School*, New York: Teachers College Press.

Eggen, P. and Kauchak, D. (2004) *Educational Psychology: Windows on Classrooms*, 6th edn, Upper Saddle River, NJ: Pearson.

Eraut, M. (1995) 'Schön shock: A case for reframing reflection-in-action?', *Teachers and Teaching: Theory and Practice*, 1(1): 9–22.

Erchul, W. and Raven, B. (1997) 'Social power in school consultation: A contemporary view of French and Raven's power model', *Journal of School Psychology*, 35(2): 137–171.

Eskes, T.B., Duncan, C.M. and Miller, M.M. (1998) 'The discourse of empowerment: Foucault, Marcuse and the women's fitness texts', *Journal of Sport and Social Issues*, 18: 317–344.

Evans, J. (1992) 'A short paper about people, power and educational reform. Authority and representation in ethnographic research. Subjectivity, ideology and educational reform: The case of physical education', in A. Sparkes (ed.) *Research in Physical Education and Sport: Exploring Alternative Visions*, London: Falmer Press.

Evans, J. (2004) 'Making a difference? Education and "ability" in physical education', *European Journal of Physical Education*, 10(1): 95–108.

Evans, J. and Davies, B. (1993) 'Equality, equity and physical education', in J. Evans (ed.) *Equality, Education and Physical Education*, London: Falmer Press.

Evans, J. and Roberts, G. (1987) 'Physical competence and the development of children's peer relationships', *Quest*, 39: 23–35.

Fairs, J. (1987) 'The coaching process: Essence of coaching', *Sports Coach*, 1(1): 9.

Fasting, K. (1997) 'Sexual stereotypes in sport: Experiences of female soccer players', Play the Game. Available at http://www.playthegame.org/knowledge%20Bank/Articles/Sexual%20Stereotypes%20in20%Sport%20_%20Experiences%20of%20Female%20Soccer%20Players.aspx (accessed 18 June 2007).

Faulkener, G. and Finlay, S.J. (2002) 'It's not what you say, it's the way you say it! Conversation analysis: A discursive methodology for sport, exercise and physical education', *Quest*, 54: 49–66.

Fernandez-Balboa, J.-M. (2000) 'Discrimination: What do we know and what can we do about it?', in R.L. Jones and K.M. Armour (eds) *Sociology of Sport: Theory and Practice*, London: Longman.

Field, B. and Field, T. (eds) (1994) *Teachers as Mentors: A Practical Guide*, London: Falmer Press.

Figone, A. (2001) 'The historical evolution of the teacher–coach dual roles: Time for a new model', *CAHPER Journal California*, 63(6): 20–22.

First Steps (1996) Issue No. 15: 4.

Fitzgerald, H. (2005) 'Still feeling like a spare piece of luggage? Embodied experiences of (dis)ability in physical education and sport', *Physical Education and Sport Pedagogy*, 10(1): 41–59.

Fleming, N. (1991) 'Sport, schooling and Asian male youth culture', in G. Jarvie (ed.) *Sport, Racism and Ethnicity*, London: Falmer Press.

Fleming, N. and Bonwell, C. (2001) *How Do I Learn Best? A Student's Guide to Improved Learning*, Christchurch, NZ: Fleming & Bonwell.

Fletcher, S. (2000) *Mentoring in Schools: A Handbook of Good Practice*, London: Kogan Page.

Fortanasce, V., Robinson, L. and Ouellete, J. (2001) *The Official American Youth Soccer Organization Handbook: Rules, Regulations, Skills and Everything Else Kids, Parents*

and Coaches Need to Participate in Youth Soccer, Hawthorne, CA: American Youth Soccer Organization.

Foucault, M. (1972) *The Archeology of Knowledge*, trans. A. Sheridan, New York: Random House.

Foucault, M. (1977) *Discipline and Punish: The Birth of the Prison*, New York: Pantheon Books.

Foucault, M. (1979) *The History of Sexuality*, Vol. 1: *An Introduction*, London: Allen Lane Penguin Press.

Franklin, S. (1996) 'Postmodern body techniques: Some anthropological considerations in natural and post-natural bodies', *Journal of Sport and Exercise Psychology*, 18: 95–106.

Fraser-Thomas, J. and Côté, J. (2006) 'Youth sports: Implementing findings and moving forward with research', *Online Journal of Sport Psychology*, 8(3). Available at http://www.athleticinsight.com/Vol8Iss3/YouthSports.htm (accessed 21 March 2007).

Fraser-Thomas, J., Côté, J. and Deakin, J. (2005) 'Youth sport programs: An avenue to foster positive youth development', *Physical Education and Sport Pedagogy*, 10(1): 19–40.

French, J.R.P., Jr. and Raven, B. (1959) 'The bases of social power', in D. Cartwright (ed.) *Studies in Social Power*, Ann Arbor, MI: University of Michigan Press.

Friedrichsen, F. (1956) *Study of the Effectiveness of Loop Films as Instructional Aids in Teaching Gymnastic Stunts*, Eugene, OR: University of Oregon.

Furlong, J. and Maynard, T. (1995) *Mentoring Student Teachers*, Routledge: London.

Gagne, M., Ryan, R. and Bargmann, K. (2003) 'Autonomy support and need satisfaction in the motivation and well-being of gymnasts', *Journal of Applied Sport Psychology*, 15: 372–390.

Galipeau, J. and Trudel, P. (2006) 'Athlete learning in a community of practice: Is there a role for the coach?', in R.L. Jones (ed.) *The Sports Coach as Educator. Re-conceptualising Sports Coaching*, London: Routledge.

Geddis, A. and Wood, E. (1997) 'Transforming subject matter and managing dilemmas: A case study in teacher education', *Teaching and Teacher Education*, 13(6): 611–626.

Geertz, C. (1973) *The Interpretation of Cultures*, New York: Basic Books.

George, L. and Kirk, D. (1988) 'The limits of change in physical education: Ideologies, teachers and the experience of physical activity', in J. Evans (ed.) *Teachers, Teaching and Control in Physical Education*, Lewes, UK: Falmer Press.

Giddens, A. (1984) *The Constitution of Society: Outline of a Theory of Structuration*, Cambridge: Polity Press.

Giddens, A. (1990) *The Consequences of Modernity*, Cambridge: Polity Press.

Giddens, A. (1991) *Modernity and Self-identity: Self and Society in the Late Modern Age*, Cambridge: Polity Press.

Giddens, A. (1993) *New Rules of Sociological Method*, Cambridge: Polity Press.

Giddens, A. (1997) *Sociology*, 3rd edn, Cambridge: Polity Press.

Giddens, A. (1998) *The Third Way: The Renewal of Social Democracy*, Cambridge: Polity Press.

Gilbert, W. (2002) 'An annotated bibliography and analysis of coaching science', unpublished report sponsored by the Research Consortium of the American Alliance for Health, Physical Education, Recreation and Dance.

Gilbert, W. and Trudel, P. (1999) 'An evaluation strategy for coach education programmes', *Journal of Sport Behavior*, 22: 234–250.

Gilbert, W. and Trudel, P. (2001) 'Learning to coach through experience: Reflection in model youth sport coaches', *Journal of Teaching in Physical Education*, 21(1): 16–34.

Gilbert, W. and Trudel, P. (2005) 'Learning to coach through experience: Conditions that influence reflection', *Physical Educator*, 62(1): 32–43.

Gilbert, W. and Trudel, P. (2006) 'The coach as reflective practitioner', in R.L. Jones (ed.) *The Sports Coach as Educator: Re-conceptualising Sports Coaching*, London: Routledge.

Gilbert, W., Trudel, P., Gaumond, S. and Larocque, L. (1999) 'Development and application of an instrument to analyse pedagogical content interventions of ice hockey coaches', *Sociology of Sport Online*, 2(2). Available at http://physed.otago.ac.nz/sosol/v2i2/v2i2.htm (accessed 27 August 2003).

Glasby, T. (2006) 'Assessment and reporting of learning outcomes in PE', in R. Tinning, L. McCuaig and lisahunter (eds) *Teaching Health and Physical Education in Australian Schools*, Frenchs Forest, NSW: Pearson.

Goodwin, C. (2007) 'The weight-loss crusade: The life of an elite female distance runner', unpublished honours dissertation, University of Otago, Dunedin, New Zealand.

Gould, D., Giannini, J., Krane, V. and Hodge, K. (1990) 'Educational needs of elite U.S. national team pan-American, and Olympic coaches', *Journal of Teaching in Physical Education*, 9: 332–344.

Grace, G. (1998) 'Critical policy scholarship: Reflections on the integrity of knowledge and research', in G. Shacklock and J. Smyth (eds) *Being Reflexive in Critical Educational and Social Research*, London: Falmer Press.

Green, K. (2000) 'Exploring the everyday "philosophies" of physical education teachers from a sociological perspective', *Sport, Education and Society*, 5: 109–129.

Green, K. (2002) 'Physical education teachers in their figurations: A sociological analysis of everyday philosophies', *Sport, Education and Society*, 7: 65–83.

Griffin, L. (1996) 'Tactical approaches to teaching games: Improving net/wall game performance', *JOPERD*, 67(2): 34–37.

Griffin, L., Mitchell, S. and Oslin, J. (1997) *Teaching Sport Concepts and Skills*, Champaign, IL: Human Kinetics.

Griffin, P. (1998) *Strong Women, Deep Closets: Lesbians and Homophobia in Sport*, Champaign, IL: Human Kinetics.

Gronn, P. (2000) 'Distributed properties: A new architecture of leadership', *Educational Management and Leadership*, 28(3): 317–338.

Halas, J. and Hanson, L. (2001) 'Pathologizing Billy: Enabling and constraining the body of the condemned', *Sociology of Sport Journal*, 18: 115–126.

Haleem, H. (2005) 'Running in pain: An autoethnography of power, coercion and injury in a coach–athlete relationship', unpublished PhD dissertation, University of Otago, Dunedin, New Zealand.

Hall, S. (1996) 'Introduction: who needs identity?', in S. Hall and P. DuGay (eds) *Questions of Cultural Identity*, London: Sage.

Hall, S. and DuGay, P. (eds) (1996) *Questions of Cultural Identity*, London: Sage.

Haralambos, M. and Holborn, M. (2000) *Sociology: Themes and Perspectives*, 5th edn, London: HarperCollins.

Hardy, C. (1995) 'Introduction', in C. Hardy (ed.) *Power and Politics in Organizations*, Aldershot, UK: Dartmouth.

Hardy, C. and Mawer, M. (1999) *Learning and Teaching in Physical Education*, London: Falmer Press.

Hargreaves, J. (2007) 'Sport, exercise, and the female Muslim body: Negotiating Islam, politics, and male power', in J. Hargreaves and P. Vertinsky (eds) *Physical Culture, Power, and the Body*, London: Routledge.

Hay, P. (2005) 'Making judgements: Student ability and assessment in physical education', *Journal of Physical Education New Zealand*, 38(1): 41–50.

Hay, P. (2006a) 'Assessment for learning in physical education', in D. Kirk, D. Macdonald and M. O'Sullivan (eds) *The Handbook of Physical Education*, London: Sage.

Hay, P. (2006b) 'Assessment for accountability', in R. Tinning, L. McCuaig and lisahunter (eds) *Teaching Health and Physical Education in Australian Schools*, Frenchs Forest, NSW: Pearson.

Hay, P. and lisahunter (2006) 'Please Mr Hay, what are my poss(abilities)? Legitimation of ability through physical education practices', *Sport, Education and Society*, 11(3): 293–310.

Heider, F. (1958) *The Psychology of Interpersonal Relations*, New York: Wiley.

Hellison, D. and Templin, T. (1991) *A Reflective Approach to Teaching Physical Education*, Champaign, IL: Human Kinetics.

Heritage, J. (1984) *Garfinkel and Ethnomethodology*, Cambridge: Polity Press.

Heywood, L. (1998) *Bodymakers: A Cultural Anatomy of Women's Bodybuilding*, New Brunswick, NJ: Rutgers University Press.

Hickey, C. and Fitzclarence, L. (1997) 'Masculinity, violence and football', *Changing Education*, 4(2/3): 18–21.

Hoffman, S. (1971) 'Traditional methodology: Prospects for change', *Quest*, 15: 51–57.

Hohepa, M., McNaughton, S. and Jenkins, K. (1996) 'Mäori pedagogies and the role of the individual', *New Zealand Journal of Educational Studies*, 31(1): 29–40.

Hokowhitu, B. (2003) '"Physical beings": Stereotypes, sport and "physical education" of New Zealand Mäori', *Culture, Sport and Society*, 6(2/3): 192–218.

Hokowhitu, B. (2004) 'Challenges to state physical education: Tikanga Mäori, physical education curricula, historical deconstruction, inclusivism and decolonization', *Waikato Journal of Education*, 10: 71–83.

Hollembeak, J. and Amorose, A. (2005) 'Perceived coaching behaviors and college athletes' intrinsic motivation: A test of self-determination theory', *Journal of Applied Sport Psychology*, 17: 20–36.

Horne, J. and Jary, D. (2004) 'Anthony Giddens: Structuration theory, and sport and leisure', in R. Giulianotti (ed.) *Sport and Modern Social Theorists*, Basingstoke, UK: Palgrave.

Horne, J., Tomlinson, A. and Whannel, G. (1999) *Understanding Sport: An Introduction to the Sociological and Cultural Analysis of Sport*, London: E & FN Spon.

Huang, C.J. and Brittain, I. (2006) 'Negotiating identities through disability sport', *Sociology of Sport Journal*, 23: 352–375.

Hussain, A. and Trudel, P. (2007) 'Coaches' learning pathways: A collaborative study with triathlon', poster presented at International Council for Coach Education Global Coach conference, Beijing Sport University, Beijing, September.

Ingvarson, L. and Rowe, K. (2007) 'Conceptualising and evaluating teacher quality: Substantive and methodological issues', paper presented at the Economics of Teacher Quality Conference, Australian National University, 5 February.

Irwin, G., Hanton, S. and Kerwin, D. (2004) 'Reflective practice and the origins of elite coaching knowledge', *Reflective Practice*, 5(3): 425–442.

Jackson, L. (2002) *Freaks, Geeks and Asperger Syndrome: A User's Guide to Adolescence*, London: Jessica Kingsley.

Jarvie, G. (1991) 'Introduction: Sport, racism and ethnicity', in G. Jarvie (ed.) *Sport, Racism and Ethnicity*, London: Falmer Press.

Jobson, G. (1998) *Sailing Fundamentals: The Official Learn-to-Sail Manual of the American Sailing Association and the United States Coast Guard Auxiliary*, New York: Fireside.

Johns, D.P. (1998) 'Fasting and feasting: Paradoxes of the sport ethic', *Sociology of Sport Journal*, 15: 41–63.

Johns, D.P. and Johns, J. (2000) 'Surveillance, subjectivism and technologies of power: An analysis of the discursive practice of high-performance sport', *International Review for the Sociology of Sport*, 35: 219–234.

Johnson, D.W. (1996) *Reaching Out: Interpersonal Effectiveness and Self-Actualization*, 6th edn, Needham Heights, MA: Allyn & Bacon.

Jones, A. (1991) *'At School I've Got a Chance': Culture/privilege: Pacific Islands and Pakeha Girls at School*, Palmerston North, NZ: Dunmore Press.

Jones, C.R., Hardman, A. and Jones, R.L. (in press) 'Sports coaching, ethics and the virtues of emulation', *Sport, Ethics and Philosophy*.

Jones, R.L. (2000) 'Toward a sociology of coaching', in R.L. Jones and K.M. Armour (eds) *The Sociology of Sport: Theory and Practice*, London: Addison Wesley Longman.

Jones, R.L. (2001) 'Applying empowerment in coaching: Some thoughts and considerations', in L. Kidman (ed.) *Innovative Coaching: Empowering Your Athletes*, Christchurch, NZ: Innovative Communications.

Jones, R.L. (2002) 'The Black experience in English semi-professional soccer', *Journal of Sport and Social Issues*, 26(1): 47–65.

Jones, R.L. (ed.) (2006a) *The Sports Coach as Educator: Re-conceptualising Sports Coaching*, London: Routledge.

Jones, R.L. (2006b) 'How can educational concepts inform sports coaching?', in R.L. Jones (ed.) *The Sports Coach as Educator: Re-conceptualising Sports Coaching*, London: Routledge.

Jones, R.L. (2006c) 'Dilemmas, maintaining "face" and paranoia: An average coaching life', *Qualitative Inquiry*, 12(5): 1012–1021.

Jones, R.L. (2007) 'Coaching redefined: An everyday pedagogical endeavour', *Sport, Education and Society*, 12(2): 159–173.

Jones, R.L. (in press) 'Coaching as caring ("The smiling gallery"): Accessing hidden knowledge', *Physical Education and Sport Pedagogy*.

Jones, R.L. and Armour, K. (2000) *Sociology of Sport: Theory and Practice*, London: Addison Wesley Longman.

Jones, R.L. and Standage, M. (2006) 'First among equals: Shared leadership in the coaching context', in R.L. Jones (ed.) *The Sports Coach as Educator: Re-conceptualising Sports Coaching*, London: Routledge.

Jones, R.L. and Turner, P. (2006) 'Teaching coaches to coach holistically: Can Problem-Based Learning (PBL) help?', *Physical Education and Sport Pedagogy*, 11(2): 181–202.

Jones, R.L. and Wallace, M. (2005) 'Another bad day at the training ground: Coping with ambiguity in the coaching context', *Sport, Education and Society*, 10(1): 119–134.

Jones, R.L., Armour, K.M. and Potrac, P. (2002) 'Understanding the coaching process: A framework for social analysis', *Quest*, 54(1): 34–48.

Jones, R.L., Armour, K.M. and Potrac, P. (2003) 'Constructing expert knowledge: A case study of a top level professional soccer coach', *Sport, Education and Society*, 8(2): 213–229.

Jones, R.L., Armour, K.A. and Potrac, P. (2004) *Sports Coaching Cultures: From Practice to Theory*, London: Routledge.

Jones, R.L., Glintmeyer, N. and McKenzie, A. (2005) 'Slim bodies, eating disorders and the coach–athlete relationship: A tale of identity creation and disruption', *International Review for the Sociology of Sport*, 40(3): 377–391.

Jones, R.L., Standage, M., Cushion, C. and Potrac, P. (2006) 'First among equals: Shared leadership in the coaching context', paper presented at the Association for the Advancement of Applied Sport Psychology (AAASP) Conference, 27–29 September, Miami, FL.

Jones, R.L., Harris, R. and Miles, A. (in press) 'Mentoring in sports coaching: A review of the literature', *Physical Education and Sport Pedagogy*.

Jowett, S. and Lavallee, D. (2007) *Social Psychology in Sport*, Champaign, IL: Human Kinetics.

Kemmis, S. and McTaggart, R. (eds) (1992) *The Action Research Planner*, 3rd edn, Geelong, Victoria, Australia: Deakin University Press.

Kemmis, S. and Stake, R. (1988) *Evaluating Curriculum*, Geelong, Victoria, Australia: Deakin University Press.

Kenway, J. and Fitzclarence, L. (1997) 'Masculinity, violence and schooling: Challenging "poisonous pedagogies"', *Gender and Education*, 9(1): 117–133.

Kew, F. (2000) *Sport: Social Problems and Issues*, Oxford: Butterworth-Heinemann.

Kidd, B. and Donnelly, P. (2000) 'Human rights in sport', *International Review for the Sociology of Sport*, 35: 131–148.

Kidman, L. (2001) *Developing Decision Makers: An Empowerment Approach to Coaching*, Christchurch, NZ: Innovative Press.

Kidman, L. (2005) *Athlete-Centred Coaching. Developing Inspired and Inspiring People*, Christchurch, NZ: Innovative Print Communications.

Kidman, L. and Hanrahan, S. (1997) *The Coaching Process: A Practical Guide to Improving Your Effectiveness*, Palmerston North, NZ: Dunmore Press.

Kipnis, D. (2001) 'Using power: Newton's second law', in A. Lee-Chai and J. Bargh (eds) *The Use and Abuse of Power: Multiple Perspectives on the Causes of Corruption*, Philadelphia: Taylor & Francis.

Kirk, D. (1986) 'Beyond the limits of theoretical discourse in teacher education: Towards a critical pedagogy', *Teaching and Teacher Education*, 2(2): 155–167.

Kirk, D. (1992) 'Physical education, discourse, and ideology: Bringing the hidden curriculum into view', *Quest*, 44: 35–56.

Kirk, D. (1998) *Schooling Bodies: School Practice and Public Discourse, 1880–1950*, London: Leicester University Press.

Kirk, D. (2000) 'A task-based approach to critical pedagogy in sport and physical education', in R.L. Jones and K.M. Armour (eds) *Sociology of Sport: Theory and Practice*, London: Addison Wesley Longman.

Kirk, D. and Colquhoun, D. (1989) 'Healthism and physical education', *British Journal of Sociology of Education*, 10: 417–434.

Kirk, D., Nauright, J., Hanrahan, S., Macdonald, D. and Jobling, I. (1996) *The Sociocultural Foundations of Human Movement*, Melbourne: Macmillan.

Kleiber, D. (1980) 'The meaning of power in sport', *International Journal of Sport Psychology*, 11: 34–41.

Knowles, Z., Gilbourne, D., Borrie, A. and Nevill, A. (2001) 'Developing the reflective sports coach: A study exploring the process of reflective practice with a higher education coaching programme', *Reflective Practice*, 2(2): 185–207.

Knudson, D. and Morrison, C. (2002) *Qualitative Analysis of Human Movement*, 2nd edn, Champaign, IL: Human Kinetics.

Kohen, D. (1994) *The Ground of Professional Ethics*, London: Routledge.

Kozulin, A., Gindis, B., Ageyev, V. and Miller, S. (2003) *Vygotsky's Educational Theory in a Cultural Context*, Cambridge: Cambridge University Press.

Krane, V. and Barber, H. (2003) 'Lesbian experiences in sport: A social identity theory perspective', *Quest*, 55: 328–346.

Kretchmar, R.S. (1994) *Practical Philosophy of Sport*, Champaign, IL: Human Kinetics.

Langley, D. (1997) 'Exploring student skill learning: A case for investigating the subjective experience', *Quest*, 49: 142–160.

Lave, J. and Wenger, E. (1991) *Situated Learning: Legitimate Peripheral Participation*, Cambridge: Cambridge University Press.

Lawson, H. (1993) 'Dominant discourses, problem setting, and teacher education pedagogies: A critique', *Journal of Teaching in Physical Education*, 12: 149–160.

Layder, D. (1996) *Understanding Social Theory*, London: Sage.

Layton, R. (2005) *Making Mentors: A Guide to Establishing a Successful Mentoring Program for Coaches and Officials*, Canberra: Australian Sports Commission.

Lee Chai, A. and Bargh, J. (2001) *The Use and Abuse of Power: Multiple Perspectives on the Causes of Corruption*, Philadelphia: Taylor & Francis.

Lefrançois, G. (2000) *Theories of Learning*, 4th edn, Belmont, CA: Wadsworth/Thomson Learning.

Light, R. (1999) 'Social dimensions of rugby in Japanese and Australian schools', unpublished doctoral dissertation, University of Queensland, Australia.

Locke, L. (1985) 'Research and the improvement in teaching: The professor as the problem', in G. Barette, R. Feingold, R. Rees and M. Pieron (eds) *Myths, Models and Methods in Sport Pedagogy*, Champaign, IL: Human Kinetics.

Lukes, S. (1993) 'Three distinctive views of power compared', in M. Hill (ed.) *The Policy Process: A Reader*, London: Harvester Wheatsheaf.

Lusted, D. (1986) 'Why pedagogy?', *Screen*, 27(5): 2–14.

Lyle, J (1998) *The Coaching Process*, Leeds: National Coaching Foundation.

Lyle, J. (1999a) 'Coaching philosophy and coaching behaviour', in N. Cross and J. Lyle (eds) *The Coaching Process: Principles and Practice for Sport*, Oxford: Butterworth-Heinemann.

Lyle, J. (1999b) 'The coaching process: An overview', in N. Cross and J. Lyle (eds) *The Coaching Process: Principles and Practice for Sport*, Oxford: Butterworth-Heinemann.

Lyle, J. (2002) *Sports Coaching Concepts: A Framework for Coaches' Behaviour*, London: Routledge.

McCallister, S.G., Blinde, E. and Weiss, W.M. (2000) 'Teaching values and implementing philosophies: Dilemmas of the youth sport coach', *Physical Educator*, 57: 33–45.

McCarthy, D., Jones, R. and Potrac, P. (2003) 'Constructing images and interpreting realities: The representation of black footballers in top-level English football', *International Review for the Sociology of Sport*, 38(2): 217–238.

McCaughtry, N. (2004) 'The emotional dimensions of a teacher's pedagogical content knowledge: Influences on content, curriculum, and pedagogy', *Journal of Teaching in Physical Education*, 23: 30–47.

McCullick, B., Belcher, D. and Schempp, P. (2005) 'What works in coaching and sport instructor certification programs? The participants' view', *Physical Education and Sport Pedagogy*, 10(2): 121–137.

McDonald, M. and Birrell, S. (1999) 'Reading sport critically: A methodology for interrogating power', *Sociology of Sport Journal*, 16: 283–300.

Macdonald, D. and Tinning, R. (1995) 'Physical education teacher education and the trend to proletarianization: A case study', *Journal of Teaching in Physical Education*, 15: 98–118.

McGannon, K.R. and Mauws, M.K. (2000) 'Discursive psychology: An alternative approach for studying adherence to exercise and physical activity', *Quest*, 52: 148–165.

MacLean, J. and Zakrajsek, D. (1996) 'Factors considered important for evaluating Canadian university athletic coaches', *Journal of Sport Management*, 10(4): 446–462.

McMillan, B. (1991) 'All in the mind: Human learning and development from an ecological perspective', in J. Morrs and T. Linzey (eds) *Growing Up: The Politics of Human Learning*, Auckland: Longman Paul.

McNamee, M. (1998) 'Celebrating trust: Virtues and rules in the ethical conduct of sport coaches', in M. McNamee and J. Parry (eds) *Ethics and Sport*, London: E & FN Spon.

Markula, P. and Pringle, R. (2006) *Foucault, Sport and Exercise: Power, Knowledge and Transforming the Self*, London: Routledge.

Marsh, C. (1997) *Perspectives: Key Concepts for Understanding Curriculum 1*, London: Falmer Press.

Martens, R. (1988) 'Helping children become independent, responsible adults through sports', in E. Brown and C. Branta (eds) *Competitive Sport for Children and Youth: An Overview of Research and Issues*, Champaign, IL: Human Kinetics.

Martens, R. (1996) *Successful Coaching*, Champaign, IL: Human Kinetics

Martens, R. (1997) *Successful Coaching*, 2nd edn, Champaign, IL: Human Kinetics.

May, R. (1972) *Power and Innocence*, New York: W.W. Norton.

Mayall, B. (ed.) (1994) *Children's Childhoods: Observed and Experienced*, London: Falmer Press.

Ménard, J.-F., Trudel, P. and Werthner, P. (2007) 'An analysis of Canadian elite coaches' learning experiences', poster presented at International Council for Coach Education Global Coach conference, Beijing Sport University, Beijing, September.

Merriam, S. (1983) 'Mentors and protégés: A critical review of the literature', *Adult Education Quarterly*, 33: 161–173.

Merriam, S., Caffarella, R. and Baumgartner, L. (2007) *Learning in Adulthood: A Comprehensive Guide*, 3rd edn, San Francisco: John Wiley.

Messner, M.A. (1996) 'Studying up on sex', *Sociology of Sport Journal*, 13(3): 221–237.

Messner, M.A., Duncan, M.C. and Jensen, K. (1993) 'Separating the men from the girls: The gendered language of televised sports', *Gender and Society*, 7: 121–137.

Metzler, M. (1979) 'The measurement of academic learning time in physical education', unpublished doctoral dissertation, Ohio State University, Ann Arbor.

Metzler, M. (1989) 'A review of research on time in sport pedagogy', *Journal of Teaching in Physical Education*, 8: 87–103.

Metzler, M. (2000) *Instructional Models for Physical Education*, Needham Heights, MA: Allyn & Bacon.

Middlethon, A. and Aggleton, P. (2001) 'Reflection and dialogue for HIV prevention among young gay men', *AIDS Care*, 13(4): 515–526.

Miedzian, M. (1991) *Boys Will Be Boys: Breaking the Link between Masculinity and Violence*, London: Virago Press.

Mitchell, S. (1996) 'Tactical approaches to teaching games: Improving invasion game performance', *JOPERD*, 67(2): 30–33.

Moll, L. (1990) *Vygotsky and Education: Instructional Implications and Applications of Socio-historical Psychology*, Cambridge: Cambridge University Press.

Moon, J. (2004) *A Handbook of Reflective and Experiential Learning. Theory and Practice*, London: Routledge.

Morss, J. (1991) 'After Piaget: Rethinking "cognitive development"', in J. Morss and T. Linzey (eds) *Growing Up: The Politics of Human Learning*, Auckland: Longman Paul.

Morss, J. (1996) *Growing Critical: Alternatives to Developmental Psychology*, London: Routledge.

Morss, J.R. (2001) 'A rainbow of narratives: Childhood after developmentalism', in B. van Oers (ed.) *Proceedings of European Early Childhood Education Research Association Conference*, Alkmaar, the Netherlands, 29 August–1 September.

Mosston, M. (1966) *Teaching Physical Education*, Columbus, OH: Merrill.

Mosston, M. (1972) *Teaching: From Command to Discovery*, Belmont, CA: Wadsworth Publishing.

Mosston, M. (1992) 'Tug-o-war, no more: Meeting teaching–learning objectives using the spectrum of teaching styles', *Journal of Physical Education, Recreation and Dance*, 56: 27–31.

National Occupational Standards (n.d.) http://www.skillsactive.com/training/standards/?searchterm=standards (accessed 28 November 2007).

Nelson, L. and Cushion, C. (2006) 'Reflection in coach education', *The Sports Psychologist*, 20(2): 174–184.

New Zealand Ministry of Education (1999) *Health and Physical Education in the New Zealand Curriculum*, Wellington: Learning Media.

Nias, J., Southworth, G. and Yeomans, R. (1989) *Staff Relationships in the Primary School: A Study of Organizational Cultures*, London: Cassell.

Nicholls, J. (1984) 'Achievement motivation: Conceptions of ability, subjective experience, task choice, and performance', *Psychological Review*, 91: 328–346.

Nicholls, J. (1989) *The Competitive Ethos and Democratic Education*, Cambridge, MA: Harvard University Press.

Nicholls, J. (1992) 'The general and the specific in the development and expression of achievement motivation', in G. Roberts (ed.) *Motivation in Sport and Exercise*, Champaign, IL: Human Kinetics.

Nixon, H. (1984) 'The creation of appropriate integration opportunities in sport for disabled and nondisabled people: A guide for research and action', *Sociology of Sport Journal*, 1: 184–192.

Nixon, H. and Frey, J. (1998) *A Sociology of Sport*, Boston: Wadsworth.

Nyberg, D. (1981) *Power over Power*, Ithaca, NY: Cornell University Press.

OECD Directorate for Education (n.d.) Retrieved 20/12/07 from http://www.oecd.org/document/43/0,3343,en_2649_33723_2674027_1_1_1_1,00.html (accessed 20 December 2007).

Oliver, M. (1990) *The Politics of Disablement*, London: Macmillan.

Oslin, J., Mitchell, S. and Griffin, L. (1998) 'The game performance assessment instrument (GPAI): Development and preliminary validation', *Journal of Teaching in Physical Education*, 17: 231–243.

Oxford (1991) *Concise Oxford Dictionary*, 8th edn, Oxford: Oxford University Press.

Paraschak, V. (2000) 'Knowing ourselves through the "other": Indigenous peoples in sport in Canada', in R.L. Jones and K.M. Armour (eds) *Sociology of Sport: Theory and Practice*, London: Longman.

Parker, I. and Shotter, J. (eds) (1990) *Deconstructing Social Psychology*, London: Routledge.

Paul, R.W. (1993) 'Critical thinking and the way we construct the meaning of things', *General Semantics Bulletin*, 55: 24–37.

Payne, G. and Isaacs, L. (1987) *Human Motor Development: A Lifespan Approach*, Mountain View, CA: Mayfield.

Penney, D. (2000) 'Physical education . . . in what and whose interests?', in R.L. Jones and K.M. Armour (eds) *Sociology of Sport: Theory and Practice*, London: Longman.

Penney, D. (2006) 'Coaching as teaching: New acknowledgements in practice', in R.L. Jones (ed.) *The Sports Coach as Educator: Re-conceptualising Sports Coaching*, London: Routledge.

Penney, D., Clarke, G., Quill, M. and Kinchin, G. (eds) (2005) *Sport Education in Physical Education*, London: Routledge.

Placek, J. (1983) 'Conceptions of success in teaching: Busy, happy and good?' in T. Templin and J. Olsen (eds) *Teaching in Physical Education*, Champaign, IL: Human Kinetics.

Potrac, P. (2001) 'A comparative analysis of the working behaviours of top-level English and Norwegian soccer coaches', unpublished doctoral thesis, Brunel University, London.

Potrac, P. and Cassidy, T. (2006) 'The coach as a "more capable other"', in R.L. Jones (ed.) *The Sports Coach as Educator: Re-conceptualising Sports Coaching*, London: Routledge.

Potrac, P., Jones, R.L. and Armour, K.M. (2002) 'It's about getting respect: The coaching behaviours of a top-level English football coach', *Sport, Education and Society*, 7(2): 183–202.

Potrac, P., Brewer, C., Jones, R.L., Armour, K.M. and Hoff. J. (2000) 'Towards an holistic understanding of the coaching process', *Quest*, 52(2): 186–199.

Poynor, R. (1994) 'Building bridges between theory and practice', *ID*, 41: 40–42.

Prain, V. and Hickey, C. (1995) 'Using discourse analysis to change physical education', *Quest*, 47: 76–90.

Pronger, B. (1999) 'Fear and trembling: Homophobia in men's sport', in P. White and K. Young (eds) *Sport and Gender in Canada*, Toronto: Oxford University Press.

Purdy, L. (2005) 'Coaching in the current: The climate of an elite men's rowing training programme', unpublished doctoral dissertation, University of Otago, Dunedin, New Zealand.

Purdy, L., Potrac, P. and Jones, R.L. (in press) 'Power, consent and resistance: An autoethnography of competitive rowing', *Sport, Education, and Society*.

Raffel, S. (1998) 'Revisiting role theory: Roles and the problem of the self', *Sociological Research Online*, 4(2). Available at http://www.socresonline.org.uk/4/2/raffel.html (accessed 20 April 2008).

Raven, B. (1992) 'The bases of social power: Origins and recent developments', *Journal of Social Issues*, 49(4): 227–251.

Readhead, L. (1997) *Men's Gymnastic Coaching Manual*, British Amateur Gymnastics Association.

Reddiford, G. (1998) 'Cheating and self-deception in sport', in M. McNamee and J. Parry (eds) *Ethics and Sport*, London: E & FN Spon.

Reel, J. and Gill, D. (2001) 'Slim enough to swim? Weight pressures for competitive swimmers and coaching implications', *The Sport Journal*, 4(2). Available at http://www.thesportjournal.org/article/slim-enough-swim-weight-pressures-competitive-swimmers-and-coaching-implications (accessed 20 April 2008).

Reiman, A. (1999) 'The evolution of the social role-taking and guided reflection framework in teacher education: Recent theory and quantitative synthesis of research', *Teaching and Teacher Education*, 15: 597–612.

Reiss, S. (2000) *Who Am I? The 16 Basic Desires That Motivate Our Actions and Define Our Personality*, New York: Tarcher/Putnam.

Riemer, H. and Chelladurai, P. (1998) 'Development of the athlete satisfaction questionnaire (ASQ)', *Journal of Sport and Exercise Psychology*, 20: 127–156.

Roberts, C. (2001) 'China, china', *Ceramic Review*, 189: 40–41.

Roberts, G., Spink, K. and Pemberton, C. (1999) *Learning Experiences in Sport Psychology*, 2nd edn, Champaign, IL: Human Kinetics.

Rogoff, B. (1998) 'Cognition as a collaborative process', in W. Damon (ed.-in-chief) vol. 2, D. Kuhn and R. Siegler (eds) *Handbook of Child Psychology*, 5th edn, New York: Wiley.

Rokeach, M. (1968) *Beliefs, Attitudes and Values*, San Francisco: Jossey-Bass.

Rokeach, M. (1973) *The Nature of Human Values*, New York: Free Press.

Rossi, T. and Cassidy, T. (1999) 'Knowledgeable teachers in physical education: A view of teachers' knowledge', in C. Hardy and M. Mawer (eds) *Learning and Teaching in Physical Education*, London: Falmer Press.

Rotella, R. and Murray, M. (1991) 'Homophobia, the world of sport, and sport psychology consulting', *The Sport Psychologist*, 5: 355–364.

Rothig, P. (1985) 'Reflections on researching sport pedagogy', in G. Barette, R. Feingold, R. Rees and M. Pieron (eds) *Myths, Models and Methods in Sport Pedagogy*, Champaign, IL: Human Kinetics.

Rovegno, I. (1995) 'Theoretical perspectives on knowledge and learning and a student teacher's pedagogical content knowledge of dividing and sequencing subject matter', *Journal of Teaching in Physical Education*, 14: 284–304.

Royal Tangaere, A. (1997) 'Mäori human development learning theory', in P. Te Whäiti, M. McCarthy and A. Durie (eds) *Mai I Rangiätea: Mäori Wellbeing and Development*, Auckland: Auckland University Press.

Rushall, B. and Pettinger, J. (1969) 'An evaluation of the effect of various reinforcers used as motivators in swimming', *Research Quarterly*, 40: 540–545.

Rutherford, J. (2004) 'Key competencies in the New Zealand curriculum: A snapshot of consultation', paper prepared for New Zealand Ministry of Education New Zealand Curriculum/Marautanga Project. Available at http://www.nzcurriculum.tki.org.nz/references (accessed 14 June 2005).

Ryan, J. (1995) *Little Girls in Pretty Boxes: The Making and Breaking of Elite Gymnasts and Figure Skaters*, New York: Doubleday.

Rynne, S., Mallett, C. and Tinning, R. (2006) 'High performance sport coaching: Institutes of sport as sites for learning', *International Journal of Sports Science and Coaching*, 1(3): 223–234.

Sabo, D. and Jensen, S.C. (1994) 'Seen but not heard: Images of Black men in sports media', in M.A. Messner and D.F. Sabo (eds) *Sex, Violence and Power in Sports: Rethinking Masculinity*, Freedom, CA: The Crossing Press.

Sage, G. (1998) *Power and Ideology in American Sport*, 2nd edn, Champaign, IL: Human Kinetics.

Sage, G. (1989) 'Becoming a high school coach: From playing sport to coaching', *Research Quarterly in Exercise and Sport*, 60(1): 81–92.

Salter, G. (2000) 'Deciding between cultural identity or "success" in physical education: Describing attitudes and values', *Journal of Physical Education New Zealand*, 33(3): 67–83.

Sanders, N. (1966) *Classroom Questions. What Kinds?*, New York: Harper & Row.

Saury, J. and Durand, M. (1998) 'Practical knowledge in expert coaches: On-site study of coaching in sailing', *Research Quarterly in Exercise and Sport*, 69(3): 254–266.

Schempp, P. (1998) 'The dynamics of human diversity in sport pedagogy scholarship', *Sociology of Sport Online*, 1(1): Available at http://physed.otago.ac.nz/sosol/v1i1/v1i1a8.htm.

Schempp, P. and Oliver, K. (2000) 'Issues of equity and understanding in sport and physical education: A North American perspective', in R.L. Jones and K.M. Armour (eds) *The Sociology of Sport: Theory and Practice*, London: Addison Wesley Longman.

Schön, D. (1983) *The Reflective Practitioner: How Professionals Think in Action*, New York: Basic Books.

Schön, D. (1987) *Educating the Reflective Practitioner: Toward a New Design for Teaching and Learning in the Professions*, San Francisco: Jossey-Bass.

Schunk, D. (2004) *Learning Theories: An Educational Perspective*, 4th edn, Upper Saddle River, NJ: Pearson.

Scraton, S. (1990) *Gender and Physical Education*, Geelong, Victoria, Australia: Deakin University Press.

Seaborn, P., Trudel, P. and Gilbert, W. (1998) 'Instructional content provided to female ice hockey players during games', *Applied Research in Coaching and Athletics Annual*, 13: 119–141.

Seedhouse, D. (1997) *Health Promotion. Philosophy, Prejudice and Practice*, Chichester, UK: John Wiley.

Seymour, W. (1998) *Remaking the Body: Rehabilitation and Change*, London: Routledge.

Sfard, A. (1998) 'On two metaphors for learning and the danger of choosing just one', *Educational Researcher*, 27: 4–13.

Sheilds, D. and Bredemeier, B. (1995) *Character Development in Physical Activity*, Champaign, IL: Human Kinetics.

Shetty, Y. (1978) 'Managerial power and organisational effectiveness: A contingency analysis', *Journal of Management Studies*, 15: 176–186.

Shilling, C. (1991) 'Educating the body: Physical capital and the production of social inequalities', *Sociology*, 25(4): 653–672.

Shilling, C. (1993) 'The body, class and social inequalities', in J. Evans (ed.) *Equality, Education and Physical Education*, London: Falmer Press.

Shogan, D. (1999) *The Making of High-Performance Athletes: Discipline, Diversity and Ethics*, Toronto: University of Toronto Press.

Shulman, L. (1986) 'Those who understand: Knowledge growth in teaching', *Educational Researcher*, 15(2): 4–14.

Siedentop, D. and Tannehill, D. (2000) *Developing Teaching Skills in Physical Education*, 4th edn, Mountain View, CA: Mayfield.

Sigelman, C.K. and Rider, E.A. (2006) *Life-Span Human Development*, 5th edn, Melbourne: Thomson.

Slack, T. (1997) *Understanding Sport Organizations: The Application of Organization Theory*, Champaign, IL: Human Kinetics.

Slack, T. (2000) 'Managing voluntary sports organizations: A critique of popular trends', in R.L. Jones and K.M. Armour (eds) *Sociology of Sport: Theory and Practice*, London: Longman.

Smyth, J. (1991) 'Problematising teaching through a "critical" approach to clinical supervision', *Curriculum Inquiry*, 21(3): 321–352.

Snow, C. (2001) 'Knowing what we know: Children, teachers, researchers', *Educational Researcher*, 30(7): 3–9.

Solomon, G. and Kosmitzki, C. (1996) 'Perceptual flexibility and differential feedback among intercollegiate basketball coaches', *Journal of Sport Behavior*, 19(2): 163–177.

Sparkes, A. and Templin, T (1992) 'Life histories and physical education teachers: Exploring the meanings of marginality', in A. Sparkes (ed.) *Research in Physical Education and Sport: Exploring Alternative Visions*, London: Falmer Press.

Sport England South West (n.d.) 'Long Term Athlete Development', http://www.sport england.org/sw_hubclub-buetin_no_4.pdf (accessed 12 November 2007).

Squires, G. (1999) *Teaching as a Professional Discipline*, London: Falmer Press.

Squires, N. and Sparkes, A. (1996) 'Circles of silence: Sexual identity in physical education and sport', *Sport, Education and Society*, 1(1): 77–101.

Stainton Rogers, R. and Stainton Rogers, W. (1992) *Stories of Childhood: Shifting Agendas of Child Concern*, Buffalo, NY: University of Toronto Press.

Stenhouse, L. (1975) *An Introduction to Curriculum Research and Development*, London: Heinemann.

Stewart, C. (1993) 'Coaching behaviours: "The way you were, or the way you wished you were"', *The Physical Educator*, 50: 23–50.

Strean, W. (1998) 'Possibilities for qualitative research in sports psychology', *The Sport Psychologist*, 12: 333–345.

Tauber, R. (1985), 'French and Raven's power bases: An appropriate focus for educational researchers and practitioners', paper presented at the Educational Research Association Craft Knowledge seminar, 12 April, Stirling, UK.

Templin, T., Sparkes, A., Grant, B. and Schempp, P. (1994) 'Matching the self: The paradoxical case and life history of a late career teacher/coach', *Journal of Teaching in Physical Education*, 13(3): 274–294.

Thompson, N. (1991) *Crisis Intervention Revisited*, Birmingham: Pepar.

Thompson, N. (1992) *Existentialism and Social Work*, Aldershot, UK: Avebury.

Thompson, N. (1998) *Promoting Equality: Challenging Discrimination and Oppression in the Human Services*, Basingstoke, UK: Palgrave.

Thompson, N. (2003) *Theory and Practice in Human Services*, Maidenhead, UK: Open University Press.

Thompson, S., Rewi, P. and Wrathall, D. (2000) 'Mäori experiences in sport and physical authority: Research and initiatives', in C. Collins (ed.) *Sport in New Zealand Society*, Palmerston North, NZ: Dunmore Press.

Thorpe, R. (1997) *Game Sense: Developing Thinking Players* (video recording), Belconnen, ACT: Australian Sports Commission.

Tinning, R. (1988) 'Student teaching and the pedagogy of necessity', *Journal of Teaching in Physical Education*, 7(2): 82–89.

Tinning, R. (1990) *Ideology and Physical Education*, Geelong, Victoria, Australia: Deakin University Press.

Tinning, R. (1991a) 'Physical Education and the cult of slenderness', *ACHPER National Journal* 107:10–13.

Tinning, R. (1991b) 'Teacher education pedagogy: Dominant discourses and the process of problem setting', *Journal of Teaching in Physical Education*, 11: 1–20.

Tinning, R. (1994) 'If physical education is the answer, what is the question? Ruminations on the relevance of physical education in the 1990s', *New Zealand Physical Education Journal*, 22(4): 15–24.

Tinning, R. (1995) 'We have ways of making you think, or do we? Reflections on "training" in reflective teaching', in C. Pare (ed.) *Training of Teachers in Reflective Practice of Physical Education*, Trois-Rivières, Quebec: Université du Québec à Trois-Rivières.

Tinning, R. (2002) 'Engaging Siedentopian perspectives on content knowledge for physical education', *Quest*, 21: 378–391.

Tinning, R., Kirk, D. and Evans, J. (1993) *Learning to Teach Physical Education*, London: Prentice-Hall.

Tinning, R., Macdonald, D., Wright, J. and Hickey, C. (2001) *Becoming a Physical Education Teacher: Contemporary and Enduring Issues*, Frenchs Forest, NSW: Prentice-Hall.

Tom, A. (1984) *Teaching as a Moral Craft*, New York: Longman.

Tomlinson, A. (1998) 'Power: Domination, negotiation and resistance in sports cultures', *Journal of Sport and Social Issues*, 22(3): 235–240.

Tomlinson, A. (2004) 'Pierre Bourdieu and the sociological study of sport', in R. Giulianotti (ed.) *Sport and Modern Social Theorists*, Basingstoke, UK: Palgrave.

Tonkiss, F. (1998) 'Analysing discourse', in C. Seale (ed.) *Researching Society and Culture*, London: Sage.

Town, S. (1999) 'Queer(y)ing masculinities in schools: Faggots, fairies and the First XV', in R. Law, H. Campbell and J. Dolan (eds) *Masculinities in Aotearoa/New Zealand*, Palmerston North, NZ: Dunmore Press.

Trudel, P. and Gilbert, W. (2004) 'Communities of practice as an approach to foster ice hockey coach development', in D.J. Pearsal and A.B. Ashare (eds) *Safety in Ice Hockey: Fourth Volume*, West Conshohoken, PA: ASTM International.

Trudel, P. and Gilbert W. (2006) 'Coaching and coach education', in D. Kirk, D. Macdonald and M. O'Sullivan (eds) *The Handbook of Physical Education*, London: Sage.

Tsai, S.D., Pan, C.-Y. and Chiang, H.-Q. (2004) 'Shifting the mental model and emerging innovative behaviour: Action research of a quality management system', *Emergence, Complexity and Organization*, 6(4): 28–39.

TV3 (2003) Interview with Daniel Carter, 24 May (video recording).

UK Sports Institute (2002) 'Leadership', paper presented at the World Class Coaching Conference, The Belfry, Birmingham, 25–27 November.

UKCC (n.d.) http://www.coachingcertificate.org/ images/UKCC%20overview%20 document-070305.doc (accessed 28 November 2007).

Valsiner, J. (1998) 'Dualisms displaced: From crusades to analytical distinctions', *Human Development*, 41, 350–354.

Van Manen, M. (1977) 'Linking ways of knowing with ways of being practical', *Curriculum Inquiry*, 6: 205–228.

Van Manen, M. (1995) 'On the epistemology of reflective practice', *Teachers and Teaching: Theory and Practice*, 1(1): 33–50.

VARK questionnaire (n.d.) http://www.vark-learn.com (accessed 10 December 2007).

Vialle, W., Lysaght, P. and Verenikina, I. (2005) *Psychology for Educators*, Melbourne: Thomson.

Vygotsky, L. (1978) *Mind in Society: The Development of Higher Psychological Processes*, trans. M. Cole, V. John-Steiner, S. Scribner and E. Souberman, Cambridge, MA: Harvard University Press.

Wacquant, L. (1995) 'Pugs at work: Bodily capital and bodily labour among professional boxers', *Body and Society*, 1(1): 65–93.

Walkerdine, V. (1984) 'Development psychology and the child-centred pedagogy: The insertion of Piaget into early education', in W. Henriques, C. Hollway, C. Urwin, C. Venn and V. Walkerdine (eds) *Changing the Subject: Psychology, Social Regulation and Subjectivity*, London: Methuen.

Walkerdine, V. (1993) 'Beyond developmentalism?', *Theory and Psychology*, 3: 451–469.

Wallace, M. (1996) 'A crisis of identity: School merger and cultural transition', *British Educational Research Journal*, 22(4): 459–472.

Ward, P. (2006) 'The philosophy, science and application of behavior analysis in physical education', in D. Kirk, D. Macdonald and M. O'Sullivan (eds) *The Handbook of Physical Education*, London: Sage.

Warner, M. (1993) *Fear of a Queer Planet*, Minneapolis: University of Minnesota Press.

Weeks, J. (1986) *Sexuality*, London: Methuen.

Wenger, E. (1998) *Communities of Practice: Learning, Meaning and Identity*, Cambridge: Cambridge University Press.

Wenger, E., McDermott, R. and Snyder, W. (2002) *Cultivating Communities of Practice: A Guide to Managing Knowledge*, Cambridge, MA: Harvard University Press.

Werner, P., Thorpe, R. and Bunker, D. (1996) 'Teaching games for understanding: Evolution of a model', *JOPERD*, 67(1): 28–33.

Werthner, P. and Trudel, P. (2006) 'A new theoretical perspective for understanding how coaches learn to coach', *The Sport Psychologist*, 20: 198–212.

Wikeley, F. and Bullock, K. (2006) 'Coaching as an educational relationship', in R.L. Jones (ed.) *The Sports Coach as Educator: Re-conceptualising Sports Coaching*, London: Routledge.

Wilcox, S. and Trudel, P. (1998) 'Constructing the coaching principles and beliefs of a youth ice hockey coach', *Avante*, 4: 39–66.

Wilkinson, S. (2000) 'Women with breast cancer talking causes: Comparing content, biographical and discursive analyses', *Feminism and Psychology*, 10: 431–460.

Williams, R. (1977) *Marxism and Literature*, New York: Oxford University Press.

Willis, P. (1977) *Learning to Labour*, Farnborough, UK: Saxon House.

Wine, S. (2003, 23 September) 'Billy Bean: "I'm as out as you could be"'. Queery.com. Available at http://www.queery.com/sybfusion.cgi?templ=q-item2.tpl&category= Q-indepth-feature&idx=69252.

Wink, J. and Putney, L. (2002) *A Vision of Vygotsky*, London: Allyn & Bacon.

Wood, L.A. and Kroger, R.O. (2000) *Doing Discourse Analysis: Methods for Studying Action in Talk and Text*, Thousand Oaks, CA: Sage.

Woog, D. (1998) *Jocks: True Stories of America's Gay Male Athletes*, Los Angeles: Alyson Books.

Wright, J. (1997) 'Fundamental motor skills testing as problematic practice: A feminist analysis', *ACHPER Healthy Lifestyles Journal*, 44(4): 18–29.

Wright, J. (2000) 'Bodies, meanings and movement: A comparison of the language of a physical education lesson and a Feldenkrais movement class', *Sport, Education and Society*, 5: 35–49.

Wright, J. and Burrows, L. (2006) 'Re-conceiving ability in physical education: A social analysis', *Sport, Education and Society*, 11(3): 275–291.

Wright, T., Trudel, P. and Culver, D. (2007) 'Learning how to coach: The different learning situations reported by youth ice hockey coaches', *Physical Education and Sport Pedagogy*, 12(2): 127–144.

Zakus, D.H. and Malloy, D.C. (1996) 'A critical evaluation of current pedagogical approaches in human movement studies: A suggested alternative', *Quest*, 48: 501–517.

Zeichner, K.M. (1980) 'Myths and realities: Field-based experiences in preservice teacher education', *Journal of Teacher Education*, 31: 237–244.

Zeichner, K.M. (1983) 'Alternative paradigms of teacher education', *Journal of Teacher Education*, 34(3): 3–9.

Zeichner, K.M. (1987) 'Preparing reflective teachers: An overview of instructional strategies which have been employed in preservice teacher education', *International Journal of Educational Research*, 11(5): 565–575.

Zeichner, K.M. and Liston, D.P. (1987) 'Teaching student teachers to reflect', *Harvard Educational Review*, 1: 23–48.

Zeichner, K.M. and Liston, D.P. (1996) *Reflective Teaching: An Introduction*, Mahwah, NJ: Lawrence Erlbaum Associates.

▼ INDEX

Routledge Sport

Sport, Culture and Society
Grant Jarvie, Stirling University, UK

An exciting new textbook exploring all of the key themes covered in undergraduate sport studies and introducing students to critical thinking about the complex and symbiotic relationship between sport and its wider social context.

PB :978-0-415-30647-8: **£28.99**

Sports Development, 2e
Kevin Hylton and *Peter Bramham, Leeds Metropolitan University, UK*

This popular course text examines the roles of those working in and around sports development and explores how professionals can devise better and more effective ways of promoting interest, participation or performance in sport.

PB :978-0-415-42183-6: **£24.99**

Psychology of Physical Activity, 2e
Stuart J H Biddle, Loughborough University, UK and Nanette Mutrie, Strathclyde University, UK

This text covers the field of exercise psychology in detail. Issues covered include motivation, attitudes, wellbeing, depression and mental illness, clinical populations, interventions and research consensus.

PB :978-0-415-36665-6: **£27.99**

The Sport Studies Reader
Alan Tomlinson, University of Brighton, UK

This reader collects several pieces of valuable, interesting and, in some cases, classic essays and extracts that have been widely recommended over the years, yet which are not always readily available.

PB :978-0-419-26030-1: **£26.99**

This is a selection of our new and bestselling titles.
Visit www.routledge.com/sport for more information.

Routledge
Taylor & Francis Group